YOUNG LIONS

CULTURAL EXPRESSIONS OF WORLD WAR II
INTERWAR PRELUDES, RESPONSES, MEMORY

PHYLLIS LASSNER, SERIES EDITOR

Young Lions

How Jewish Authors Reinvented the American War Novel

Leah Garrett

NORTHWESTERN UNIVERSITY PRESS | EVANSTON, ILLINOIS

Northwestern University Press
www.nupress.northwestern.edu

Annotations by Joseph Heller from his copy of *Catch-22* in the Robert D.Farber
University Archives and Special Collections Department at Brandeis University are
quoted by permission of the Heller Estate.

Various unpublished archival letters by Norman Mailer copyright © 1944, 1945, 1948
by the Estate of Norman Mailer are used by permission of The Wylie Agency LLC.

Extracts from the letters of Leon Uris are reproduced by permission of the Harry
Ransom Center at the University of Texas at Austin.

Extracts from the letters of Herman Wouk from the Herman Wouk archive at the Rare
Book and Manuscript Library of Columbia University are reproduced by permission of
the BSW Literary Agency.

Printed in the United States of America

10 9 8 7 6 5 4 3 2 1

Library of Congress Cataloging-in-Publication Data

Garrett, Leah, 1966– author.
    Young lions : how Jewish authors reinvented the American war novel / Leah
Garrett.
    pages cm. — (Cultural expressions of World War II)
    ISBN 978-0-8101-3144-6 (cloth : alk. paper) — ISBN 978-0-8101-3175-0 (pbk. :
alk. paper) — ISBN 978-0-8101-3145-3 (ebook)
    1. American literature — Jewish authors — History and criticism. 2. American
literature — 20th century — History and criticism. 3. World War, 1939–1945 —
United States — Literature and the war. 4. Holocaust, Jewish (1939–1945), in
literature. I. Title. II. Series: Cultural expressions of World War II.
    PS153.J4G37 2015
    810.98924 — dc23
                                                         2015017601

CONTENTS

ACKNOWLEDGMENTS

As a child I heard the stories of my relatives' service in World War II: my grandfather, Abraham Klein, who attended medical school in Vienna and then found himself a member of the Medical Corps (U.S. Army) as well as the Jewish chaplain stationed in Arles, France; my great-uncle Sig Lichterman, who was a dentist in the United States Navy; and my other great-uncle Jake Lichterman, who also served in the Medical Corps. My grandmother, Irene Klein, was a staunch liberal who would nevertheless get angry if any of her grandchildren said a negative word about the United States, because its military had "saved the Jews of Europe." This book was written as a means to understand that generation of American Jews and its relationship to World War II.

Several of my colleagues and friends generously read parts or all of the manuscript and I am very grateful to them for comments and suggestions. Deborah Dash Moore read the full manuscript and offered me a series of excellent suggestions for improving the work. Moore's book *GI Jews: How World War II Changed a Generation* was a huge inspiration, and I am extremely grateful that she was so generous about working with me. Werner Sollors also offered a series of thoughtful recommendations that greatly helped me. Victoria Aarons had great advice for incorporating Saul Bellow's work into my analysis. Hasia Diner and Derek Penslar also gave me invaluable suggestions on improving chapters in the book. Julian Levinson was my reader for an essay on Jewish war literature that appeared in the journal *Jewish Social Studies*, and his comments were extremely insightful. At Monash University, David Garrioch kindly shared many insights about strengthening my overall arguments. I also received helpful guidance and suggestions from Michael Hau, Daniella Doron, Adam Clulow, Paula Michaels, Clare Corbould, and Julie Kalman. It goes without saying that I alone am responsible for any shortcomings that still remain in the book.

My greatest debt goes to my readers at Northwestern University Press for their guidance in revising the text and bringing out its strengths. Profound thanks as well to Phyllis Lassner for her assistance and support of the work. And deep thanks to Henry L. Carrigan Jr. at Northwestern University Press for his guidance of this project, Anne Gendler for her astute editorial suggestions, and Rudy Faust, Marianne Jankowski, and Gianna Mosser for intelligently and carefully overseeing the publication process.

The faculty and staff of the Australian Center for Jewish Civilization at Monash have made the university a great home for me: Mark Baker, Andrew Marcus, Daniella Doron, Noah Shenker, Helen Midler, and Nathan Wolski. Thank you as well to my wonderful students, whose passion for American literature always inspires me.

My father, John Garrett, offered useful insights into American literature generally. My friends Bettina Wachsmuth and Mette and Leif Aiken-Pettersen have been sources of strength over the course of writing this book. My mother, Susan Vladeck, has been a staunch supporter of all my work and read through several drafts of this book with enthusiasm and intelligence.

I was lucky to conduct my research at archives with extremely helpful librarians. The staff of the Harry Ransom Center at the University of Texas at Austin helped me immeasurably as I worked my way through the Norman Mailer, Leon Uris, and James Jones archives. At Columbia University I was assisted greatly by the librarians at the Rare Book and Manuscript Library. And special thanks to Anne Woodrum, head research librarian of the Robert D. Farber University Archives and Special Collections Department at Brandeis University, for her help in navigating me through the Joseph Heller collection.

I presented lectures on this book at a number of forums and am grateful to Jeremy Dauber and Ruth Wisse for organizing talks at Columbia University and Harvard University, where I learned much from lengthy question-and-answer sessions with the highly informed audience. Thank you to Steve Zipperstein for his long-standing support of my work. I continue to learn from my mentors at the Jewish Theological Seminary, David Roskies and Raymond Schiendlin. And I would like to take the opportunity here to thank Herman Wouk, who kindly responded to my queries about his service in the United States Navy and his attitude toward World War II fiction.

This book is dedicated to my husband and best friend, Adrian, and to my daughters Sophie and Arwynn, who I hope will always love their Jewish American heritage as do I.

Young Lions

Introduction

> I've personally ended the career of at least 2 (definitely 2
> more, probably) Nazis, and the idea of knocking more out
> does not make me in the least squeamish . . . The first one
> I got was for Papa's brother that was killed in Poland. The
> second was for a boy in our outfit who was killed.
> —OCTOBER 6, 1944, LETTER FROM CPL. ALEX NUTKOWITZ TO HIS MOTHER

On December 5, 1948, the *New York Times* cultural correspondent
Charles Poore offered an overview of the year's major literary trends in
which he noted, "Nineteen Forty-eight will go down in literary history
as the year that America rediscovered the war."[1] Remarkably, the five
books about the war that dominated the *New York Times* best seller list in
1948, and which together created the new genre of World War II fiction,
were all written by Jews and made Jewish soldiers central protagonists:
Norman Mailer's *The Naked and the Dead*, Irwin Shaw's *The Young Lions*, Ira Wolfert's *An Act of Love*, Merle Miller's *That Winter*, and Stefan
Heym's *The Crusaders*.[2] A sixth book about a Jewish soldier also sold well
that year (although it did not make the best seller list), Martha Gellhorn's
Point of No Return.[3]

The critical and popular dominance of Jewish-authored war novels
in America extended throughout the 1950s and into the early 1960s.
For instance, Herman Wouk's *The Caine Mutiny* (1952) was the biggest

American best seller since *Gone with the Wind*, while Joseph Heller's *Catch-22* (1961) was also a best seller and helped to initiate the literary style of satirizing and subverting America's war aims that would come into vogue in the 1960s. In much the same way that in Hollywood Jewish studio heads and directors helped shape how mainstream Americans understood cultural touchstones such as Christmas, best-selling Jewish American war novels influenced how the public came to understand the recent war.[4]

Young Lions: How Jewish Authors Reinvented the American War Novel documents how Jews, traditionally denigrated as weak and cowardly,[5] for the first time became the popular literary representatives of what it meant to be a soldier. The ability of the Jewish soldier to kill Germans, rather than be killed by them, symbolized the superiority over Germany of America, which was utilizing some of its best men and women rather than seeking to exterminate them like vermin. Intentionally or not, the Jewish American soldier stood in stark contrast to the negative stereotype of the passive Holocaust victim: America had transformed the Jew from a weak sufferer into a proactive warrior who fights and slays the enemy.[6] The popularity of these best sellers suggests that they offered a mainstream readership an exciting and new vision of the American Jew.

The novels also became a chronicle of the postwar era, documenting the concerns and fears of Jews as they sought to create a viable life in an era where they were haunted by the Holocaust and were struggling to fit into a society that now saw them as more "white" than "black." It makes sense that authors would turn to war novels as a medium to present their broader concerns about being American, since the military represented an iconic hierarchical organization, while the platoon became a symbol of an idealized American melting pot where those from a variety of different ethnicities came to live and fight together.

Young Lions fills a gap in our understanding of postwar literature by focusing on a range of best sellers that were voraciously read by the American public and whose merits were argued over in newspapers and journals. The recent war cast a shadow over 1950s America, and Jewish American war novels played a major role in showing the public how to understand the war and how to use its lessons in the postwar era. Moreover, because Jewish war novels were *the* central form of postwar Jewish American literature in terms of sales numbers and critical reception, turning to these works yields important insights into the impact and development of Jewish American discourse that extends far beyond the canonical triad of Bernard Malamud, Philip Roth, and Saul Bellow.

These novels and novelists profoundly influenced the development of mid-century American discourse in a number of ways. For example, Norman Mailer, due to the massive popularity of *The Naked and the Dead*, immediately shot to fame as a major literary figure whose views and writings would inspire everyone from the Beats to 1960s radicals. Herman Wouk and Leon Uris, after the success of their debut war novels, would continue as major best-selling novelists and their next works, *Marjorie Morningstar* and *Exodus*, respectively, would centrally impact upon how Jews defined themselves and would be defined in the postwar era.

Remarkably, the central role of Jews in fictionalizing World War II for a postwar readership has largely gone unnoticed in literary and historical studies. Usually, all American war fiction is lumped together as a cohesive whole with the aim of seeking its commonality.[7] The focus on general trends overlooks the historically specific aspects of this literature and avoids asking how much the authors were influenced by their varying backgrounds. Either the Jewishness of the writers is uncommented on, or the Jewish aspects of the text are negated. This factor is central, because as I will show, Jewish authors wrote about the war in unique ways, and since their novels were best sellers, they had a direct impact upon how Americans understood the war effort and the lessons they should take from it in the postwar era.

By revisiting these works we will also see how Jewish writers engaged with the subject of war in such a way as to teach mainstream Americans a series of important lessons about liberalism, masculinity, and pluralism. *Young Lions* will therefore advance our knowledge of American Jewish literature and culture while at the same time intervening in a range of other debates. The popularity of these books meant that the American Jewish soldier became a central icon of Jewishness in the postwar era.[8]

The Evolution of Liberalism

All of the novels I will discuss were written after the war and during a time when Jewish life in America entered a "golden age"[9] as Jews became wealthier, better educated, more mobile, and more assimilated into the broader society than they had been before. For the most part, the authors of these novels had been raised in immigrant families where liberalism was a core belief. During their childhoods in the 1920s and 1930s, the focus was on workers' rights, the New Deal, and the government's ability to rectify the worst aspects of capitalism. They were mostly the children of Yiddish-speaking, working-class East Europeans who had been raised in homes where Judaism was defined along traditional lines, and where its rituals touched all aspects of daily life.[10] Once in the United States, these immigrants raised their children to acculturate into America by learning English and attending public schools. They primarily lived in urban Jewish ethnic enclaves where their children mixed with non-Jews in school, and where they often followed a watered-down set of Jewish rituals.

The second-generation children spent their school years during the Depression when antisemitism in America was at its height, and many of the men spent their college years in the military. Returning to the United States after the war they experienced profound changes in Jewish American life. Using the GI Bill to get a free college education, fluent in English and matured in the multiethnic platoons, they found themselves uniquely prepared to enter the middle class. In the space of a generation, Jewish Americans therefore transformed from a mostly working-class population to a cohort that subsequently become one of the wealthiest ethnic groups in America. Concurrent with the massive shifts in Jewish economic life, liberalism remained a central belief while adapting to the changing times.[11]

With the economic boom brought by the Second World War it seemed that inequities were being overcome and a comfortable life was becoming a real possibility for many. There thus followed a "retreat from radicalism"[12] in some intellectual circles, although on the ground in day-to-day Jewish life liberalism and the fight against racial injustice remained a shared principle. In the two central Jewish intellectual journals the *Partisan Review* and *Commentary*, there was a swing to the right as some thinkers began voicing a type of Cold War consensus that in a time of world crisis it was better for all Americans to unite against Communism than to fight for individual rights.[13] Jews in all facets of American cultural and political life created complex ways of dealing with the dual pressure of opposing Stalinism while remaining loyal to their liberal beliefs.[14] For many, one could be a liberal and assert a belief in pluralism and equality for all, while at the same time being opposed to international Communism. By the early 1960s, Americans in general shifted leftward as evident with the consolidation of the civil rights movement and the rise of both the New Left and beatnik, bohemian culture which reasserted the primacy of individualism as against the conformism of the suburban organization man.

Since liberalism was the core outlook of Jewish Americans during the twentieth century, central to the story of the evolution of the war novels was the manner in which the authors used their works to mediate their varied and changing concepts about liberalism in the postwar era. In 1948, for example, when the hearings of the House Un-American Activities Committee (HUAC) against Communism in Hollywood were well under way, all the authors of the best-selling Jewish war novels stood out by being either the victims or active opponents of HUAC's anti-Communist witch hunts: Ira Wolfert was labeled a Communist-by-association by HUAC; Irwin Shaw and Merle Miller were part of the Hollywood blacklist; Stefan Heym moved permanently to East Germany to escape the witch hunts; and Martha Gellhorn wrote pieces for the *New Republic* that were highly critical of the "bigots, reactionaries, and racists" who ran the HUAC hearings.[15] Moreover, the second novels of Norman Mailer (*Barbary Shore*), Irwin Shaw (*Trouble in the Air*), and Merl Miller (*The Sure Thing*) were about the dangers of the Red Scare and were three of only five major novels of the late 1940s and early 1950s that shared this theme.[16]

Because the first wave of Jewish war novelists were in public and private opposition to the oppressive intentions of the HUAC hearings, their novels can be seen as part of a backlash against the anti-Communists. While they can be read from a number of angles, of central importance is how the novelists used the motif of war to shape their readers' perceptions about liberal concepts. The liberalism espoused by the authors in their novels included assertions that a basic American value is pluralism, and by implication, all communities, including African Americans, Jews, and Mexicans, needed to be valued in postwar life.[17] Jewish literature had always had a strong moralistic intention, and war novels carried this tradition into mainstream America in an attempt to shape the ethical stance of the reading public.[18] The authors' calls for liberal pluralism were also self-serving because if America treated its minorities better, then Jews would be direct beneficiaries of a more tolerant country.[19]

The liberal agenda was evident in the novels' assertions that Jews could be true American heroes at a time when many were being stained with the blight of being "red." Norman Mailer in *The Naked and the Dead* presents this common conflation of the "Jew" and the "Communist" when his racist character, the Irish Catholic Bostonian, Gallagher, recalls his activities to highlight the public turn against "foreigners": "We gotta stick together, or we'll be havin' our women raped, and the Red Hammer of Red Jew Fascist Russia WILL BE SMASHING YOUR DOOR DOWN."[20]

In the 1950s, the general shift to the right played out forcefully in the two central best-selling war novels of that era, Herman Wouk's *The Caine Mutiny* and Leon Uris's *Battle Cry*. These war novels share a call for conformism, loyalty to American doctrines, and patriotic faith in the actions of the military while at the same time castigating American racism. By the 1960s, with the return of liberalism and the beginnings of beatnik culture, there was a renewed call for individualism and rebellion. Joseph Heller's *Catch-22* tapped straight into the Zeitgeist with the dichotomy it established between the negative military-as-corporation and the positive individual-as-rebel.

Jewish American war novels were also postwar responses to the Marshall Plan, which was instituted in Europe from 1948 onward under the guidance of General George Marshall, who had been the chief of staff of the U.S. Army during World War II and was the secretary of state from 1947 to 1948 during the Truman administration. The aim of the Marshall Plan was to lead Europe's postwar recovery along capitalist lines as a buffer against the spread of Communism. When authors composed their novels about World War II, it was under the shadow of this new, central role of the military in Europe's postwar recovery. Therefore the manner in which the authors rendered the armed forces can be read as presenting their varied stances on how the military should best institute American values in Europe during the postwar era.

The Soldier as Male Icon

The tension the authors felt between being defined (and defining themselves) as minority Jews or mainstream Americans played out in all of the Jewish American war novels as "Jewishness" went beyond an ethnic and religious definition and took on "universal" aspects. Well read in American and European literature, these authors replayed stock themes of modernist writing in their works, while at the same time giving them a "Jewish" flavor. This balancing act between being a "minority" writer and an "American" one helped to bring a shift in American letters to a more multicultural framework.[21] While many Jewish American authors had been raised on the Yiddish writings of Sholem Aleichem, Mendele Moycher Sforim, and I. L. Peretz, and the short stories of the largest circulation Jewish newspaper, *Forverts*, the war novelists instead sought to emulate mainstream American popular writing, and they were so successful at this they are now primarily thought of as "American" writers.

The conformist suburbs where Jews moved en masse during the time period of this study reflected the "aggressively assimilationist milieu of the mid-1950s" that brought some to feel a sense of shame about the East European behavior patterns of their parents.[22] Moreover, the dominant Jewish core belief in liberalism which argued for civil equality by stressing commonalities over differences tied in with the assimilationist pressures. Jews in suburbia faced a number of changes in their social patterns in contrast to how life had been conducted in cities, where Jewish neighborhoods created a strong sense of being part of an ethnic enclave. Jews in the suburbs therefore created "new Jewish spaces" where they could make connections with one another, leading to the dominance of the synagogue in suburban cultural life.[23] Although suburbanization brought on a newfound sense of economic security, it also meant for some a deep dissatisfaction with its bland materialism, the pressures to conform, and its anti-intellectual strains.[24]

Part of the popularity of the Jewish-penned war novels may have come about because the soldier was seemingly the opposite of the suburban man, and provided Jewish and non-Jewish readers alike with access to areas of their lives that they had sublimated to fit into that norm.[25] War novels became a place where postwar readers could enter an exciting, hyper-masculine world that was free of the bland and watered-down masculinity of suburbia.

Where the suburban man succeeded or failed by his ability to be a breadwinner, the soldier received a regular paycheck and never faced this problem.[26] Where the suburban man was paradigmatically defined as a father, the soldier was free of any and all familial concerns. Where the suburban man lived the unexciting life of the nine-to-five worker, the soldier's day was filled with the excitement of warfare. Where the suburban man had to negotiate his life with a wife, the soldier was free to have sex with a number of women and was not tied down to anyone. They were similar, however, by having to fit into a corporate, hierarchical world that demanded they dress and act in a way deemed proper by the strict rules of the bureaucracy: either wearing a gray flannel suit and following the codes of office life, or wearing a soldier's uniform and following military protocol. But of course, as the suburban man knew only too well, the stakes of his current life were as nothing compared to the life of the soldier whose actions could lead to the life or death of himself and others.

Jewish war novels also gave postwar mainstream readers a chance to visit a multiethnic America that was exciting but not fearsome, since it did not include African Americans (who were segregated in the military), and which was a contrast to the suburban neighborhood. The "multiethnic platoon" offered a stark contrast to the segregated middle-class suburban world where the aim was to mirror one's neighbors, be it in one's dress, home, and lawn, social and religious practices, or child rearing. In the war novel's platoon, however, the story was all about difference: a group of men from a variety of classes, ethnicities, and regions who live, fight, and die together.

While the war novels therefore established a paradigm of masculinity that contrasted with the suburban man, the specific depictions of Jewish soldiers evinced complex portraits of gender. The Jewish soldier, in distinction to his Anglo brother-in-arms, feels intense fear and angst about military life. He is drawn as both tough and sensitive, and his humanity is evident in his emotional soul searching. He is therefore a paradigm that blurs gender notions and suggests to readers that the modern man can be strong *and* emotional *and* intellectual. It is precisely by being a member of a culture typically ascribed with unique gender concepts — intellectualism is a central attribute of Jewish masculinity — that the Jewish soldier works as a bridge between contrasting ideas about masculinity in the postwar era.[27] The popularity of Jewish-penned novels about Jewish soldiers in the late 1940s and 1950s suggests that many readers were seeking complex renditions of manhood at a time when there was pressure to conform to suburban norms.

Jewish war novels also described women who were the opposite of the suburban wife.[28] This reflected what had been documented in the 1948 best sellers based on the Kinsey Report that showed that American men (and women) were far more sexually promiscuous than had been previously recognized.[29] The discussion of sex in war novels backed these findings, showing American soldiers frequently having sex with a range of women they were not married to, and also describing homosexual encounters. In the war novels, while women do not play central parts, since war was clearly the arena of men, they do fulfill certain roles: they are the ones the men left behind and whom they think about with longing; almost always they are fiancées or girlfriends, rather than wives with children. Or they are the women met in Europe or in the Pacific who are frequently prostitutes or are very willing to have sex with them. The simple domestic housewife does not generally exist in these novels, and for both male and female readers, these exotic, sexual women who are single and free may have been quite an appealing counter-image to the suburban mother whose life is focused on running the home and raising the children.

Many of the authors I will discuss came from sexually conservative families, and through war service for the first time came into contact with young men who talked freely (and bragged) about sex. The way that many soldiers discussed women — as prostitutes they frequented while in service, or as wives at home that they feared were having affairs — were viewed by many Jewish men as representative of what modern women were like. In the works of Philip Roth, Saul Bellow, Joseph Heller, Norman Mailer, and others, women often are hypersexual, untrustworthy, promiscuous, lusty, and unintelligent. Thus the female counterpart of the new soldier man of postwar Jewish literature is often a sexualized, all-body being, without intellect, soul, or substance.

Most of the authors who became central during this time period were men, although in the previous generation of Jewish American immigrant writing, there were numerous women writers such as Emma Lazarus, Anzia Yezierska, and Anna Margolin. And when the literature became dominated by male voices Jewish writing became critically acclaimed. In large measure, the postwar years, and the reintegration of American soldiers, meant that this time period lent itself to masculine voices.[30]

The Holocaust as Central Motif

As the center of Jewish life shifted to America after the extermination of the Jews of Europe, the Shoah cast its shadow over the prosperous postwar years in Jewish American life generally, and war fiction specifically. Jewish American war novels of 1948 argued forcefully that the Nazi killings of Jews were a central, rather than ancillary, aspect of the war experience. Even though few American GIs — mostly members of the 157th Infantry Regiment — were at the liberation of the camps, all the Jewish soldiers of the European novels are placed there to witness the machinery of mass killing.[31] This counteracts the prevalent, although mistaken, view that the sole literature about the Holocaust that became popular with American readers of the late 1940s and 1950s was *The Diary of Anne Frank*, which was published in 1952.[32] And even recent analysis of Jewish American Holocaust literature focuses almost entirely on Saul Bellow, Philip Roth, and Cynthia Ozick and by so doing misses out on most of the much earlier discourse.[33] Moreover, because Saul Bellow did not write about the Holocaust in the 1940s, there is a mistaken belief that Jewish American literature did not take on this subject, as Bellow's 1987 letter to Cynthia Ozick makes clear:

> It's perfectly true that "Jewish Writers in America" (a repulsive category!) missed what should have been for them the central event of their time, the destruction of European Jewry. I can't say how our responsibility can be assessed. We (I speak of Jews now and not merely of writers) should have reckoned more fully, more deeply with it.[34]

While Bellow was avoiding the subject because, as he wrote in the same letter, he "was too busy becoming a novelist to take note of what was happening in the Forties," for Jewish authors of World War II novels, the Holocaust was already a central focus right after the war.

There is also an erroneous view that Jewish American authors wrote *either* about the war *or* about the Holocaust.[35] But in Jewish American war novels both were given focus by authors intent on reminding their mainstream readers that World War II and the Holocaust (which as yet had no name) were being conducted at the same time and in many of the same places. America's victory was therefore not only against the German fascist but against the Nazi antisemite.

Although the novels I consider were primarily about World War II and the experiences of American soldiers, *all* the European-based novels describe in often graphic and extremely extensive detail the machinery of the death camps and the trauma of the Jews in Europe. This fact is crucial and requires us to reconsider how we understand the development of Holocaust literature in America, since it moves the starting point four years earlier than previously recognized. By turning our gaze to Jewish American popular literature, we discover a series of early attempts by Jewish authors to tell mainstream readers about the Shoah, and this rebuts the notion that Jewish American authors were largely silent about the Holocaust until the 1950s.[36] The manner in which war novelists wrote about the Holocaust, and their intentions for doing so, were however different than how it would be presented by later writers. As Lillian Kremer has documented, later Jewish American Holocaust literature focused on the Jewish victims and their modes of survival after the war. Moreover, this type of "survivor" protagonist sought ways to keep his or her Judaism alive in America and to maintain a rich connection with the Jewish past.[37]

By contrast, the war novel protagonists are soldiers who have a very different take on their Jewishness than do the survivor heroes. Since the authors of the war novels were composing their works for mainstream readers, their "use" of the Holocaust highlighted their liberal notions about pluralism and equality, as I discussed earlier. In their rendering, the Jewish soldier is a fighter against, rather than a victim of, the Germans and because of this he serves as an emblem of the American war against totalitarianism. By reinventing him as a mainstream American hero, his Jewish religious and cultural aspects are negated. The sole aspect of his identity that remains "Jewish" is that he is victimized by other soldiers. He thus becomes a symbol of all victims of hate, a wakeup call to American readers that in the postwar era they must treat all members of society equally. Because, after all, don't they want to transform America into a country that is completely different than totalitarian Germany?

In Jewish American Holocaust literature, Germans are erased from the landscape, with the sole focus on the Jewish victims; in war novels, the Germans are central figures and they are drawn as the embodiments of pure evil. By setting their works in the landscape of war, the authors extended their attention beyond the Jews, to show that Germans were the absolute enemies of the United States, regardless of American propaganda which had generally drawn the Japanese as devils and the Germans as misguided European brothers.[38]

Finally, the intention of detailing the machinery of the death camps was different for this first wave of writers than it would be for later authors. The war novels of 1948 use a journalistic voice to document what happened in the death camps since the aim was to get the news out to mainstream readers.[39] Hasia Diner has labeled this a strategy of "presenting" versus "memorializing" the Holocaust since it privileges "the acquisition and diffusion of knowledge."[40] By contrast, for later writers facing a public already saturated with images of piles of Jewish corpses, writing about the Holocaust was an act of "memorialization" that served cultural, artistic, and political purposes beyond disseminating information.

By cloaking reportage about the Holocaust within a novel meant for popular consumption Jewish authors thus were able to get the details of the Shoah across to large numbers of readers. And by putting the story into readable, exciting narratives, as readers came to the sections on the Holocaust, they were already deeply invested in the characters and could vicariously experience the Jewish soldier's horror as he confronts the dying and dead Jews of Europe.

The Rise of the "Middlebrow"

Although there were quite a large number of novels published by and about Jewish soldiers in the postwar years, I will focus only on books that were best sellers because they give us such an interesting insight into mainstream culture.[41] Also, these works shed light on the changing notions about the role of novels during the paperback boom in the United States, when print culture massively expanded. Many of the authors discussed in this book, from Norman Mailer to Joseph Heller, saw their novels become instant best sellers as soon as the paperback edition came out.[42] While some of these texts, such as *The Naked and the Dead* and *Catch-22*, are considered to be critical masterpieces, the majority were negatively characterized as "middlebrow" fiction.

In mainstream America, book reading had been the domain of the rich, but during the 1930s and 1940s it became a standard way that the middle class experienced "cultural" life.[43] As mainstream American readers showed their enthusiasm for the written word by joining reading clubs, enrolling in book of the month clubs, buying books, subscribing to *Reader's Digest*, and joining libraries, some members of the intellectual elite felt under attack as their protected realm was infiltrated by American readers who confused the "middlebrow" novel with art.[44]

The disgust felt by intellectuals toward this new reading public was evident in the use of the term "middlebrow" for their reading habits. "Middlebrow" was a derogatory expression from the dubious "science" of phrenology which asserted that a "low" brow was a facial trait of the immigrant poor in contrast to those who came from the higher strata and had "high brows." The "middlebrow" was the term for those who were somewhere in between. It quickly took on negative characteristics for those "upstart readers" who lacked the cultural background that was necessary to understand art and who were attempting to sneak their way into the sacred domain of the intelligent, refined elite.[45] Or, as Jonathan Freedman notes about this "vexed and contested term," the "middlebrow, whatever else it is, is what the academic or intellectual critic is not."[46] Generally, however, it is a term similar to "nouveau riche," applied to those who try to change their social status by acquiring the products that connote wealth. The disdain felt by critics toward the "middlebrow" matched their "disdain for suburbia" which they viewed as conformist, simplistic, trashy, and dull.[47]

Matching this disdain for popular writing was the postwar dominance of New Criticism that perpetuated the canonical division of high and low, excluding "genre" and "middlebrow" writing from artistic consideration. The movement was largely led by Southern, white intellectuals such as John Crowe Ransom and Allen Tate who took an elitist stance, asserting that it was only trained academics who could do the type of close readings that were necessary to discern the real meaning of literature. They, moreover, argued against biographical or historical readings and saw art as a pure artifact that should not be dirtied by evoking its ties to real life. Jewish critics of the time such as Alfred Kazin and Leslie Fiedler by contrast argued against reading literature in a vacuum, asserting that biography and historical context were important factors that should be considered in analyses.[48]

For many Jews, their relationship to literature and their reading habits were different from other Americans. Unlike mainstream America where the paperback boom brought print culture to a broad range of the public, for Jews since the early modern era the consumption of books, journals, and newspapers was a central facet of cultural life regardless of one's class status.[49] There was a democratic rather than hierarchical concept of the role of literature in daily life. Although Jewish intellectuals had, since the Enlightenment two hundred years previously, attacked the "shund" or trash reading of the Jewish public, there was never the sense that reading was a protected realm of the elite. Rather, the aim of the critics was to "elevate" what the public read.[50] Since the attack on the "middlebrow" in the United States and Britain frequently came from critics who sought to "protect" the status of good art from the non-Anglo herds, Jewish writers, working on the margins of elite literary traditions, had much to gain by discrediting the false binary of "high" and "low" literature that would naturally exclude them because of their outsider status.

Moreover, Jewish American culture in the twentieth century was dominated by immigrants from Eastern Europe who did not have the long tradition of class stratification which underlay the concept of the "middlebrow" reader. These differing notions of literature played out in the contrasting views of the "middlebrow" put forth by two of the central Jewish critics of the postwar era, Clement Greenberg and Leslie Fiedler, in a 1948 forum entitled "The State of American Writing" in the *Partisan Review*. The forum, a major cultural moment in American intellectual life, documented the views of nine prominent male American writers and critics, including John Berryman, Lionel Trilling, and John Crowe Ransom, as they responded to seven questions on American literature in the postwar era posed to them by the editors. Clement Greenberg spoke for the majority opinion when he asserted that earlier writers such as William Faulkner and F. Scott Fitzgerald had produced dynamic, "highbrow" works, while the current crop of novels were tepid "middlebrow" productions:

> It must be obvious to anyone that the volume and social weight
> of middlebrow culture, borne along as it has been by the great
> recent increase of the American middle class, have multiplied
> at least tenfold in the past three decades. This culture presents a
> more serious threat to the genuine article than the old-time pulp,
> dime novel, Tin Pan Alley, Schund variety ever has or will . . .

> Middlebrow culture attacks distinctions as such and insinuates itself everywhere, devaluating the precious, infecting the healthy, corrupting the honest, and stultifying the wise.[51]

Greenberg went on to ask where were the major writers such as Hemingway and why was weak writing in the ascendant? How were critics to protect "true art" from the infection of "middlebrow" mediocrity?

For the poet John Berryman, the decline of good literature was caused by the recent war:

> It has been a bad decade so far. If the twenties were Eliot's decade, and the thirties Auden's, this has been simply the decade of Survival. Wider military operations, their prolongation, their involvement of civilians, above all the preceding and accompanying genocide, distinguish wholly this war from the last. Everybody lost years, and many seem to have lost their nerve. There is a political, perhaps a moral, paralysis.[52]

The war had been such a cataclysmic event that writers felt frozen and unsure how to proceed.

Leslie Fiedler was the sole respondent who offered a different and more positive take on the times. He asserted that "the real Jew and the imaginary Jew between them give to the current period its special flavor." In the 1940s, therefore, "Jewishness is the condition of the Artist." Fiedler goes on to discuss how the writing of the era is dominated by "typically urban, second-generation Jews, chiefly ex-Stalinist, ambivalently intellectual."[53] These writers and critics have come to dominate the current literary climate to such a degree that Gentile writers are now trying to emulate them.

While the ascendancy of Jewish writing may have been one of the unspoken aspects of the era that so troubled the other critics, for Fiedler it was clearly thrilling that in the late 1940s the Jewish author was moving into the center of cultural life and was relegating the Gentile writer to the margins. Jewish writers, according to Fiedler, were dominant for two reasons. First, as second-generation immigrants they were uniquely positioned to straddle the literary traditions of America and Europe, creating a symbiosis between the two. Second, they were able to reinfuse intellectual concerns back into literature, which had taken an anti-intellectual stance during the era dominated by Ernest Hemingway. Jewish authors were also working for the freedom of the individual against repression, since the sheer act of writing was an assertion of a fight for truth, creativity, and individualism.

Greenberg and Fiedler present opposing notions of the role of literature: Greenberg clearly believes that art needs to be protected from the dumb herd while Fiedler views the opening of the gates as positive for Jewish literature. Where for Greenberg art is the domain of the educated against the "middlebrow" masses, Fiedler argues for a reorientation of dogma to ascribe to the Jewish urban writer a positive status. Jewish American World War II novels, as I will show, take on these two contested perspectives: the urban liberal stance of the city Jew, and the populist "middlebrow" voice of mainstream America. By so doing, Jewish literature subverts the destructive dichotomy of high and low that devalues the work of the non-Anglos, by bringing the perspectives and narrative forms of the Jew into the domain of "worthy" literature.

War novels were a type of discourse that would be widely disseminated and read and could therefore have an impact upon American life.[54] During the war, American GIs had voraciously read the paperbacks circulated by the military, and they brought their taste for books back with them to America as they sought out works that were both literary and exciting. Keenly aware of their inherent popularity, publishers created cheap volumes for mass consumption. Their great popularity therefore made these novels suspect for critics who viewed them as a central genre of the unworthy "middlebrow" literature. As Malcolm Cowley bemoaned in 1955: "war novels as a class have been reaching an extremely wide public that doesn't listen to what the critics say."[55]

As I chart the evolution of war novels between 1948 and 1961, I will therefore also discuss the changing attitudes of the authors, the readers, and the critics toward the virtues or vices of "middlebrow" texts. When I use the word "middlebrow" I use it as a self-referential marker that extends beyond its negative use as a term for the sentimental, popular, and inartistic literature of the middle-class masses. I also employ it to connote the shifting class relations in postwar America.[56] As noted, for the Jewish authors of war novels, the "middlebrow" was interchangeable with "popular" and connoted art forms that could reach broader audiences. For them, to quote Joan Shelley Rubin in her book *The Making of Middlebrow Culture*, "the promise that middlebrow ventures would put more books in the hands of more people is a highly attractive one."[57] As Rubin further notes, part of the reason for the great neglect in literary and historical studies of populist and "middlebrow" literature was that American academics, often unwittingly, mimicked the stance of figures such as Virginia Woolf who dismissed it utterly when they asserted that critical focus should only be on the modernists who had small, educated, and elite reading audiences.[58] Jewish novelists in America created the genre of the popular World War II novel and dramatized significant messages using a range of interesting narrative voices and forms. As feminist and cultural critics have taught us,[59] we need not negate or ignore these forms simply because they were popular because by so doing we overlook the hidden literary and cultural value embedded in these forms of cultural production.

Jewish literary studies has at times also insisted upon strict canonical forms that neglect best sellers and "genre" writing from consideration and by so doing has established artificial boundaries between the books that some critics admire and those that have had the greatest cultural and literary impact. Arnold Band writes of best-selling American novels generally that "they contributed significantly to the identity, circulation, and agenda setting of the Post World War II American Jewish community. . . . As such, they have been historical events of major import and deserve our serious study."[60] Yet except for the case of Laurence Roth's *Inspecting Jews: American Jewish Detective Stories*, Jewish American popular literature has been largely absent from any serious study of Jewish American discourse.[61] Leon Uris or Merle Miller seldom come up in critical discussions these days, whereas Norman Mailer's *The Naked and the Dead* is safer ground for the serious critic because of Mailer's largely uncontroversial canonical status.

The overarching structure of this book is chronological. My methodology is interdisciplinary, although my primary emphasis is on the impact of the changing historical milieu of postwar American life on the manner in which Jewish writers described the war. I therefore situate all my analysis within the historical context of American life generally, and Jewish life specifically, to present a chronological narrative of the interplay between postwar life and the changing ideological imperatives of Jewish authors. I mine the journals, newspapers, and popular media of the time to see how the intellectual and popular environment affected the authors and reciprocally how the war novels were received in those cultural sites. I have chosen a chronological methodology because *Young Lions* is the first book on Jewish American war novels and therefore its purpose is both to give a general survey of the field and to document the specific ways in which the novels changed over time in response to external trends. My intention is to consider all the novels as more than simply works of art: they were a means for writers to disseminate their ideas to mainstream readers about the recent war and the role of Jews in America. My analysis will therefore consider the fictional tropes that the authors invented to serve these aims.

I have labeled books as "Jewish American" not because I assume that there is some sort of monolithic type of identity called "Jewish" to which the authors ascribe. In fact, it is impossible to pinpoint the meaning of the term "Jewish" when it has been contested, particularly over the last two hundred or so years, on religious, cultural, artistic, political, and social grounds. And this issue is particularly complicated in the postwar era when many authors were uncomfortable labeling themselves or their work as "Jewish-American," preferring to drop the hyphen and claim themselves as part of the great American literary tradition. The authors I will discuss had extremely varied ideas about what "Jewish" meant, from Norman Mailer, who did not want his children raised as Jews, to Herman Wouk, who was Orthodox. So when I use the term "Jewish," I apply it less to the author's identity, and more to a genre of war writing that made the topic of Jewishness, in its many and varied forms, a central lens through which the war was filtered. By so doing I hope to avoid normative assumptions about what Jewish literature is and how it should or should not work in the postwar era.

In the first chapter of *Young Lions: How Jewish Authors Reinvented the American War Novel*, I give an overview of the American war novel and discuss how certain literary precedents were established in terms of how the war and Jewish soldiers were represented. I also discuss Jewish American World War II military service by concentrating on the experiences of the best-known and central writer of the genre, Norman Mailer. In chapter 2 I analyze the two major best-selling Pacific set novels of

1948, Norman Mailer's *The Naked and the Dead*, generally considered the first major work of World War II fiction, and Ira Wolfert's *An Act of Love*. In chapter 3 I discuss the best sellers of 1948 that were set in the European theater of the war, focusing in particular on the role that the Holocaust plays in the narratives. In the fourth chapter my analysis moves to the 1950s, looking at the impact of the Cold War, the Korean War, and McCarthyism on how Herman Wouk and Leon Uris wrote about World War II in their novels *The Caine Mutiny* and *Battle Cry*. In the fifth chapter I consider how Joseph Heller's *Catch-22* gave expression to the changing situation of Jews in the mid and late 1950s.

The character of the Jewish soldier was an ideal symbol for the shifting concerns of postwar America. As a member of the armed services, he could evoke issues related to individuals facing the pressure to conform to military standards. As a young person, he could show how youth interacted with their elders at a time when there was a great deal of intergenerational conflict. And as a Jew, he could symbolize the minority against the majority and what that meant in the broader American arena.

CHAPTER 1

The Jewish Soldier and Literary and Historical Precedents

I was brought up on those war hero novels. Of course, all the war ideals you had were quickly lost about a week after you got into the Army.

—NORMAN MAILER, 1948

Crouched on a hillside in Luzon in the Philippines during a massive rainstorm on May 3, 1945, just five days before VE day, a young conscript, Norman Mailer, contemplated the torrential rain and how his experiences in the Pacific had transformed him and his view of the world. Mailer had been raised in a loving home in Brooklyn where "everybody around us was Jewish,"[1] and educated at Harvard University where he majored in aeronautical engineering while taking numerous English literature electives.[2] Mailer was drafted in April 1944, six months after his college graduation. Until his military service Mailer had little experience of the "dark undercurrents" of life. But now each rainstorm reminded him of the new terrain of death and violence that is war:

> Each different type of storm seems to have a different connotation in man's experience. This was a storm of black lusts, of the old words, or murder and passion. Somewhere in the rain-swollen thickets you would not be surprised to run across a body with a knife in it.[3]

Mailer, like countless others, viewed his military service as a grand adventure that would give him the opportunity to undertake a range of new experiences far different from what life in the United States offered.[4] And near the end of his life, Mailer would assert that "those two years" of war service "were the most valuable in my life in making me a better writer than I would have been . . . It gave me a great deal of balance and a great deal of healthy cynicism, I'd say, about the military."[5]

Like his literary idol Ernest Hemingway, Mailer used his wartime experiences to nourish his artistic side and become a tough soldier writer. Therefore, while most men viewed service in the Pacific as more dangerous and less desirable than being in the European theater, Mailer was glad to be sent there since he believed it was a better setting for a great war novel.[6] Also, although his Harvard degree would have enabled him to undergo officer training, according to his wife Bea "he preferred to go in as a private because he felt that if he was made an Officer, he would be put behind a desk and never see combat."[7] Yet regardless of his desire to see combat, Mailer, like most men in arms, was never on the front lines[8] although this did not hamper his literary efforts. While he served on the periphery of battle, as a cook, office clerk, and fence patroller, Mailer jotted down the stories he heard from others about close combat. And in order to understand the inner life of soldiers from different backgrounds, he also conducted detailed interviews with his fellow draftees about a number of things, including their sex lives.[9] One of his fellow conscripts in basic training, Clifford Maskovsky, found Mailer's interviews and obsession with the sex lives of others to be so sordid that he recalled: "In 1948 I was out of the Army, in college, it was final exam time, and I was flipping through the back pages of *Time Magazine* and I saw a picture of Norman Mailer with a smoking cigarette in his hand — a sort of sophisticated picture — and my first thought was, Oh, my God, Norman's been arrested for rape."[10] Throughout the span of Mailer's war service, he would write up his notes and insert them into his letters to his wife Bea, telling her to save them so he could use them later to write his great American war novel.[11]

For the wave of Jewish writers this book focuses on, going to war was a rite of passage that turned them into adults, and also provided them with the impetus to author grand, adventurous, and heroic novels rather than the parochial "Jewish" tales of immigration that had dominated the literature of their parents' generation. For Mailer, close combat was something he both craved and feared because of the danger. Unlike the boys' stories that Mailer had been brought up on, being in the actual war forced him to confront his innermost fears and to look directly at how he viewed himself as a man. Mailer was just one of more than 16 million Americans, and more than 500,000 Jewish men — nearly half of the Jewish American male population between the ages of 18 and 40 — who served in World War II.[12] Military conscription started on February 16, 1942, for men between the ages of 20 and 44. Mailer, typical of most Americans, served in the U.S. Army. This was the branch of the military that had the highest percentage of Jews. (And a disproportionately large number of Jews served as medical and dental officers and as USAAF fliers.)[13] Just over 11,000 Jews were killed, in comparison with just over 400,000 general American war casualties.[14] Although Mailer had been drafted, Jews in general volunteered at a higher percentage than the general population for a range of demographic reasons.[15] They also served at more than three times the rate of American Jews during the first World War.[16]

World War II military service had a profound effect on American Jewish life. As Deborah Dash Moore writes: "The war had changed everything, although it would take time for American Jews to assimilate the breadth of the transformation."[17] The majority of second-generation Jewish American writers underwent war service, and for those who did not, the cultural impact of having their family and friends in arms was immeasurable. Since World War II enlistees were younger than those in the First World War, for many their stints in the military occurred during the years when they were coming of age and transforming from boys into men. For an entire generation, being in the armed forces served as their college education where they learned about what it meant to be a Jew, a man, and an American.

World War II had a much greater impact on Jewish American life than World War I for a variety of reasons, most centrally because so many more Jews served in the latter war than the former one. Fewer Americans in general served in the First World War because the country only participated for one year, and there was no full-scale conscription. Moreover, the first war broke out when most American Jews had recently emigrated from Europe and when few wanted to enlist and return there. Also, there was broad distrust by first-generation Jewish immigrants of the armed services because they were familiar with the stories of the Cantonists: Russian Jewish boys who were snatched up by the Czarist police to serve in the Russian Army for much of their adult life, with the aim of making them convert to Christianity. Many did not want to return to Europe to fight on the side of the hateful Russians.[18] Despite Jewish cultural fears, during World War I many Jewish men found that due to staunch efforts by the Jewish Welfare Board and the Union of Orthodox Rabbis, they were allowed to practice their Judaism while in uniform. For instance they could be granted leave to attend services on the major Jewish holidays, and even received Passover matzoh in training camps.[19] By the time of the Second World War, Jews in America were more comfortable with the whole idea of service in the military.

When Jewish Americans volunteered or were drafted into World War II, even though procedures were in place to support their religious practices, they nevertheless found that enlistment often meant entering an entirely new world. The transition began in the hundreds of training camps spread all over the United States, but mostly concentrated in the South, where Jews, like all conscripts, were taught how to transform from civilians into combatants.[20] In training camp, many Jews found themselves for the first time living and working with a range of ethnic, socioeconomic, and regional groups, including Jews from all over the country, rather than those with whom they had grown up.[21] The training of a division lasted for about a year, and by the end of it, the group was deeply bound to one another. In camp, all the men lived an extremely regimented life, meant to toughen them up and to learn the skills necessary to undertake their roles in the war. For many Jewish men, having grown up in an intellectual tradition, the transformation was hard, and their intelligence was looked down upon rather than rewarded.

In camp, the men also had to shed their personal idiosyncrasies to work for the sake of the unit, since in a war situation the real measure of success was not individual acts of heroism, but how well the platoon worked together. Norman Mailer described this transformation as one that wiped out his individuality and turned him into a cog of the war machine:

The Army is so horrible a mechanized thing. Slowly I can feel it encroaching upon my ego's strength — making me part of its mass-man, so gearish and cog-wheelish and axleish. You laugh in unison, groan in unison, applaud with the others, say "Private Mailer etc., etc.," when you answer and hear your own voice so foreign and apart. And then a part of me screams — "I'm being squeezed out of existence, let me live, let me live, let me live, there's so little room for me."[22]

The conflict between the long-standing members of divisions, who had trained together, and the new replacements who showed up to take over for those who had died or who were injured was a large issue particularly for enlistees such as Mailer who only started serving late in the war. Mailer found himself placed with the 112th Regimental Combat Team, a platoon primarily composed of Protestant farm boys from Texas who by the time Mailer joined them in 1945, were extremely hardened, having managed to survive some of the bloodiest campaigns of the war where they lost most of their fellow soldiers along the way. As Mailer described them:

They were tough men. Many of them were bitter . . . They would sit on the deck honing their bayonets for hour after hour with a dull glaze over their eyes. They were cold, hard men.[23]

Uneducated, hardworking, devout, loyal, and tough, they were the type of men that Mailer had read about in his favorite authors John Steinbeck, James Farrell, William Faulkner, and especially Ernest Hemingway.[24] And for the Texans, who had little previous contact with those "who represented the values of the cosmopolitan and technically diverse northern states," the arrival of soldiers like Mailer into the platoon meant for them, too, an accelerated introduction to the broader world of America from which they had been sheltered.[25]

Serving in the military with oftentimes very tough men forced many Jews to face and overcome the legacy of being viewed as "weaklings" too effeminate or fearful to be effective warriors. For instance, Norman Mailer wrote to Bea about seeing his body reflected in a mirror and feeling surprised and proud about how strong he had become: "Before I went to the bed I looked at myself in the mirror. I had not seen myself since that time we made love in Monterey before the mirror. I looked awfully good . . . I've gained a lot of weight but I've grown as well. My chest and belly are stronger and rounder, and my arms and legs heavier and muscled."[26] Turning into a soldier pushed these men to their limits, and for many, brought about a newfound confidence that they were more capable and brave than they had imagined themselves to be. Norman Mailer, desperate throughout his life to take on the guise of a tough guy,[27] found that in the army he could now assume that role, and as he wrote to Bea, become just like the other working stiffs: "I enjoy working in the chowline for I know all the guys (I've been in every platoon in the troop) and I roar at them when they bitch about the food and threaten to put them on T.P. and they sass me back. The cooks like me. I'm a tough guy from Brooklyn (the thousand roles I assume) and I work hard."[28] In this transformation, the broader perception of Jews changed since Jewish soldiers "in doing their part for America . . . had knocked down (if not out) stereotypes about Jewish men as conniving, unpatriotic cowards."[29]

Thrown into a new world where they lived and worked with a broad range of Americans, military service also could bring about a newfound awareness that in many ways Jews were similar to Christians, particularly those who came from immigrant families. Friendships were forged between Jews and non-Jews that outlasted the war. For instance, Norman Mailer's first "best friend" in the army was a fellow Jew from New York, Meyer Marotznik, but by the end of his service his closest pal was an Arkansas farmer named Francis Irby Gwaltney with whom he would remain close for the rest of his life. (And both of these friendships as I will discuss served as the basis for central characters in *The Naked and the Dead*.) As Jay M. Eidelman put it, "Serving in the military had integrated American Jews into white American society in ways that were unimaginable just five years earlier."[30] The friendships forged, could, at the same time, also bring a realization of their own differences. Enlisting in the military enabled Jews for the first time to take on a generic American identity where they were equal with other non-Jews and were just one of a whole tide of Americans defined first and foremost by their national status.

Unlike African and Asian Americans, Jews were not segregated into their own units since they were viewed as being "white" enough to serve with fellow "white" Americans.[31] However, since so many of the training camps where men began their war service were located in the deep South which had a strong legacy of antisemitism, many Jewish men were aware that while they were "white" enough to serve in mixed units, they were still marked as different.

For Norman Mailer, the military was a climate where antisemitism was regular and entrenched and unquestioned. He describes this in a letter to Bea:

> The cooks on my shift are average men. They have a mild amount of anti-Semitism. One of them made a crack about Jews, and I told him I was Jewish, and I'd prefer not to hear him talking like that when he was around. He backtracked "Oh, I didn't mean all Jews. Just a way of talking, you know." So now there's no anti-Semitic talk in the tent which doesn't mean a damn thing. The cooks like me, but they'll never bother to work out the reasoning implied. I know damn well that sometime in the future when I'm not around, they'll be talking to a guy who'll say, "aaah, the fucking Jews." "Yeah," one of the cook'll say, "They're all cocksuckers." It doesn't mean very much either way. It's a passive opinion, a way of talking about the weather. They'll argue with the trenchant anti-Semites, they'll agree with arguments for tolerance, the way we would agree with a stranger about the weather. It's too much trouble to disagree.[32]

For men like Mailer, war service complicated his understanding of what it meant to be a Jew. On the one hand, it enabled him to undergo a new range of experiences, including friendships with men he would never have known in Brooklyn or at Harvard. At the same time, however, it continually reminded him that he was different, and by many deemed to be somehow inferior. Nevertheless, in 2004 Mailer would assert in an interview that he did not face antisemitism in the military and only heard about it from others.[33] This letter to Bea, however, belies the case.

Also, being in the military forced Mailer and many Jews to confront racism against African Americans and to ask themselves if they sided more with whites, some of whom victimized Jews, or with African Americans who bore the brunt of the hatred. The realization began in training camp when Jews found that while they were placed with other "whites," African Americans were immediately segregated and given the worst work. Even in New York, with no legacy of Jim Crow, African Americans in the military were treated in ways that mimicked those laws. Norman Mailer writes about experiencing this at his first training base, Camp Upton in Long Island, New York: "The conditions for Negroes at Upton were very unfair. They were separated from us as soon as we got off the train, and we never saw them again, except at a distance. They were given all the heaviest work, seated at the rear of the theater, given special towels and soaps, and so forth."[34]

Mailer's awakening in the military to the situation of African Americans, as was typical of many Jewish soldiers, would later be a facet in the heavy Jewish involvement in the civil rights movement. Mailer's racial consciousness continued to develop when he was sent to a training camp at Fort Bragg, North Carolina, where the Jim Crow laws were in effect in the surrounding towns, and where the poverty among African Americans was extreme. Norman Mailer describes to Bea, in a rather melodramatic way, wandering into the "Negro" section of Fayetteville, the town in which his training camp of Fort Bragg was situated: "Darling, it was so painful a sight, I felt a mood of melancholy which changed later to depression. The street is a narrow, sandy road, and on either side are the shacks, two room shanties, raised on stilts a foot off the ground, their wood dry, and splintered, and very deep grey."[35] Experiencing firsthand the racism directed toward African Americans in the United States generally and in the military in particular led Mailer and many of the war authors to use their novels to remind their readers of the mistreatment of all minorities, including Mexicans, Native Americans, and homosexuals.

Through war service many Jews also came to realize that they had a better lot than African Americans, and that this would translate into their different treatment after the war. So where many Jews returned from the war having developed relationships for the first time with Christians, and would often recount those friendships in a fairly positive light, for African Americans overall the war was a long series of degradations with only small and rare victories.[36] Norman Mailer discusses this, and how his fellow soldiers planned to bring their racism home with them, since they intended to fight the "Negro threat" in the postwar era:

The Negro set up is far worse than you can begin to believe. In all the time I've been in the Army I've only known one guy who likes the Negros — Abe Goldscholl at Bragg who was a Commie — and only a few who were vaguely sympathetic. The average view ranges from instinctive dislike to phobia. Our precious Southerners after killing Japs are going to be little troubled by the value of a man's life if he has black skin. So many numberless times I've heard perfectly good guys start off talking about all the post-war problems there're going to be and then suffix the remarks with a declaration. "There's going to be one thing that's got to be settled and that's the Nigger problem. They're getting too big for their boots, one of these days we're going to have to give them a lesson."[37]

Once back in the United States after the war ended, both Jews and African Americans nevertheless expected that their service entitled them to equal treatment, and returned intent on fighting continued discrimination. In particular, many Jews felt that they had the right not only to be treated the same as "white" Americans, but also that they should be allowed to claim their Jewishness publicly rather than disappearing into the "melting pot" of the Anglo-American norm. They had fought as Americans for the good of the world, and they expected that in peacetime their efforts would be rewarded with equal treatment.

Upon returning home, Mailer and a wave of other Jewish Americans started composing their war novels in part as a way to delve into all these issues. As John W. Aldridge wrote in his influential 1951 book, *After the Lost Generation: A Critical Study of the Writers of Two Wars*, "It was not until 1948, however, when Norman Mailer's encyclopedic *The Naked and the Dead* appeared that the general public fully accepted the new war literature."[38] The three-year gap between the end of the war and the new literature was due in large measure to the fact that "by 1948 the war was far enough away for people to remember it with some detachment and to begin to speculate on its larger meaning."[39] Also, it took a necessary few years for returning servicemen to write, send off, and then have their books published. These novels would not only be exciting and moving accounts of the war, but would also serve to educate mainstream readers about the treatment of Jewish soldiers in the military and about how they, and other minorities, should be treated in the postwar era.

War fiction brought to the forefront the struggle between the individual, whose aim was to survive, and the collective, symbolized by the officers, whose intention was to win the war.[40] War novels therefore explored young men coming up against those in power and trying to choose their own path. Having left the safety of their homes and their own ethnic and class enclaves, and been thrust into the deeply regimented world of the military just at the time in their lives when they were beginning to create their own identities, the setting of war enabled authors to explore the tensions felt by youth between their own individualistic impulses and societal constraints.

War novels could also delve into a host of issues of concern to mainstream Americans since "for all their surface realistic grit, the best war novels were really parables about American life."[41] These topics included the tension between a conservative culture and those who sought to rebel against it, the desire for or rejection of a more multicultural society as symbolized by the multiethnic platoon, the marginalization and invisibility of black Americans as shown by their segregation, and the confusion about the role of women in an era dominated by new ideas about masculinity.

War novels therefore filled a crucial role for returning soldiers generally as they tried to negotiate the relationship between their war service and the new demands of peacetime life, although only a small proportion of veterans had actually engaged in combat in a direct way, and even fewer had been responsible for saving their fellow soldiers.[42] Upon their return, however, soldiers were lauded as heroes who had fought valiantly for their country. In war novels, the disjunction between the ideal of brave front-line combat and the reality of not having experienced it is unpacked as soldiers who are engaged in or facing direct combat do not feel heroic and are often terrified. Reading war novels likely gave the men who had missed out on imminent danger the opportunity to fulfill their curiosity about what it had really been like at the front. And for those who had done fierce fighting, the novels discussed how hard this could be.

War novels delineated as well peak situations of fear where the soldier had to confront the meaning of life and of death. War novels therefore showed the rite of passage of young men, but in extremely tense situations where they inevitably sought out the "momentary gratifications" that would ease their burdens.[43] The setting of war also enabled authors to write about a range of generally taboo topics such as casual sex and homosexuality. All of this made for good reading as war novels offered readers both existentially deep moments and sordid and exciting descriptions of bodily pleasures.

Literary Precedents

When Jewish American writers took up their pens to compose their novels they did so as part of a well-established literary tradition of war writing in the United States, initiated with Stephen Crane's Civil War novel *The Red Badge of Courage* (1895). The most critically acclaimed and central novels of World War I were John Dos Passos's *Three Soldiers* (1921), E. E. Cummings's *The Enormous Room* (1922), and Ernest Hemingway's *A Farewell to Arms* (1929). Moreover, before the large wave of Jewish war novels of 1948, there were four best-selling World War II novels, Harry Brown's *A Walk in the Sun*, Thomas Heggen's *Mister Roberts*, James Michener's *Tales of the South Pacific*, and John Horne Burns's *The Gallery*. There were also two hugely popular nonfiction works: Marion Hargrove's *See Here Private Hargrove* and Ernie Pyle's *Brave Men*.

The Red Badge of Courage was rediscovered by critics in the 1920s and had a large impact on later war novelists.[44] The novel describes in detailed and explicit naturalistic prose ferociously close battles during the Civil War as experienced by the young Unionist foot soldier, Henry Fleming, who overcomes his fears to prove himself in battle. The novel is a violent and lyrical tale that fluctuates between moments of extreme terror, as young men face direct combat, and moments of extreme joy, when they survive the battle.

With the authors of the American World War I novel, there is a marked shift in tone from Crane's tale of a young man's heroic rite of passage. John Dos Passos's *Three Soldiers* presents a deeply negative view of the military bureaucratic hierarchy that would be reiterated in Mailer's *The Naked and the Dead* and Joseph Heller's *Catch-22*.[45] Using a naturalistic and gritty prose style, also later employed by Norman Mailer, Dos Passos describes the experience of war service through the eyes of a small group of American "types." The war is its own character and is a brutal, inhuman, industrial machine that consumes everything in its wake and stands in opposition to individual initiatives. The chapter headings symbolically evoke the transformation of the soldier into a cog in the industrial war machine: "Making the Mold," "The Metal Cools," "Machines," "Rust," "The World Outside," and "Under the Wheels."

Ernest Hemingway was a great fan of *The Red Badge of Courage* and initially an admirer of *Three Soldiers*, and his semi-autobiographical *A Farewell to Arms* picks up on some of the same themes. Hemingway had the largest impact of any of the writers on Jewish World War II novelists, and he took on an almost mythic role in defining how "masculinity" was to be understood by this generation of Jewish writers.[46] Although *A Farewell to Arms* takes place in the heart of World War I battles, its protagonist Frederic is on the periphery: he is an American in the Italian Army and he is an ambulance driver rather than an infantryman. Not only a portrait of war, the book is also a story of one man's search for, and loss of, love. Europe, even when at war, remains an exotic and interesting setting where Frederic undergoes adventures, eats wonderful food, and see the sights. Frederic is certainly stoic and brave: he expresses no fears of battle and barely complains even when he is wounded. In fact he suffers almost no emotions about anything, including the deaths of fellow soldiers. As Ernest Hemingway would state in 1942, "A good soldier does not worry."[47] The war itself is devoid of any heroic aspects: no one is fighting for any good reason and everyone is always complaining about how it goes on endlessly. The war comes across as a perplexing and pointless event that everyone is sucked into without really understanding why.

E. E. Cummings's semi-autobiographical *The Enormous Room* is considered the third major American World War I novel, although the theater of war is not directly covered. Instead the novel focuses on the day-to-day lives of a group of prisoners crammed together in a French prison cell. The style of the prose is typical of Cummings's poetics, often utilizing a series of short staccato-like sentences, and interlaying large numbers of French words into the prose. It is a high modernist take on the landscape of war as a chaotic and destabilizing force.

In the World War I novels of Dos Passos, Cummings, and Hemingway, the main critique is against the chaotic and often totalitarian nature of the war machine. These novels were composed in response to a war that was seen as so unprecedented in its hugeness that it obliterated the progress and reforms that the new century was meant to herald in. In fact, for these writers, this war was being used to suppress dissent in all forms, particularly the fights for workers' rights, as the government's propaganda machine sought to make Americans into docile soldiers who followed the rules and supported all the actions of the military.[48]

World War I was therefore viewed cynically by many American artists as an effort that benefited the rich and corrupt and that broke the will of the masses.[49] In this Great War, the mechanized traits of the modern world had been turned into machines of destruction that killed individual initiative, and the shock of this type of totalizing warfare was evident in the novels written in response to it. As Ernest Hemingway wrote, the war was "the most colossal, murderous, mismanaged butchery that has ever taken place on earth."[50] The novels about the war therefore were about the "mismanaged butchery" without describing any larger redemptive purpose.

Moreover, since the Great War was seen as being used to suppress individual rebellion, the central authors of American World War I novels, Hemingway, Dos Passos, and Cummings, were all self-consciously artful writers who infused their war novels with a modernist aesthetic that argued for the individual as against the mass docility the war machine required for its effective running. And even the "middlebrow" writers of the popular, critically reviewed novels of World War I, while outlining some good *effects* of the war such as that it brought Americans back to a more united path, avoided describing it as being conducted for positive reasons.[51]

Jews in the war novels of Dos Passos and Cummings are drawn in an extremely negative light. This reflects the increase of xenophobia, racism, and antisemitism during the 1920s and 1930s in America. In *Three Soldiers*, for instance, Eisenstein is a "little man of thirty with an ash-colored face and a shiny Jewish nose" who speaks with a "squeaky voice."[52] He is depicted throughout as a weak, sniveling "kike" who the other soldiers do not trust because he is a Polish-born "foreigner" who is always complaining about the war. In Cummings's *The Enormous Room*, also riddled with antisemitism, there are myriad hateful and repulsive descriptions of the Jewish soldier character who is labeled "The Fighting Sheeney."[53]

The American novels of World War I contrasted starkly with those composed by Europeans because the war was far away from the home audience they were addressing. Readers in America did not have the direct experience of being in or near the battles and did not understand the daily fears of life in a war zone as did European readers. A case in point is the hugely best-selling 1929 German novel *All Quiet on the Western Front* by Erich Maria Remarque that argued so forcefully and intimately against a sentimental or patriotic view of war that it was one of the first novels banned by the Nazis. There is nothing heroic nor grand in the efforts of the soldier the book focuses on, Paul Bäumer. Rather, the novel shows the corrosive evil of front-line battle where bodies and minds are destroyed under continual yet unpredictable fighting. While evoking the chaotic and intense battle scenes in Crane's *The Red Badge of Courage*, the book at the same time erases from the war any possibility for heroic action since in this landscape the individual becomes reduced to nothing but the will to survive. By undergoing war the soldier does not become a heroic man but a dead corpse. Remarque's anti-nostalgic, harsh, and brutal take reaches its pinnacle in the final scene when the character whom the reader has learned to care deeply for is killed:

> I am very quiet. Let the months and years come, they can take nothing from me, they can take nothing more. I am so alone, and so without hope that I can confront them without fear. The life that has borne me through these years is still in my hands and my eyes. Whether I have subdued it, I know not. But so long as it is there it will seek its own way out, heedless of the will that is within me.
>
> He fell in October 1918, on a day that was so quiet and still on the whole front, that the Army report confined itself to the single sentence: All quiet on the Western Front.
>
> He had fallen forward and lay on the earth as though sleeping. Turning him over one saw that he could not have suffered long; his face had an expression of calm, as though almost glad the end had come.[54]

In this German novel the war destroys everything in its wake, including the civilians who discover that their family members who have served have become mere shells of their former selves. The war infects all who come into contact with it, while in the American novels there is a distance between the location of the readers and the places where the terrible action unfolds.

By the time we get to the literature of the Second World War, a huge, cataclysmic, all-encompassing war was already an old story. According to the Jewish authors of World War II novels, this new war, while similarly large, differs because it includes the extermination of European Jews. Because of this, the American war effort in this case matters and it serves a greater good. Rather than being merely representative of a chaotic, corrupt, and anarchic form of mass violence, this war is being fought for a noble reason and the soldiers are on the side of good. For Jews, in particular, the war against the Nazis was personal, and the larger aim of the Allied efforts was nothing less than the salvation of Jewish life in Europe.[55]

Moreover, because American military involvement was much more extensive in the Second World War, the literature shifts from being primarily an expression of individual dissent against the military complex to a moralistic discourse encouraging readers to a greater appreciation of the positive role of the war in both destroying the evil enemy and in making America more pluralistic. This shift is mapped out in the evolution of war writing from the earlier modernist, literary, tone of Dos Passos and E. E. Cummings to the populist voice evident in the best-selling Jewish novels of the late 1940s and 1950s. Where the World War I authors used their works as "acts of artistic non-conformity,"[56] the Jewish World War II novel reaches its pinnacle with Herman Wouk's *The Caine Mutiny*, which expresses disgust with the selfishness of the individual and is a call for mass conformity.

The four best-selling World War II novels that preceded the Jewish-authored ones of 1948 were Harry Brown's *A Walk in the Sun* (1944), Thomas Heggen's *Mister Roberts* (1946), James Michener's *Tales of the South Pacific* (1947), and John Horne Burns's *The Gallery* (1947). *A Walk in the Sun* depicts the stressful and deadly day when a group of American GIs make their way from an Italian beach landing to a farmhouse held by Germans six miles inland. With their officers dead and their map lost, the group uses their wits to advance, even as many of them are killed. The novel is important because it establishes the archetypal platoon of the war novel, showing how men from a variety of backgrounds through their experiences transform into a cohesive group.[57]

Thomas Heggen's *Mister Roberts* was the largest best seller of the pre-1948 novels and had such lasting importance in American popular culture that it became a 1955 John Ford movie starring Henry Fonda, and ten years later in 1965 a television show that ran for two years. A comic novel, it is in many ways the opposite of the standard war novel, because in this case all the action takes place on a navy cargo transport ship far outside the realm of battle: "for the most part it stays on its regular run, from Tedium to Apathy and back; about five days each way" (*Mister Roberts*, 6). The men on board, in contrast to soldiers on the front lines, are "unheroic men only because they are non-combatant" (8). The novel tells in a comic way the daily life on the ship, where rather than battling the Japanese or German enemy, the men face off against the much despised, petty-minded Captain Morton, a precursor of Herman Wouk's Captain Queeg in *The Caine Mutiny*. The huge popularity of the novel suggests that it spoke to the majority of servicemen, who never saw combat and appreciated a comic account of what life in the backwaters was like.

None of the characters are described as ethnic or Jewish and there is no suggestion of the multiethnic setting found in Jewish-authored renditions of the war. The protagonist, Lieutenant Roberts, sticks out from the others because he alone cares about the war, rejoices when it ends in Europe, and longs to be on the front lines of the battle where he can experience "real" war firsthand. Quite unexpectedly, going against the whole comic tenor of the book, Roberts is killed in the final pages of the novel. This fact is discovered when one of his fellow servicemen receives a letter that tells that after leaving the cargo ship Roberts volunteered for service on a destroyer in the Pacific where he was shortly thereafter killed in a Japanese kamikaze attack. The real war, which had been in the distance throughout the rest of the novel, took the protagonist's life.

James Michener's *Tales of the South Pacific* established a literary trend that would be repeated in Norman Mailer's *The Naked and the Dead* and Ira Wolfert's *An Act of Love*, of drawing the landscape of the Pacific theater as a mixture of the exotic and the horrible, the beautiful and the terrifying. Michener's stories depict life on the ground for Pacific-based soldiers as long spells where little happens and the men dabble in native life, dating exotic and beautiful local women, drinking, and taking stock of their lives. The extended moments of calm are broken up by intense, often horrific, close-combat battles with the Japanese who will go to any length to kill them. Overall the men are depicted as tough, resolute, and decent.

In Michener's collection, as will be evident in most of the Jewish-authored novels, there is an underlying critique of race relations in the military. For instance, one of the tales focuses on an American nurse from the deep South who forces herself to try and overcome her racism. And the collection ends with a story about visiting an American military cemetery on the island of Konura and encountering two African American gravesite workers who describe a racist and antisemitic commander who torments them. The black men, while hating the racist, admire and are deeply grateful to all the dead in the cemetery who became heroes by fighting for the American cause. The message is clearly that the best aspect of the military is that it encourages brotherly respect, and that those who are racist and antisemitic are giving the armed forces a bad name. *South Pacific*, the Broadway musical and movie based on the book, created an even larger audience for this work.

The fourth of the novels, John Horne Burns's *The Gallery*, presents an extraordinary portrait of a Jewish soldier and was a direct precedent of Joseph Heller's rendition of Italy as found in *Catch-22*. The novel was published just before the Jewish novels of 1948 so it would not have had any influence on that group of authors. However, it would have helped to shape the reading public who took up the Jewish-authored novels in the following months.

The Gallery gives a series of portraits of individuals who congregated in an arcade in the heart of Naples in August 1944. Burns presents the war through a gallery of types, but crosses the traditional Axis vs. Allied divide by showing the internal lives of Italians as well as Americans: the book is separated into chapters that encompass nine portraits, most of GIs, but also of a couple of Italian women. There are also several chapters that render the different locations where the author himself had served. The portraits are a chorus of voices giving a series of impressions from different angles of the war and its impact on current life. The descriptions of Italian civilians are deeply empathetic, and show from their viewpoint the great suffering they have undergone and the current terrors they still face. They also describe the deep animosity many feel toward the American servicemen who exploit them for goods and sex.

The portraits of Italians contrast markedly with how Heller would paint them in *Catch-22*, even though Heller was deeply impressed with the novel.[58] As we will see, Heller's depictions of Italian women show them mostly as playthings for the Americans with whom they willingly have sex. In Burns's novel, by contrast, the women speak angrily about how this makes them feel and how it breaks their will: "And we will yield to your desires, no matter how beastly they may be . . . for a price, you understand. But you should hear how we talk about you among ourselves. We sear you and we scald you. Because we hate you."[59] This acknowledgment of the burden that the civilian women undergo because of their poverty never comes to light in Heller's rendition of Rome as a city where the women sleep happily with the men because they are naturally lusty. Moreover, Burns gives extensive and compassionate treatment to homosexual soldiers, depicting in detail an afternoon at a bar where the men congregate and make connections with one another.

The novel concludes with the final portrait, "Moe," short for Moses Shulman, about a second lieutenant from Brooklyn who has recently been wounded and has a day in Naples before returning to the front line, where he has a premonition that he will be killed. We find out that Moe is Jewish when a fellow serviceman calls someone a "kike" and he responds "I'm a kike" (*The Gallery*, 313). The first half of the chapter is devoted to his day in Rome where he comes across as far and away the most decent, ethical, philosophical, and intelligent GI in the book. Where other soldiers scheme to take all they can from the impoverished Italian locals, Moe spends the day giving back to the weakest and most vulnerable: feeding a homeless Italian girl, giving cigarettes to a young man who is used to trading sex for goods, buying coffee and donuts for a store worker. His day ends with a beautiful and loving interaction with a local Italian woman. She recognizes immediately that he is different from all the other American soldiers because he is kind and good and decent.

Moe's Jewishness in Burns's rendition comes from his ability as an outsider to have a broader perspective and to try and reach an ethical and moral stance during a time when darkness is overshadowing everything. Like Burns's portraits of women and homosexuals, the Jew is an outsider to the dominant and abusive pathos of the heterosexual, American, non-Jewish GIs. The Italians notice that the Jew is different and therein more akin to them, and respect that he is seemingly disconnected from the dumb soldier pack that exploits them. As an Italian notes of Moe, "You're the first man today who treated me like a human being." "Take a look at my nose and my dark skin," Moe said. "I might almost be a Napolitano" (314).

During Moe's wanderings through Naples he meets another Jewish soldier, an immigrant from Vienna who went to the United States in 1938 after the Nazis killed his father and is currently a captain in the U.S. Army. When the captain starts to complain about the extent of the antisemitism he must face in the military, Moe cuts him off, saying, "The country took you in. As you said yourself, it even gave you a commission in its Army. No other country in the world except the United States" (321). He then tells the captain that he should move on and let his rage go, although the captain's plan is to return to Vienna and kill the Nazis who murdered his father.

Moe then is a voice for moderation, an acceptable vision of the Jew as the ennobled sufferer who brings others back to their own humanity. It is an extremely positive yet subtle binary that Burns draws between the GI-as-exploiter and the Jew-as-humanitarian. This plays out in the second half of the chapter when the scene shifts to Moe back in combat leading a platoon through northern Italy as they try and root out the retreating Germans. The reader understands from Moe's constant prophetic insights that this will be his final day on earth.

The platoon has captured three German infantrymen, one of whom keeps saying "over and over again that Roosevelt was a Jude" (332). For the reader, who has discovered that the "Jude" Moe is the most decent American in Italy, it is a compliment to have Roosevelt compared with such an ethical figure, although that clearly is not the intention of the German. In fact, even though the German is constantly spitting out antisemitic slurs, Moe is the only American who gives him food, and when one of the others kills the German in a fit of rage, it is Moe who admonishes the GI that he must remember that he is still a human and cannot merely kill a prisoner (336).

As the readers expect, the chapter, and in fact the book, end with Moe's death: he is shot by a German lieutenant and the last words he hears as he dies are "Heil Hitler" (341). In Burns's rendition, the Jew shows the best aspects of humanity and reminds Americans of their moral responsibilities to act in a dignified and ethical way, in marked contrast to the stupid and hateful Germans. Burns, who was himself gay, and who certainly felt his "otherness" in America and in the military, uses outcasts in his novel to show readers that those in the position of weakness often have finely tuned moralistic visions. He is also reminding all Americans that they must treat the "others" in their midst better because, as he has depicted with Moe, some of America's most heroic and ethical soldiers are from the outcast groups. Moreover, initiating a pattern that we will see with all the novels of 1948, the work reaches its pinnacle with the murder of the Jewish soldier whose death will hopefully bring other American GIs back to a more ethical stance.

In January 1948, the year of the first wave of Jewish war novels, J. D. Salinger's extraordinary story "A Perfect Day for Bananafish" was published in the *New Yorker*, foreshadowing many of the themes that would arise in the other novels. The tale takes place in a hotel in Miami where Muriel and Seymour Glass are on their honeymoon. (We know all the characters are Jewish because of their names.) While Muriel is painting her nails and unpacking her clothes from Saks Fifth Avenue, Seymour is at the beach playing with a young girl and joining her to look for "bananafish." After their interaction Seymour goes back to the hotel room, pulls out a gun, and blows his head off while Muriel is napping in the bed. For some the story was disturbing not only because of the suicide, but also because Seymour may have been sexually attracted to the young girl as shown by his flirtatious behavior with her and the phallic referencing of "bananafish." I do not think Salinger's intention was to suggest that Seymour kills himself because he is attracted to children. Instead every facet of the story points to the impossible situation of the returning soldier who is trying to reintegrate into a middle-class Jewish world that is shallow, materialistic, and vapid.[60] Seymour is an intellectual young man, a reader of German poetry, who has just lived through a series of horrific campaigns in Europe (as had Salinger himself). He is returning to a Jewish world that is becoming more middle class and less intellectual. In the postwar setting he is utterly and completely lost. Suicide seems to be his only option.

There were also two nonfiction works that were major best sellers before 1948: Marion Hargrove's nonfiction account of his basic training entitled *See Here, Private Hargrove* and Ernie Pyle's collection of war writing, *Brave Men*.

See Here, Private Hargrove was the number one nonfiction best seller of 1942.[61] Marion Hargrove was an editor of the *Charlotte News*, and during the war he sent the paper thrice weekly dispatches about his life in basic training at Fort Bragg, which were compiled together into his 1942 book. The work describes Hargrove's daily life as he undergoes three months of basic training, and ends with the announcement of the attack on Pearl Harbor and the realization by the men at Fort Bragg that the United States is about to enter a deadly serious war. The final scene is of a train pulling out with the soldiers heading off to war and a sergeant yelling after them "Give 'em hell, boys . . . Give 'em hell!" (*See Here, Private Hargrove*, 192).

This extremely popular comedic book offered an interesting take on the Jewish soldier which undoubtedly influenced the novels that would be written a few years later, as well as preparing the mainstream American readership to view Jewish soldiers in positive ways. Three Jewish soldiers are all described quite affectionately, and Hargrove's best friend is a "smart and likeable Jewish boy from Columbus, Ohio" named Maury Sher (101). In fact, as it turns out, Marion Hargrove knows Yiddish and proceeds to teach it to Maury, and he even has a better stock of Jewish jokes:

> We started an acquaintance when I topped all his Jewish jokes
> and began teaching him how to speak Yiddish. I was attracted
> by his native intelligence, his pleasant personality, his sense of
> humor, the similarity of his likes and dislikes to mine. (101)

In fact, Hargrove is so in tune with Jewish culture that he even jokingly calls himself Jewish: "Yeah," I sighed wearily. "And selt gornisht helfen, as we Jewish people say — nothing will help you, Maury, you're a disgrace to the tribe of Israel. They yank you into the Army to make a man of you — and now look at you. A softie" (159). *See Here, Private Hargrove*, read broadly and widely by Jews and non-Jews alike, is narrated by a man so comfortable with all things Jewish that he calls himself one, speaks Yiddish, and has a best friend who is a Jew.[62] It likely helped lay the groundwork with some segments of the American reading public to feel affection for the Jewish soldier and to see him as a true brother in arms, while also instituting the American literary trend of comically describing the war.

Ernie Pyle was one of the most important American war correspondents, whose accounts of life on the front lines were published in all the major American papers and whose 1945 death by Japanese machine gun fire while covering the Pacific campaign solidified his fame as a journalist who put the story above his own personal safety.[63] In 1944 Pyle published *Brave Men* with Henry Holt and it was an instant best seller and remained one through all of 1945 and into the first half of 1946. The title of the book says it all, and is devoted to Pyle's folksy accounts of serving with a number of different "brave men" during the Italian and French campaigns. Published when the war was still well under way in the Pacific, but winding down in Europe, the book's dedication sets the stage that this is a memorial to the heroic men who died fighting for their country: "In solemn salute to those thousands of our comrades — great, brave men that they were — for whom there will be no homecoming, ever."[64]

Embedded with the foot soldiers, Pyle shows the war from their perspectives, recounting all aspects of their daily life both during battle and in the moments of calm. Throughout *Brave Men* Pyle writes up brief biographies on all the men with whom he serves so that the readers will understand that they are typical American men doing brave service for their country. Only rarely does Pyle describe the terror that some men experience in battle. Generally, all the men are from Anglo stock and come from the small towns and cities of middle America. Only in one instance does Pyle describe a couple of "Negro" cooks.[65] Beside that one foray into a multiethnic portrait, the brief biographies do not include descriptions of Jewish or ethnic soldiers. Also, overall the military is drawn in highly positive tones, from the officers who lead wisely and intelligently, to the hospital staff that perform their duties with exemplary professionalism. The book concludes with a call to American readers to remember to respect one another and to be aware that the men who return will be scarred from battle.

When the Jewish war novelists of 1948 composed their novels they were certainly reacting in part to the way Jewish soldiers specifically, and warfare generally, had been depicted in previous American discourse. For instance, in Thomas Heggen's *Mister Roberts* and Ernie Pyle's *Brave Men*, the platoons are almost entirely composed of non-Jewish men. Since in the United States at that time Jews were just over 3 percent of the population, it is possible that neither Heggen nor Pyle intentionally wrote Jews out of the picture, but that both had encountered them only rarely in the military. By contrast, in Jewish-authored novels, this marginal group would become the central one through which the story of the war was told. Another example is that the negative portraits of Jewish soldiers in the novels of Dos Passos and E. E. Cummings would be redrawn into idealized visions of heroic leaders. Or that the positive images of officers in the works of Burns and Pyle would in the case of Norman Mailer and Joseph Heller be redrawn in largely negative ways.

1948

The first wave of Jewish American war novels was published in a year when there were momentous changes in Jewish life worldwide. Foremost was that on May 14, 1948, the State of Israel was established. In America, most Jews and Christians alike viewed the Jewish state with deep pride.[66] In the United States, as well, there were hopeful signs that Jews were becoming accepted into mainstream life. Foremost was the radical decrease in public acts of antisemitism as charted by Leonard Dinnerstein in his seminal study *Anti-Semitism in America*.[67] And the previous year's Academy Award nominations for two movies about antisemitism, *Gentleman's Agreement* and *Crossfire*, showed that leaders of culture viewed antisemitism as a blight that America needed to distance itself from.[68]

Not only was antisemitism becoming taboo, but overt Christian propagandizing was deemed to be against American principles. In March 1948, *McCollum vs. Board of Education* brought the Supreme Court to assert that religious instruction in schools violated the Constitution, effectively meaning that there was no place for Christianity in the public schools. America was proclaiming that it was a pluralistic society with no room for religious discrimination. That year Jewish Americans even created their own nonsectarian Jewish university, Brandeis. In November 1948 the surprise defeat of the Republican Thomas Dewey by the

Democrat Harry Truman, who was overwhelmingly supported by Jewish Americans, seemed a clear sign that Americans in general were supporting liberal principles rather than conservative ones.

Yet there were some troubling signs that Jews still had major battles to face. This was especially evident as Congress debated how many refugees to let into the country from the displaced persons camps where Holocaust survivors were confined. In June, Truman signed into effect the Displaced Persons Act which allowed for 205,000 refugees to be admitted (if they had sponsorship). Even though the number was far too small to match the need, it was still opposed by many congressmen for a range of antisemitic reasons. The upsurge in political antisemitism that was made evident in the opposition to the act reminded Jews of the closed-door policy that had excluded Jewish refugees in the years leading up to and during the Holocaust.[69] This was a real slap in the face to American Jews who thought that things were finally going to change. The disgust is evident in the 1948–49 *American Jewish Year Book*'s description of the "meticulous care taken by the legislators in so framing the Displaced Persons Act of 1948 as to keep to a minimum the number of qualifying Jewish displaced persons."[70]

In 1948 Joshua Bloch, writing his yearly review of Jewish American books for the *Jewish Book Annual*, noted that "our current Jewish literary output, when it does not attempt to escape from it altogether, reflects the acute bewilderment of the contemporary Jew; his frightening loss of direction."[71] For American Jews seeking to comprehend the news of the destruction of Jewish life in Europe, the extremes of loss in Europe and the economic boom in America meant their "bewilderment" was profound. Jewish authors were therefore describing a deep sense of discomfort and confusion at a time when Americans in general were supposed to be buoyant in light of the recent success at war and the booming economy. No wonder Jewish American literature was becoming mainstream: it was tapping into the general fears of the postwar era as men returned from war and sought to integrate their often harrowing experiences into postwar life.

It was a complicated time to be a writer, and some Jewish American authors felt intense pressure to hide their Jewishness, while for others it came into central focus. These competing impulses were personified by Arthur Miller's changing artistic direction after the war. In 1945 he published his first novel, *Focus*, that directly confronted antisemitism in America when the protagonist, the non-Jew Newman, gets new glasses that make him appear to be Jewish.[72] By November 1947, however, five months before he started *Death of a Salesman*, Arthur Miller gave a watershed talk at the "Jewish Committee of Writers, Artists and Scientists" which was republished in March 1948 in the journal *Jewish Life*.[73] In the speech entitled "Concerning Jews Who Write," Miller states that his writing changed once his awareness of antisemitism made him realize "I was a Jew." He then decided to no longer "go on writing about Jews." This radical decision came about because of "Hitler . . . I felt for the first time in my life that I was in danger." Miller added that "I think I gave up [on] the Jews as literary material because I was afraid that even an innocent allusion to the individual wrong-doing of an individual Jew would be inflamed by the atmosphere, ignited by the hatred I was suddenly aware of, and my love would be twisted into a weapon of persecution." Miller thus made the decision to turn "away from the Jews as material for my work." When he published *Death of a Salesman* in 1948, he therefore changed the Jewish family of "Schoenzeit" to the ethnically vague "Millers."[74] Even though Miller distanced himself from a "Jewish" perspective in his work, he, like the authors of the Jewish war novels, was an intellectual who remained true to his prewar liberalism by outwardly challenging the oppressive acts of the anti-Communists.[75]

The year 1948 was therefore a time when American Jews were receiving a confusing range of signs about their role in postwar life. On one side there were positive trends, such as a newfound confidence after having served in a successful war, a large decline in public displays of antisemitism, greater earning power, pride in the establishment of Israel, higher education rates, and social mobility. On the other side were the reactionary forces and latent hostilities that were gaining power, as was evident in the debates over the Displaced Persons Act and the rise of the Red Scare, and tensions about how to continue a liberal ethos in an age of consumerism and the ascendancy of corporate culture.[76] All of these tensions would be evident in the Jewish-authored war novels of 1948.

CHAPTER 2

1948 and the Pacific Theater: *The Naked and the Dead* and *An Act of Love*

I can see where it was possible that a lot of combat men in
Europe did take a certain crude appreciation of the values of
the war, and perhaps if I were in Europe I would have written
a somewhat different novel. But in the Pacific I really think . . .
that there were virtually no positive values and no positive
people.

—NOVEMBER 10, 1948, LETTER FROM NORMAN MAILER

In the Pacific, in contrast to the European theater, the warfare itself
tended to be short bouts of dangerous close combat on subtropical terrain, followed by periods of waiting on bases. Not only did the soldier in
the Pacific battle a Japanese enemy that he had been taught to view as
intent on killing him in the most brutal way possible, but he also had
to fight in a wild jungle landscape filled with deadly insects and malaria, one that was sweltering and difficult to navigate. In war writing,
the physical landscape of the Pacific was therefore drawn as contrasting starkly with Europe, where soldiers found a setting that was familiar:
towns, churches, paved roads, and locals who often knew English. It was
a similar geography to home, although it was Europeanized. In the Pacific, by contrast, the terrain was shown as being utterly foreign: fecund
and primal and overgrown; the locals were "exotic primitives" in tune
with nature and considered "childlike"; there were no symbols of "civili-

zation" such as schools, houses of worship, and shops. In Pacific-set war novels, the landscape therefore takes on its own life as a primitive and deadly force at battle with the modern American war machine.

For Jewish servicemen in the Pacific, Jewishness did not take on the elevated status that it did for those serving in Europe who were confronting Nazis who wanted to kill Jews.[1] The Pacific war, therefore, could be seen as an anarchic force of destruction, and to write about it meant employing dark and harsh tones. Norman Mailer's novel *The Naked and the Dead*, then, would resonate with World War I novels that depicted warfare as a deadly, all-consuming machine, rather than how it would be portrayed in the European-set novels as a force for good against an evil regime.

When it was published in early 1948, *The Naked and the Dead* was hailed as "THE novel of our War"[2] and it is still considered a groundbreaking and seminal work of war literature. The novel challenges the notion that war is a noble event conducted by heroic Anglos, instead showing it to be a dirty and nasty business which can only be described by subversively using coarse language.[3] In order to convey the vulgar talk of soldiers (and to avoid possible obscenity charges), Mailer used "fug" throughout the book in place of "fuck."[4] Nevertheless, readers got the picture, as we see in Raymond Rosenthal's 1948 review in *Commentary*:

> *The Naked and the Dead* can be regarded as the inevitable reaction to the pallid, neatly trimmed literary commodities turned out by the graduates of *Yank, Stars and Stripes*, and *OWI*. It is the exposing of the Army's underside, the sewer of hostility and fear and petty annoyance and boredom that until now has been either covered up by banalities or avoided altogether.[5]

Mailer's novel thus refutes idealized portraits of battle which negate the gritty, horrible realities of military service.

By placing his Jewish characters into a "broader America" of the platoon, Mailer's novel explores how minority groups respond to and are treated by those outside the context of their own ethnic enclaves. The World War I novels of Hemingway, Dos Passos, and Cummings had drawn the Anglo protagonists, and in particular working-class GIs, in positive and heroic ways. In *The Naked and the Dead*, by contrast, they are often depicted in negative ways, while the ethnic characters often take on much more positive attributes.[6] Moreover, Mailer shows that the interactions between the non-Jews and the ethnic soldiers are often fraught with bad feelings and that Jews, Mexicans, homosexuals, and other minorities often become the whipping boys for stressed-out members of the military. Mailer, like other Jewish authors, was able to expose the negative aspects of service because he had experienced firsthand the antisemitism prevalent both among the enlisted men and in the officer corps. Having returned home to discover that Americans were now increasingly uncomfortable with public displays of antisemitism, he had little to fear by documenting the many ugly aspects of the American military.

The Naked and the Dead also exposes how the officers enabled the proliferation of "chickenshit," as Paul Fussell labeled it, the innumerable, petty rules that wore out enlistees and which were the domain of small-minded officers seeking anything with which to chastise their men. As Fussell noted, "the literature of chickenshit is extensive, and not surprisingly, since so many authors-to-be were, in the services, precisely the types that are chickenshit's external targets, bright Jewish boys like Norman Mailer and Joseph Heller."[7]

Using the type of naturalism made popular by James Farrell and John Dos Passos, The Naked and the Dead describes war through a chorus of voices that represent a vast array of American 'types': the racist redneck, the Mexican with broken English, the physically weak Jewish intellectual.[8] Mailer's book paints a damaged portrait of America as the opposite of the idealized "melting pot": here we see platoons that are not unified but are riddled with petty hatreds.

To showcase the range of men, Mailer creates an extraordinarily varied template of colloquial speech where each man talks and is described with a voice that imparts where he comes from, his race, and his general attitude. This multiplicity of narratives is further exemplified in each of the "Time Machine" chapters that work like short-story templates of each main character. The "Time Machines" are a literary tour de force, an "anthology of literary echoes," where Mailer takes up narrative styles straight out of Dos Passos, James Farrell, Herman Melville, and others.[9] These chapters depict individuals as being profoundly influenced by their ethnic and social class. Like Mailer himself, whose family was deeply affected by the Great Depression, most of the men are weary or permanently broken from having undergone those difficult years.[10]

Mailer's masterful use of a range of voices means that the characters become known to the readers in a variety of ways: how they act in battle, how others describe them in their own voices, how they speak with others, how they conduct their internal dialogues, how the narrator describes them. For instance, the "Time Machine" for the tough he-man, Sam Croft, begins with a nickname that establishes his character type as "The Hunter." It then follows with an external, third-person physical description of Croft that shows how he always aims to seem big: "A lean man of medium height but he held himself so erectly he appeared tall." This is followed by a third-person description of Croft's psychological bearing: "he was efficient and strong and usually empty and his main cast of mind was a superior contempt toward nearly all other men. He hated weakness and he loved practically nothing." Then in order to draw a full-sided portrait of Croft, the narrative voice switches again to a chatty discussion: "Why is Croft that way? Oh, there are answers. He is that way because of the corruption-of-the-society. He is that way because the devil has claimed him for one of his own." After delving into some of the reasons for Croft's toughness, suddenly the narrative voice switches again to a sketch of Croft as a boy hunting that fluctuates between third-person descriptions of him in the forest looking for a deer, and Croft's internal voice that highlights his country roots: "Ah'm fugged if Ah'll wait for any ole deer. Ah'm gonna track 'em." This is followed by ruminations about "The Education of Sam Croft" or, in other words, how he became such a hard and mean adult, which brings up other episodes in Croft's prewar life such as "It ended with him going to town alone, and taking a whore when he was drunk, beating her sometimes with a wordless choler" (*Naked and the Dead*, 162). The "Time Machine" concludes with a list that seeks to account for how Croft became so tough and which enters Croft's mind to have him also seek to explain it:

> His ancestors pushed and labored and strained, drove their
> oxen, sweated their women, and moved a thousand miles.
> He pushed and labored inside himself and smoldered with
> an endless hatred.
> (You're all a bunch of fuggin whores)
> (You're all a bunch of dogs)

(You're all deer to track)
I HATE EVERYTHING WHICH IS NOT IN
MYSELF. (164)

The chapter therefore imparts who Croft is by using a vast range of narrative voices to depict Croft from a multiplicity of angles and temporal locations. He is the product of his childhood, where he lived, his internal psychology, the racism he learned while young. Nothing is wasted in Mailer's rendition, and the hunt for the deer which opens the chapter is brought up at the end to describe Croft's warrior stance. Remarkably, Mailer does this with all the main characters in the book.

Mailer's adept and assured choreography of an extensive range of narrative types in *The Naked and the Dead* gives a kaleidoscopic portrait of the landscape of the battlefield in two ways. First, we get a full portrait of *individual soldiers* in each "Time Machine" chapter with its tour de force of narrative voices that describes the men: first- and third-person descriptions, internal and external evocations, spoken words, internal speech, colloquial speech, chatty questions put forth by the narrator, descriptive imagery. Second, we get a full picture of *war*: landscape descriptions of the island, kaleidoscopic "Time Machines" showing the men in a range of ways, accounts of dialogues between the men where they each speak in a colloquial manner, internal descriptions of the men's fears, biographical flashbacks, real-time moments of terror. The book's encyclopedic structure therein aims to render the full scope of the internal and external world of soldiers while also showcasing an entire generation of young American men.

As the narrative fluctuates between intense and horrific battle scenes and small moments in daily life, it depicts the psychological reality of war as that of abrupt shifts between serious and mundane moments. The portrait of the battlefield is unrelentingly disturbing. In one of many shocking scenes, Croft shoots a defenseless Japanese captive in the head, a war crime, in part to toughen up his men who have felt empathy toward the captive after he showed them pictures of his children. Mailer subverts the ideal of the heroic soldier in a range of ways, showing him to act inhumanely or at times to cry or wet himself from fear.

The Naked and the Dead describes the battle for the imaginary Japanese-held Pacific island of Anopopei. The first section of the book is about an American counterattack on the Japanese-held island where the enemy is deadly yet nearly invisible. The soldiers are divided by class lines: the racist and corrupt General Cummings who "controls everything" (85); officers who rule their men with terrifying and often selfish determination; and foot soldiers who hold no real power over the life and death decisions being made about them. The lush island is its own presence: a fertile landscape that readily hides the enemy and that is riddled with the corpses of the dead. Showing the violence and decay of the battlefield, Mailer also offers extremely lyrical descriptions that imbue the terrible backdrop with a dark and haunting beauty:

> The foliage of the jungle was churning turbulently, and the leaden-green sky painted it with greens so varied and brilliant that Ridges thought it looked like the Garden of Eden. He felt the throbbing of the jungle as a part of himself, the earth, which had turned to a golden mud, seemed alive to him. He kept looking at the fantastic green of the jungle and then at the orange-brown earth, febrile and pulsing as though the rain were cutting wounds into it. (97)

The second part of the novel shifts from a general portrait of the invading Americans to an account of a single reconnaissance mission's terrifying foray into the jungle overrun by the Japanese, in order to see if the island can be attacked on its south side. Mailer based the account in part on an eight-day patrol he had heard about while serving in the Philippines.[11] In contrast with *The Naked and the Dead*, in Mailer's actual war experience, the "recons" were always searching for, but never finding, Japanese soldiers.[12] In *The Naked and the Dead*, however, the recon patrol is deadly serious and committed to its mission, and the Japanese are everywhere and dangerous.

When the account moves to the reconnaissance squad, the narrative focuses more intensely on a small group of men. The squad is led by the most even-tempered, insightful, and intelligent character in the book, Lieutenant Hearn. Hearn, like Mailer himself, attended Harvard, where he loved taking English classes. At Harvard, Hearn became aware that he had transformed from a Midwestern upper-class WASP into a Jew of sorts: "As he passes a store front, he stares at himself for a moment, regarding his dark hair and hooked blunted nose. I look more like a Jew-boy than a Midwestern scion" (343). Hearn became Judaized through his education, where he developed liberal sympathies that put him in opposition to the conservative, wealthy WASPs with whom he was raised. Hearn, the WASP who has turned into a Jew, is a liberal who dislikes the offhand racism of his soldiers, and seeks to be a fair leader. However, he also flip-flops easily and lacks the backbone of Cummings and Croft. Hearn represents the younger officer as tolerant and even-handed, if weak, in stark contrast to his nemesis, the career soldier General Cummings, who is autocratic, deeply racist, antisemitic, and snobby.

As Nigel Leigh correctly points out, Mailer is making Hearn, the character with whom he has the deepest sympathies, a hidden Jew who is both an insider and an outsider to the surrounding culture.[13] Hearn can act like Mailer's vision of a Jew — having liberal sympathies, a deep sense of fairness, and a dislike of racism — while at the same time being an all-American Anglo hero. Whether or not it was intentional on Mailer's part, it may have been easier for his general readers to relate to an Anglo liberal than a Jewish one. Hearn is a "crypto-Jew" in contrast to the overtly Jewish characters Roth and Goldstein, who at times become ethnic caricatures and whose background defines them. Hearn, instead, can move around freely and take up different personas since he is not weighed down by any single one.

Yet in the end, Hearn's hidden identity cannot be sustained, and he is killed off quite suddenly by the combined malice of the two most aggressive WASP warriors in the book, Cummings who sends him out on the "recon" patrol because he ignores Cummings's homosexual advances and is not properly deferential, and Croft, who tricks him into a suicidal mission. The three American and two Japanese deaths brought about by the mission are pointless, and Hearn, who had been against the patrol in the first place, had been correct to try and bring the group home.

Even though issues of Jewishness pervade the entire text, almost no critics have discussed this.[14] Antisemitism (and racism) are everywhere and anti-Jewish comments are a constant chorus from the opening onward as when we are first introduced to the Irish Catholic Gallagher: "He looked at one of the orderlies, Levy, who was shuffling the cards, and Gallagher's throat worked. That Jew had been having a lot of goddam luck, and suddenly his bitterness changed into rage" (6). In *The Naked and the Dead* it is clear that Jewish soldiers are considered by the others to be (barely) a notch above African Americans, and certainly it is acceptable to despise and discriminate against them.

Mailer depicts the catastrophic effect of antisemitism on Jewish servicemen in the central characters, Roth and Goldstein. Mailer's portrait of Roth often falls into disturbing caricatures about Jews such as: "a small man with an oddly hunched back and long arms. Everything about him seemed to droop; he had a long dejected nose and pouches under his eyes; his shoulders slumped forward" (52). Yet while Roth and Goldstein evince traditionally negative Jewish stereotypical traits, such as fearfulness and a lack of physical adeptness, they also have a range of qualities that are positive in comparison to some of the brutal warriors with whom they serve: extreme empathy, intellectualism, an attempt to be fair and honest. Moreover, nearly alone of all of the characters, Roth and Goldstein have loving wives and good stable families to whom they want to return. By contrast, for the non-Jewish soldiers, women are viewed as those "they abuse and who abuse them."[15]

Roth and Goldstein are not clones but come from different life situations and have different perspectives on life: Roth is educated, agnostic, pessimistic, snobby, tends to see the worst in situations, and views himself as an American first and a Jew second. (Mailer's closest friend in service commented that "Mailer had put more than a little of himself into" Roth.)[16] Goldstein is working class, religious, always tries to put a positive spin on things, and is desirous of ingratiating himself with everyone by wearing his "stupid outsider grin" (485). Goldstein's attempts to always try to please the Christians are based on an upbringing where Goldstein's grandfather stressed that antisemitism was permanent and even "this America is not so different. They beat you because you're a Jew" (482). By being ingratiating he aims to deflect any hatred. Goldstein tries to build strong friendships, but discovers in the army that this does not always work because for many he is first a Jew:

> "Aw, shut up, ya dumb Jew bastard." Stanley spoke with fury.
> "You can't say that to me," Goldstein piped. He was quivering
> with anger now too, but back of it was the shattering realization
> that Stanley had been so friendly the night before. You can't trust

any of them, he thought with a certain bitter pleasure. At least this time, he was certain. (626)

Roth and Goldstein's friendship reflects the complicated reality of war service for Jews. Although they immediately recognize one another as fellow Jews that they can rely on, they also feel anxiety that the other one will do something to cast blame on all the Jewish soldiers. Or as Goldstein states: "he was always chagrined that Roth was Jewish, for he felt he would give a bad impression to Gentiles" (477). Once in battle, and for the first time living and working with Christians, both characters must directly confront what it means to be a Jewish American man. Their first conversation together awkwardly addresses the antisemitism they are facing. Of war service, Goldstein says: "Aaah, I don't know, they're just a bunch of Anti-Semiten." "Who, the Germans?" [asks Roth]. "Goldstein didn't answer right away. . . . 'Yes.' " (53). Dealing with the constant antisemitism in the military is harder than battling the Japanese, since their fellow soldiers often treat them worse than the enemy. After an antisemitic taunt by Gallagher, Mailer describes Goldstein's reaction:

> Goldstein was still quivering. His sense of shame was so intense that a few tears welled in his eyes . . . for Gallagher's words had pitched Goldstein so taut that he needed some issue desperately now. He was certain, however, that he would start weeping with rage if he opened his mouth, and so he remained silent, trying to calm himself. (128)

Both Roth and Goldstein lose their innocence about the American dream and become weaker: "[Goldstein] was changing. He realized it suddenly. His confidence was gone, and he wasn't sure of himself" (206).

For Roth, the intellectual with the college education who sees himself as "modern" and "agnostic" and not very Jewish, it is a shock to discover that in the army his deepest friendship is with the religious, uneducated Goldstein:

> Goldstein was a kindred soul, a friend. Roth sighed. He supposed a Jew always had to go to a fellow Jew to find understanding.

The thought depressed him. Why should things be that way? He was a college graduate, educated, far above nearly all the men here, and what good did it do him? The only man he could find who was worth talking to sounded a little like an old Jew with a beard. (57)

War service has had a leveling effect on Roth who believed himself to be modern and educated, causing him to realize that when thrust into the broader America of the armed services, his ethnicity overrode everything and he was first and foremost a Jew. The United States, perhaps, is not the land of limitless reinvention where anyone can fulfill their dreams.

Mailer's portraits of Roth and Goldstein give readers a full expression of the complex questions faced by Jewish American soldiers: How to live and work with fellow soldiers who can be antisemitic? How to be friends with members of one's platoon when they come from vastly different cultural worlds? How to confront antisemitism — is it better to ignore it for troop unity or to fight back? What is the relationship between Jews and other ethnic groups, such as Mexican Americans? How does one define positive masculinity, when one's culture stresses intellectualism, and American culture instead stresses physicality?

Roth and Goldstein seek different answers to these questions about how they can fit into combat culture, and Roth ends up making a catastrophic choice. During the reconnaissance patrol he is continually belittled by Gallagher for being a weak Jew. Roth, who is highly sensitive, finally breaks. After being chastised for being too cowardly to leap across a large crevice, he jumps it to prove to the others that he is not a weak Jew but a tough soldier (666). It is a suicidal jump and he falls into the crevice and dies. The pressure placed upon him as a Jewish soldier is too much to bear, and he takes a symbolic last stand that kills him. Although he brings on his death by a suicidal jump, the end result is that, like Jesus, he is sacrificed for the humanity of the platoon, and soon thereafter, they turn back from their patrol.

Goldstein, by contrast, seeks out a completely different solution. Where Roth kills himself by becoming the symbolic tough guy, Goldstein instead is saved through his friendship with a fellow soldier. The final section of the book shows Goldstein becoming good friends with the poor Arkansas farmer Ridges as they both struggle to carry the body of their comrade, Wilson, back to base. It is a sort of religious fellowship that grows between the two men; a spiritual quest for meaning that arises while burdened with the body.[17] The scene also resonates with Faulkner's *As I Lay Dying*, as Mailer wrote in a March 8, 1946, letter where he said of the scene that "I want to be Faulknerian the soldier wounded and then dead becomes a burden that they couldn't leave, an albatross."[18]

As they make their way, both ruminate on their tough backgrounds: Ridges's family barely survived the Depression, and Goldstein as a Jew has the burden of the "gas chambers" on him: "All the suffering of the Jews came to nothing . . . All the ghettos, all the soul cripplings, all the massacres and pogroms, the gas chambers, lime kilns — all of it touched no one, all of it was lost" (682). For the Jewish soldier in the Pacific, he suffers a particular type of frustration at not being in the European campaign where he can fight the Nazis. This is the only time in the novel that the Holocaust casts a shadow over the events in the Pacific. Although the Holocaust is occurring over there in Europe, here in the Pacific Jewish soldiers still have to deal with being despised for being a Jew. The constant chorus of antisemitism in *The Naked and the Dead* is therefore a reminder to readers that the type of hatred inspiring the Nazis is also found in some segments of the American population. This is not to say that the antisemitic soldiers in Mailer's work are as evil as Nazis. Rather, as he portrays it, they are stuck in an outdated way of relating to others, and in order to realize their full potential as Americans they need to discard their hatreds.

As the two men bond to one another during the difficult passage back, Mailer shows that the poor rural non-Jew and the urban Jew have found through war that they have much in common and that they are true brothers. This matches Mailer's own experience where his best friend was also a working-class Protestant from Arkansas, Francis Irby Gwaltney.[19] Mailer attempts to show that the friendship between Goldstein and Ridges, like his own with Gwaltney, is an effective means of fighting antisemitism, since in Mailer's case Gwaltney stood up for him against the Jew haters.

Mailer, who was writing a war novel about a vast range of Americans, and who never evinced much interest in "Jewish" themes, creates here a remarkable, moving account of the difficulties of being an American Jew during World War II. Roth and Goldstein paradoxically were the last characters in Mailer's corpus of work who addressed head-on the topic of Jewish life in America.[20]

It is important to note that Roth and Goldstein were composites of Mailer's first "best friend" in the military, Meyer Marotznik, with whom Mailer served in training camp in both Fort Upton and at Fort Bragg.[21] In letters from training camp, Mailer was clearly intrigued with Meyer, and wrote constantly about him, even sharing with his wife Bea Meyer's full biography.[22] The amount of time he spends discussing Meyer in his letters suggests that Meyer was intended as a character study that Mailer planned to use later in his great American novel.

Goldstein and Meyer are similar family men with young children. Moreover, like Goldstein, Meyer is a "shy, gangling youth"[23] who is one of "these extremely good hearted generous guys."[24] And like Goldstein too, Meyer is "strictly old-country Jew."[25] Yet it is Roth who receives the most important aspects of Meyer, since Roth's suicidal leap is based directly on an incident that occurred with Meyer at Fort Bragg which Mailer described in detail in an April 26, 1944, letter to Bea. Meyer, who was physically unfit and had a bad knee, was continually the victim of abuse by their drill sergeant, and like Roth, he finally broke:

> When the Sergeant would read the roll call he would spit out Marotznik as if it were foreign and distasteful to him. Meyer took his riding quietly and painfully, his face containing so many sorrows as he walked along . . . This kept going on and on. Each day would come a few more turns of the screw, and Meyer's knee was no better than it had been a week ago. Yesterday we went over the obstacle course for the first time, and Meyer tried to follow along . . . At one obstacle you had to climb a nine foot fence and then jump into a pit. Meyer halted before it and looked rather dubious. The Sergeant gave his tight little sneer and said to Meyer, "Do you think you can do it Marotznik?" Meyer, without saying a word, climbed up, poised at the summit, and jumped. He couldn't land on his bad leg so he took the entire shock on his good one, so slim and frail. The damn thing crumbled under him, and he lay on the ground almost unconscious. The Sergeant rushed up worried, because it looked as if Meyer had broken his leg. "My God, man, why did you jump? Who told you

to? I didn't mean you should," the Sergeant said. Meyer didn't answer. He opened his tired eyes for a moment and smiled, the wise Jew smile at having confounded the Goy, shown him something he didn't know. Later he got up and crawled at a minutely small pace, his right knee wrenched, his left ankle sprained. But victorious.[26]

In Meyer's case, he jumps the fence as a means to enact revenge on the antisemite and survives the leap to enjoy the pleasure of his brave but foolish act. In the novel, Roth also jumps in response to the belittling of an antisemite, but there is no chance of enjoying his revenge since he dies. So while clearly impressed by Meyer's act, to have let Roth live would not have imparted the dramatic elements necessary to make it a major turning point in the narrative. Mailer therefore changes him into the neurotic, secular Jew Roth who lacks faith and the "old-country" ethos of Meyer/Goldstein and leaps a much wider crevice. By so doing, the event takes on Christological elements as the death brings on the redemption of others, particularly Gallagher, who becomes a better man afterwards. In the battlefield, where actions have larger ramifications and dangers are more intense than in training camp where Meyer's leap took place, Roth's suicidal jump becomes a symbol of all Jews whose lives are sacrificed by antisemites.

In *The Naked and the Dead*, there is a third ethnic character who struggles in the platoon: Martinez. Like so many other characters in the novel, Martinez was also based directly on a soldier, also called Martinez, with whom Mailer served in the Philippines. As in the novel, the real-life Martinez was always out to prove himself, and according to Mailer, even though Martinez hated it and it terrified him profoundly, nevertheless he "always picked himself to lead the most dangerous patrols."[27] Where Mailer's letters about Martinez do not mention race hatred, in Mailer's literary portrayal it is articulated as the main motivating factor for Martinez's heroism.

In Martinez's "Time Machine" we see this when he asks: "What can a Mexican boy do in San Antone? He can be counterman in hash house; he can be bellhop; he can pick cotton in season; he can start store; but he cannot be a doctor, a lawyer, big merchant, chief" (65). For Mexicans, according to Mailer's novel, the military is the one and only place they can succeed and become heroes, even if it leaves them feeling profoundly insecure:

> Martinez made sergeant. Little Mexican boys also breathe the American fables. If they cannot be aviators or financiers or officers they can still be heroes. No need to stumble over pebbles and search the Texas sky. Any man jack can be a hero. Only that does not make you white Protestant, firm and aloof. (67)

Throughout the book Martinez, like Roth and Goldstein, continually struggles to prove himself to the non-Jewish soldiers. While all three are emphatically patriotic and see their home as a "beautiful country" with "lots of opportunity" (450), in military service they are made to feel extremely insecure about being outsiders: "Goldstein was self-conscious when he saw himself as a Jew talking to a Gentile; then every action, every word, was dictated to a great extent by his desire to make a good impression" (451). Or as Martinez describes it, "And as he looked into Croft's cold blue eyes he felt the same inadequacy and shabbiness, the same inferiority he always knew when he talked to . . . to White Protestant" (691).

Martinez's fear of being seen as a cowardly Mexican even causes him to risk his life. In this case he attacks a Japanese soldier with a knife:

> He became conscious of the knife in his hand again. "Never trust a goddam Mex when he's got a knife." It spilled into his mind, a long-concealed fragment from a conversation he had heard between two Texans, and he felt a choked resentment. Goddam lie, and then it was lost in the realization of what he had to do. He swallowed. He had never felt so numb in all his life. (595)

This was based on a real incident Mailer wrote about to Bea when Martinez "tracked down a straggler Jap and killed him in a creek bed."[28] After the killing, the real-life Martinez was haunted and that night: "he shivered and got drunk and was moody, and said once 'I see his face, too damn much.' And then after a while, in his slow speech, as he translated from the Spanish in which he thought, 'It's no good to kill a man.'" In the novel, Martinez falls immediately to sleep the night of the killing and does not suffer like the real Martinez over the death. Instead he views the killing as something that can potentially bring him recognition for his heroism.

In order to gain any respect, all three ethnic soldiers therefore have to work twice as hard, and risk their lives twice as much, as the other combatants. As Mailer portrays it, the choices for minority combatants were extremely limited. Either they could harden up and shed their ethnic characteristics to mimic the macho culture of the fellow soldiers, or, like Goldstein they could seek out friendships with non-Jews. In neither case, however, did the soldier have the option simply to be himself. He had to change in order to survive. Yet, in Goldstein's case, by so doing he opens himself up to a broader world. I do not believe that Mailer is calling for Jews to assimilate, but rather he is stressing that war has taught Jewish Americans that there are good aspects to building friendships with non-Jews. This matches with Mailer's personal belief that hatred could only be overcome when racists got to know and work with the groups they despised and discovered that they were men just like them.[29] It does not mean that after the war Goldstein will be any less "Jewish" in thought or behavior, but that he will, for the first time, have gotten to know some Americans beyond the small world of his own ethnic enclave. For Mailer, this is certainly positive: a platoon throws together a range of Americans (except for African Americans) who must find a way to live together. The result is a deeper understanding of what it means to be part of the broader multiethnic American community. This, in turn, ideally makes the soldiers have greater compassion since the "other" is now a brother in arms. It is a fine lesson to postwar readers that they need to embrace the liberal ethos of equality for all in a pluralistic society.

Mailer uses the novel's "Time Machine" chapters to depict the haters as complex individuals with a range of positive characteristics. These chapters teach Mailer's readers that they too can shed their old prejudices, as shown emblematically with the most hate-filled character in the book, the Boston Irishman Gallagher, whose loathing of the Jews is longstanding, deep, and central to what defines him. In his "Time Machine" we learn that he beat up Jews in Boston as part of an Irish Catholic gang, and that he sold magazines and marched in support of the infamous antisemitic and racist activist, Father Coughlin. Gallagher's hatred resurfaces in the war when he blames the untimely death of his wife on the Jewish doctor who was treating her, asserting that "the Yid killed her" (265). Although Gallagher is a rabid antisemite, he also evinces deep love for his dead wife. At one and the same time, he comes off as a hateful and sympathetic figure, traumatized by the death of his spouse, but who responds to it by becoming even more antisemitic. Yet through the course of the novel he becomes more humane, and even Goldstein, who has been the brunt of much of his hatred, feels sorry for Gallagher when he shows a trace of humanity after his wife's death. In response to Goldstein's expression of sympathy, Gallagher, for a fleeting moment, is moved to like Goldstein.

Why was Mailer rendering the all-pervading antisemitism of the military while at the same time trying to make the antisemites into human and even pitiable characters? Foremost, I believe, it was his attempt, on a very personal level, to try and understand what makes people hate Jews, and to generate a complex portrait of the root causes of antisemitism. Also, by having the Jewish characters in the end evince empathy for the antisemites, it may have reflected his own transformation during the war when Mailer became close to fellow Christian combatants, and it was therefore a call to readers to move on from their own hatreds. It may as well have been a mechanism to downplay or lessen the impact of the constant antisemitism that Mailer depicts in the armed services by making the antisemitic characters have sympathetic aspects. A non-Jewish readership would potentially be more likely to take the bad (the antisemitism) with the good (even bigots have positive aspects); the sugar with the medicine. Overall, Mailer is seeking to account for the pervasiveness of antisemitism in America and in the military, and to unpack the psychology of the victimizer and turn him from a bogeyman into a human so that postwar readers would understand that it was now time to embrace a new, broader vision of brotherhood.

Mailer's novel also grapples with the macho culture of non-Jewish American men. In the "Time Machine" accounts of the soldiers, Mailer becomes an outsider looking in on a society he does not really understand, as was the case when he served with the Texas platoon. As Mailer describes it, rednecks are schooled from childhood to hate "the other": women, blacks, Jews. Having served with the hardened men of Platoon 112, Mailer uses his book to try and break down their facades and see what is inside the men he went to war with.

The Naked and the Dead concludes with the brief section entitled "Mute Chorus: On What to Do When We Get Out" where members of the platoon ruminate on what they will do when they get home. Typically, the non-Jewish soldiers think about getting drunk, catching their wives cheating, and fighting with civilians. For Goldstein, by contrast, the return home will mean a loving reunion with his wife Natalie, while for Martinez he will get to see his family, go to church, and hang out with girls. Although facing constant antisemitism and racism in the military, in the end, the Jew and the Mexican display that they are of superior cultural stock to the non-Jews: they are peaceful men seeking out the ties of family and community rather than fighting, drinking, and whoring.[30] The war has not broken either Martinez or Goldstein, and both have come out of it transformed, but not into the brutal, hate-filled warrior types of Croft and Gallagher.

How does a focus on the Jewish aspects of the text assist our understanding of the novel? The topic of Jewishness is evident in manifold ways in the novel. (1) A large amount of the book is devoted to two of the central characters' explorations of what it means to be a Jew in the military. (2) Antisemitic statements arise throughout the work. (3) The turning point of the action occurs after the Jewish soldier dies. To neglect the topic is therefore to overlook the major theme of what it means to be a Jewish American soldier and how Mailer's portrayal of it served certain ideological aims.

Mailer's focus on Jewishness also helps us to understand much of the book's preoccupation with what makes a man and a warrior. For an intellectual of small stature, questions of maleness, of toughness, were a central focus of Mailer's life, and his novel explores them from a range of perspectives that demarcate the complexities of the topic. It is his Jewish soldiers who embody the contradictory nature of masculinity, who suffer fears and doubts while aiming to appear tough, and they are positioned in opposition to figures like Gallagher who are masculine he-men. Much of Gallagher's machismo is predicated on his antisemitic posturing, which makes him into a hateful and scary man. If he discarded his prejudices, his hyper-masculinity would be tempered and he would be a deeper, more well-rounded man.

Mailer's complex renderings of masculinity divided critics about whether or not the warrior Croft was the "positive" male or whether instead it was the intellectual Hearn.[31] In the novel there is no simple answer to this; instead we see a very complicated understanding of masculinity, where the warrior and the intellectual both have good and bad traits. The positive aspects of the warrior are his steady focus, his ability to act, and his fearlessness, while for the intellectual it is his fairness, his ability to think things through, and his capacity for empathy. The negative aspects of the warrior are his lack of compassion, his selfish motivations, and his inability to admit wrong, while for the intellectual it is his flip-flopping, his lack of determination, and his propensity to overthink things. In the end, both Croft and Hearn lose because they are flawed: Hearn dies and Croft gives up on his mission. By contrast, Goldstein learns to create a better balance and survives to return to his beloved wife.

The Naked and the Dead uses the portraits of the platoon members generally, and the Jewish soldiers particularly, to teach readers that they must disavow their prewar prejudices or be stuck in the ugly mode of Gallagher before his transformation. Like Gallagher, all Americans must purge themselves of their racist impulses in order to move forward to assert a new brotherhood between all men, as exemplified by the friendship between the uber-Jew Goldstein and the uber-Gentile Ridges. By employing a complex and varied polyphonic structure, encyclopedic in nature, Mailer presents to his readers a multifaceted portrait of war that delineates how combatants must confront and reevaluate what it means to be a man and an American.

Ira Wolfert: *An Act of Love*

Where Mailer's novel was published at the beginning of 1948, Ira Wolfert's Pacific-set *An Act of Love* became a best seller late in December, leading it to be negatively compared to Mailer's much admired work.[32] Wolfert (1908–1997) was a major war correspondent who used a poetic prose style to convey the intensity of the war experience. For instance, in a dispatch he penned for the Associated Press about the fight for Guadalcanal, he wrote: "This is no banana war involving the potting of Japanese killers from trees. The prolonged Japanese effort to break the American toehold is continuing daily with their familiar tempo, but the Japanese are paying dearly for their ambitions."[33] Wolfert won the 1943 Pulitzer

Prize for three articles on the fight for Guadalcanal.[34] That year he also published the popular and critically successful novel about corporate greed during the Depression, *Tucker's People*, that was turned into the film *Force of Evil* for which he wrote the screenplay.

Wolfert was never happy with *An Act of Love*, perhaps because it was savaged by the critics.[35] Wolfert rewrote the book twice with minor changes, in 1954 and 1955.[36] The central protagonist is a Jewish soldier, Harry Bruner, who through the course of the novel realizes that he needs to stop defining himself as a minority member who must ingratiate himself into the larger majority culture, and instead become a full member of the larger world entitled to act for the benefit of mankind.

Ira Wolfert was raised in Manhattan by working-class immigrant Latvian Jews, and he worked his way through Columbia University's School of Journalism. While a student he married the poet Helen Herschdorfer, and they remained together until her death sixty-nine years later. During the 1920s and 1930s, Wolfert, like many New York Jews, was attracted to political radicalism and Communism, and his Communist beliefs are evident in the ideology underpinning *An Act of Love*. In the 1930s, Wolfert worked at the Berlin office of the *New York Post* where he experienced the rise of Nazism in Germany. Wolfert wrote three best-selling works about the Pacific campaign, all based on his firsthand experiences there as a journalist. In the 1950s, he was deemed to be a Communist-by-association by the House Un-American Activities Committee. Throughout the rest of his life, Wolfert wrote stories and essays, mostly for the *Reader's Digest*, as well as a third novel, *Married Men* (1953).

As with Norman Mailer's *The Naked and the Dead*, *An Act of Love* covers the battle between the Japanese and Americans for an imaginary South Pacific island, in this case called Templedor, during the final stages of the war. Where Mailer's novel revolves around a group of Americans, in Wolfert's work everything centers on events in the life of Harry Bruner, a 25-year-old Jewish lawyer from Newark, New Jersey. Unlike Mailer, who uses a remarkable range of narrative voices to evoke the battlefield, Wolfert relies on a more traditional third-person narrative form where the events are described by an unknown, omniscient narrator. Yet although Wolfert is employing a more standard structure, his writing has moments of beauty and depth that evoke the terror of war, as in this account of a shell exploding:

The pity hung in Harry and swayed. Thought flew through it like squashed birds blowing. Perceptions like bullets, emotions like screams, intuitions, instincts — they all pelted the spumy shape of the pity in him. But nothing shook it, nothing moved it, nothing changed it, and the noise of the guns shook his head and stung his feet and twisted at his knees and made his tongue flop up heavily and float down softly in his mouth. (148)

Since *An Act of Love* focuses on the story of a main protagonist, Harry Bruner, rather than the chorus of Mailer's novel, the war is imparted through the singular account of Harry's experiences and the psychological and spiritual mark they make upon him. Harry therefore becomes the stand-in for all men who enlist and then suffer in battle and at the end find a way to resolve and understand what they have gone through. For this reason, the account is delivered in a traditional linear manner rather than jumping around in time as occurs in Mailer's novel.

Harry Bruner is serving as a U.S. Navy pilot in the reserve, and at the start of the novel he is the sole survivor of 836 men in the Japanese sinking of the *Minot* warship. Lying nearly dead on the beach, his ripped-up leg infested with maggots, we learn through a series of flashbacks that he spent days at sea floating in shark-infested waters. Washed ashore, barely alive, Harry is rescued by a group of Solomon Island natives who nurse him back to health. At the same time that Harry is trying to live like a native, the war is a constant rumble in the distance, reminding him that if he remains with the natives he will face desertion charges. Once he has fully recovered, Harry leaves them to live with an expatriate American farming family, the Andersens, where he falls in love with their nineteen-year-old daughter, Julia. Harry stays with them for many months until the Americans send a reconnaissance mission to the island in preparation for an invasion, and Harry goes to rejoin the Americans.

In the final section of the book, Harry undertakes a terrifying mission into the jungle to try and root out the Japanese. He acts heroically, staying to try and find an American major who has disappeared, rather than rescuing himself by turning back. When he finds the major's corpse next to that of a Japanese soldier, Harry realizes that the major killed the last Japanese holdout and the battle is over. In an act symbolizing Harry's new faith in a universal humanity, he secretly buries the two together under a sign that reads "Here Lies Major Munday & His Bro. in Arms Who Was Known Only in Love" (*An Act of Love*, 544). The novel ends with the Americans winning, the Japanese retreating, and Harry and Julia reuniting. The universalist credo that all men are essentially brothers regardless of the their ethnic or national differences, which is the central message of the book, and was undoubtedly rooted in Wolfert's own earlier embrace of Communism, is the winning message.

During the course of the novel Harry searches to understand himself, his Jewishness, his view of war and love, and his relationship with the broader world. The event leading up to the war that had the largest impact on him was when his Jewish mother was too ashamed to make a fuss about him departing on the train for basic training, in contrast to an Italian American mother who refused to get off the train without her son. Harry understood his mother's quelling of her emotions as expressing her belief that quiet passivity was socially acceptable since it would not result in her sticking out as an immigrant Jew: "She wanted to sit there, too, and scream she wouldn't get off unless I did. But she was a Jew. She was a Jew's wife. And my father, the both of them, they felt they didn't have the right to behave like people" (151). This event is used to show the pressure felt by some Jewish immigrants to hide behind a veneer of respectability; to not be too loud and emotional, too "Jewish." As Wolfert portrays it, this need to hide from the majority world in a culture of shame is the albatross around Harry's neck that he must discard if he wants to live a healthy life.

In Wolfert's portrayal, Harry's understanding of his Jewishness is primarily rooted in the poor treatment of Jews: "As a Jew, he had been made to feel he was in the Reserve, too. The human race regarded Jews as a kind of foster people" (25). Growing up Jewish in America has been extremely difficult for him. For instance, Harry only became a lawyer because most of the professions which he would have preferred to pursue were closed to him:

> Harry would have preferred architecture. But Jews find success difficult in that field. He would have preferred, as next best, civil engineering, but there again the clientele was restricted. They

lived near Protestant and Catholic churches, although not because that was where God was but because that was where Jews
were not. (181)

His Jewishness also caused problems in relationships with women. For
instance, before the war he broke up with his Christian girlfriend Barbara
because, so he said, "Who knew what might become of Jews as a result
of this war? Nonsense she said, but he did not think it was fair to commit
her — perhaps to a concentration camp, perhaps to a gas chamber as a
race polluter" (24–25). In fact, for Harry there is almost nothing that is
positive about being a Jew.

Harry's negative view of his Jewishness reflects in part Ira Wolfert's own
second-generation belief that the immigrant parents want nothing more
than to escape their backgrounds. This idea played out in an interesting exchange of letters in *Commentary* between Wolfert and the famous
Yiddish poet Jacob Glatstein. In the letters Wolfert defends his negative
portraits of "Jewish life in the slums" in contrast to Glatstein, who instead
asserts that life on the Lower East Side had many positive aspects.[37]

Harry's intense awareness of his Jewishness was brought on by the rise
of Hitler and the increase in xenophobia in America during the Depression, which made him realize that he was a member of a hated minority.
Typical of the time, Harry could only view himself as a Jew or as a member of the "universal" world. He could not be both and the only way that
he was able to survive in America was to sublimate his Jewishness: "On
earth, in his own homeland, it occurred to him now, he had been permit-
ted to survive only because he had not allowed his alien-ness to intrude
on the majority. They could ignore the fact of his Jewishness in favor of
the fact that he was a man" (93). Harry is therefore seeking to figure out
how to be a man who does not have to hide his "alien-ness."

In military service, Harry had quickly discovered that although he was
aiming to show that "he belonged as an American" (182), in reality the
old order of WASP insiders and despised ethnic outsiders still reigned:
"The Navy sent him to the Pacific, where the enemy was the enemy of
his own enemies, and his own enemies — the loud mouths, the racists, the
Country Club bigots — were finding a voice in the throats of American
Admirals" (182). For Jews and other minority groups, the reign of the

WASP officer was particularly troubling since upper-class white "country club" America perpetrated an especially nasty form of antisemitism.

While his background as a child of fearful Jewish immigrants has made him feel the need to be small and quiet, his actions contradict this. In every situation, Harry is the ideal hero who always does the heroic and difficult thing. By so doing, Wolfert gives us a portrait of a man suffering profound internal insecurity about being a Jew while outwardly acting brave and confident. Harry is also an idealized portrait of a new type of masculinity that combines intellectualism with physicality: he can express his emotions but also can suppress them when necessary; he is both sexual with and respectful of women.

For other American soldiers, it is easy to kill the Japanese and difficult to kill the Germans. This is shown when an aid worker describes to Harry how much he prefers burying dead Japanese soldiers to German ones: "I can stand seeing the bugs eat them. But it's Europe where I'd hate to be. Killing Nazis would make me sick. They're white men" (544). The non-Jewish soldiers see the Germans as their European kin and it is painful to kill them, whereas the Japanese are their alien enemies. For the Jewish soldier, as Wolfert draws it, it is the opposite. Harry describes this dilemma:

> He had hated Hitler and the Nazis as a Jew rather than as a man who knows the world is one. But he knew nothing about the Japanese except that he did not like the people who were in the van of propaganda against them. The big mouthed Yellow Peril, White Man's Burden boys, those who hated the Japanese for Country Club reasons . . . Harry felt these Americans were stronger enemies of his than the Japanese could ever be. (180)

This is a reminder to postwar mainstream readers to approach American propaganda with caution and to be perceptive about the hate that can be hidden in it. At the same time it is a call to Jewish readers not to forget their long-standing mistreatment by the WASP establishment, and a reminder that they need to be cautious about aligning themselves with establishment forces in this new, conservative era.

Like *The Naked and the Dead* when the Jewish characters are contrasted with the Mexican Americans, *An Act of Love* introduces two other "ethnic" characters: the black native "Craik," whom Harry alone calls "Mr. Craik" and the Italian American Sergeant Poglese. Poglese succinctly describes the treatment of these three ethnics by the other soldiers: "Craik's an eight-ball, thought Poglese, that's what they got against him. If he was a wop, they would have that against him. If he was a kike, they would have that against him. If he was a — " (133). As we also saw in *The Naked and the Dead*, the minority soldiers feel they must work twice as hard, and take twice as many dangerous risks, in order to prove that they are as tough and as capable as the others. When Andrew Andersen asks Harry why he intends to return to the war rather than hide out with them, he therefore responds: "I guess it's the Jew in me . . . A Jew had to prove he was the same as anybody else. Those around him did not take it for granted" (149).

In Wolfert's novel the pressure to prove oneself is felt by all the outsiders to mainstream Anglo America. For instance, Commander Korn leads his men on a suicidal mission in order to show how fearsome he is and to distance himself from being labeled "a sissy" — derisive slang for a homosexual (477). Moreover, the Italian American Sergeant Poglese risks his life because he is desperate to get a medal and prove himself to American racists (509). Yet while Harry sees himself and others like Poglese as brothers, Poglese jokingly makes it clear that Italians do not view Jews as their kinsmen:

> "Medals help wops." "I know what I'm talking about. I got a medal, and besides I'm a Jew." "A Jew is not a wop." "It's the same thing." Poglese smiled. "I know wops who'd punch you in the nose for saying a Jew is the same as a wop." (508)

Even with a fellow outsider, the Jew still cannot find any brotherhood, and remains despised.

In Wolfert's universalist vision of the war, Harry comes to believe that the hatred toward the Jews is not unique, but rather it is part of the human condition for the victimized to seek to become the victimizer: "Harry realized that the world did not attack only Jews. It attacked everybody, and everybody attacked everybody because everybody felt attacked" (175). The Pacific campaign has broadened Harry's understanding of how hatred and violence works, from that of his parents' parochial viewpoint to a more global, universalist conception. As a good warrior for the brotherhood of all men, Harry has come to realize that he needs to force himself to act for the good of humanity broadly defined, even if he is despised because he is a Jew.

This shift in consciousness is played out when Harry goes on a suicidal reconnaissance mission with Major Munday whom he considers to be antisemitic: "That was a hot one, the Major saying he was full of borrowed blood. If the guy woke up to find he'd been given a transfusion by some Jew buddy of his, he'd cut his wrists to let the blood out and keep the Munday line pure" (521). In the final scene when Harry buries Major Mundy with the Japanese soldier he asserts his belief in the transcendence of universal love over nationalistic and ethnic divisions.

Harry's long quest, with myriad symbolic moments of loss and rebirth, ends with him moving out of his Jewishness into being a universal man. This occurs after he selflessly risks his life to save a soldier he has just met:

> Then, when Harry had done this, an act of human will became an act of love. Harry as no longer a minority of one on earth, seeking a cave in which to hide from both organic and inorganic life, from the hostilities of man and nature . . . He was not of a warring herd any longer, warring within itself and on other herds. He no longer had to be of a herd to feel secure. He had only to be of the human race. There was nothing hostile to him any more in human life. He was one with it, and so his fears ended. (534)

Unintentionally mimicking the pressures on American Jews to assimilate, Harry can only come fully into his own when he discards his Jewish particularity, embraces the world as a "universal" member of it, and goes on to successfully woo the (Christian) girl Julia. In other words, Wolfert is showing his readers that they all have the ability to become brothers to all men in the world. Even his Jewish hero protagonist will do this by gladly sacrificing his particular status for the betterment of humanity.

In combat, where men try to kill each other based solely on national origin, Harry's journey has taught him that all men are in fact united and that nationalism creates hatred. He has left his Jewishness behind in order to embrace the brotherhood of man. For Wolfert, love for a Christian woman enables Harry to finally come into his own and to fully embrace his universal status. Wolfert is showing that Harry (and all Jewish American men) can seemingly have it both ways: they can be Jews but without being bogged down by the particulars of the religion and of their ethnic distinctiveness. By embracing universalism the Jew will stop being the downtrodden insecure type of old, as embodied by Harry's worried mother. A second-generation Jewish American, he has no other option but a rebirth into Anglo American manhood which is realized in a marriage with a Christian woman. American mainstream readers need no longer fear the Jews in their midst because they are happy to reinvent themselves as Americans in the Gentile mold.

Wolfert believed that he was writing Bruner in the same tradition as the protagonists of Dos Passos, Hemingway, and Crane, who show how war is "a dramatization of the conflicts that exist in normal life."[38] If that is the case, then the transformation of Harry Bruner into the ideal soldier is a lesson that all men can change from weaklings into brave guys and that they can overcome their fears and do the right thing. Harry is proactive rather than reactive, a real American pioneer successfully pursuing his dreams. However, in the end, the only way he can fully come into his own is to drop his Jewishness and become a "universal" representative of humanity.

An Act of Love offers striking passages that show the universalistic principles of a best-selling postwar writer who used the Jewish soldier as a prop to further the aims of his ideological platform. It also delineates some of the profound insecurity faced by Wolfert as he sought to present an acceptable vision of the Jewish man to a mainstream readership. This, it seems, required that his protagonist proclaim, over and over again, that he had happily transformed from a parochial little Jew into a universal American man.

Considering the widespread dehumanization of the Japanese enemy in America during the war, both Ira Wolfert, and to a lesser extent Norman Mailer, wrote groundbreaking portraits of the Japanese. In An Act of Love, perhaps inspired by his Communist "internationalist" background, Wolfert made his boldest statement against the anti-Japanese racism so prominent in America by having his protagonist bury a Japanese soldier with an American major as "brothers." And when Mailer portrays the soldier Croft casually shooting a Japanese captive in the head who is begging to be spared so that he can return to his family, Mailer is rehumanizing the enemy and showing the casual yet brutal racism that is a part of a soldier's life. In both cases the presentation of the Japanese as being as human as the Americans is a challenge to all forms of hatred and reinforces the liberal view of a pluralistic world. It is also a reminder that the Jewish soldier does not easily fall victim to American efforts to make the Japanese into devils, since Jews of the time acutely understood the legacy of propaganda-inspired hatred. Moreover, it overturns the typical "typecasting" by Americans that deemed brave soldiers as blond Anglos, Japanese as animal-like demons, and Nazis as sharing the European blood of whites.[39] In this reconfiguration, the brave soldiers are Jewish, the Japanese are fellow minorities, and the Nazis are subhuman monsters.

In the Pacific theater, where Jewish soldiers were about as far away as they could be from their urban neighborhoods, the subtropics were portrayed as strange, exciting, and terrifying places where soldiers sought to understood their Jewishness in light of what they encountered there. All three Jewish characters look for ways to make this foreign place feel more comfortable: Goldstein tries to build bonds with Christian soldiers; the secular Roth finds himself connecting with fellow religious Jews; and Harry establishes ties with natives and non-Jewish locals. And as Mailer and Wolfert depict it, the experience of war service in the Pacific forced these men to change in their innermost beings: for Goldstein by establishing deep friendships with Christians; for Roth by undertaking a suicidal act to prove himself; and for Harry by completely dropping his Jewishness to embrace "universalism." In both Goldstein's and Harry's cases, the change was for the better since it meant leaving behind their Jewish parochialism and embracing the shared humanity of their non-Jewish brothers. In order to do this, they had to broaden their worldview to include men who were raised outside their Jewish ethnic enclaves and by so doing their mapping of the world was extended and enriched.

Mailer's and Wolfert's novels taught lessons to their readers about how to understand the war and how to use that awareness to shape their postwar life. Looking back, they showed that the Japanese enemy had elements of humanity, and that even in the Pacific the shadow of Nazism was felt by Jewish soldiers who encountered antisemitism in their platoons. Looking forward, they presented an idealistic image where friendships could overcome class and ethnic hatreds, and where Jews could be treated as equals with others, but only as long as they were willing to discard their own specificity to embrace non-Jews as their equals.

CHAPTER 3

1948 and the Holocaust:
The Young Lions, That Winter, The Crusaders, and *Point of No Return*

> "No one will believe us," one soldier said. They all agreed.
> "We got to talk about it, see? We got to talk about it if anyone
> believes us or not."
>
> — MARTHA GELLHORN'S RECOUNT OF INTERVIEWS WITH AMERICAN
> SOLDIERS WHO HAD LIBERATED DACHAU

The four best-selling 1948 war novels set in the European theater — *The Young Lions, That Winter, The Crusaders,* and *Point of No Return* — cover events such as D-Day, the liberation of Paris, and the Battle of the Bulge, and offer a specifically Jewish American take on the events in Europe. This is evident when, remarkably, all four novels culminate in the liberation of Dachau. As Isaac E. Rontch described it in the foreword to *Jewish Youth at War: Letters from American Soldiers,* "The American Jewish soldier fights as an American and as a Jew."[1]

The Jewish soldier becomes a trope for blurring "the war" and "the Holocaust," since at one and the same time he is under fire as an American (and member of the Allied forces) and as a Jew (the enemy of the Nazis). Reciprocally, for the Jewish soldier, the German enemy is both a member of the Axis and a killer of his people. Where for others the war was distinct from the Holocaust because it took place on battlefields rather than in ghettos and death camps; between Allied and Axis soldiers versus between Jews and Nazis, for the Jewish soldier in Europe both occurred simultaneously. And where non-Jewish soldiers could look back on their war service with a sense of relief and pride in the American effort, "the joy felt by American Jews in 1945 as a result of the Allied victory over the Axis was tempered by sadness and forebodings not experienced by other Americans."[2]

When Jewish soldiers and journalists returned home and composed war novels, they discussed the Holocaust as *part* of the war experience, rather than negating the topic and focusing merely on troop movements and military campaigns. Moreover, by describing what the Nazis had done to the Jews, the war novels were perhaps attempting to sway public opinion toward deeper compassion for Jewish refugees at a time when the U.S. Congress was trying to limit the intake of Jews from displaced persons camps.

Hasia Diner recently exploded the myth that Jewish Americans were largely silent about the Holocaust until after the trial of Adolf Eichmann and the Six Day War.[3] As Diner convincingly argues, the pervasiveness of academics denying the widespread Jewish American acts of disseminating information about the Holocaust is particularly troubling because it is so historically inaccurate. She notes that one of the many reasons why researchers overlooked the prevalence of Holocaust material in the postwar years was because they had very limited notions about the meaning of the term: "From a research perspective, much of the Holocaust-related material produced in the late 1940s and into the middle of the 1960s did not appear in archives and libraries, in the indices of books or in card catalogs under the heading "Holocaust."[4] In other words, there was a range of cultural responses to the Holocaust that did not fit under any neat heading, including Jewish war novels.

My research extends Diner's concepts by considering novels that were composed primarily for large mainstream audiences. The popularity of the novels I discuss meant that the descriptions of the Shoah found in them reached broadly into American culture and this suggests that Jews and non-Jews alike were reading about the Holocaust in the years right after the war. To get the message across, Jewish writers embedded the Holocaust story within the larger framework of a war novel. However, the authors' uncertainty about whether the novelistic form was adequate for descriptions of the Holocaust was evinced by the stark shift into a journalistic mode for descriptions of the death camps. As this first wave of fiction writers attempted to tell readers about the Holocaust, they turned to the genre which had transmitted the story during the war: journalistic reports. They also used this style because it was seen as a better way to show that what they were telling about had in fact occurred and was not part of the made-up world of fiction. As Phyllis Lassner notes of Martha Gellhorn's ideological use of a nonemotional, journalistic style to describe the death camp: "Having been reduced to 'nothing,' Hitler's victims would only suffer another invasion by an artistic construction of their interior lives."[5]

All of the novels I discuss document how seeing the Holocaust first-hand forever transforms the Jewish American soldier, and results in a radical change in his life. We see this most emblematically in *Point of No Return* when the Jewish protagonist, Jacob Levy, starts the war an innocent assimilated Jew who only wants to be left alone, and ends it by murdering German civilians even though peace has been declared. He will never be the same and he will never feel safe again, even in America. Levy's response to Dachau is very different from that of Noah Ackerman in *The Young Lions*, whose experience ends up teaching him that Americans are superior to Germans. When confronted with Dachau, Noah at first suppresses his emotions, only breaking down after his senior officer, Captain Green, allows a rabbi to conduct a service for the survivors against the pleas of an Albanian Christian political prisoner who does not want it to take place.[6] The Captain's actions show him to be an ideal American, able to do the fair and good thing, to challenge antisemitism, and to stand up for what is right. Ackerman's faith in America returns. By extending the focus of their "war" novels to include the Holocaust, these writers changed the war novel genre so that it included the genocide of civilians along with the combat stories of soldiers. As I will discuss later, when "Holocaust Literature" became a distinct genre in America, the focus would contract to be solely on the Jewish victim without mention of the broader war.

By focusing on the epochal moment when forward units of General Patton's Seventh Army liberated Dachau during the German retreat, these novels offer a distinctly American perspective on the Holocaust. What was discovered in the camp was so gruesome and horrific that everyone — the soldiers, General Eisenhower, the journalists covering the event — worried that Americans would not believe what the Germans had done. Even though few American GIs — mostly members of the 157th Infantry Regiment — were at the liberation of the camps, all the Jewish soldiers of the European novels are placed there.[7] These books portray the liberation of Dachau as the moment when the Shoah is brought home to Americans generally, and Jewish Americans specifically. The novels use a Jewish soldier to show the pinnacle moment of awakening when what the Nazis did to the Jews of Europe becomes tangible and real. Once having awoken, the protagonist in each of the novels changes utterly.

Moreover, because all the authors were liberals, their portrayals of the liberation of the camps should be seen as having the intention of teaching readers to share the authors' beliefs. As Diner has shown, in postwar Jewish American life where liberalism was a core belief, linking the Holocaust with liberal principles was a common rhetorical strategy for a range of Jewish communal and cultural organizations. The Holocaust could be used to insist that African Americans be treated better, that more immigrants be allowed to enter, that the worst excesses of anti-Communism be curtailed.[8] The war novelists also used the Holocaust to remind readers that pluralism, as signified by the ideal platoon, was a counterpoint to the racist intolerance of the Germans. Moreover, when the American Jewish GI liberates the camps, he signifies this dichotomy between democracy and totalitarianism. Making the liberation of the death camps a central motif in the novels serves as a reminder to postwar mainstream readers that they must do everything possible to distance America from ideologies of hatred.

Jewish writers knew that the war was justified because the Germans were intent on killing all of them, and they therefore did not challenge the larger war aims in their writings. Instead, what they could and did critique, from a Jewish perspective, was how Americans performed in battle. Where the war was good, the way in which it was conducted needed to be reformed, much as the United States needed to improve in its treatment of its minorities.

Because most of these novels are currently out of literary fashion I will first briefly discuss their plots. This will be followed by my analysis of the important trends delineated in the novels.

Irwin Shaw: *The Young Lions*

Irwin Shaw (born Irwin Gilbert Shamforoff, 1913–1984) was in some ways Norman Mailer's nemesis: unlike Mailer who tried to act like a tough guy but was more of an intellectual, Shaw was a talented boxer, sportsman, and semi-professional football player. He attended bullfights, drank hard, womanized, and even wrote copy for the radio serial about the ultimate hard-boiled man, Dick Tracy.[9] Ernest Hemingway, who was introduced to his third wife, Martha Gellhorn, by Shaw, claimed that Shaw was one of the toughest guys around who could only be beaten in a boxing match by cheating.[10] Shaw could not only out-man Mailer, he could also out-man the paragon of literary American manhood, Ernest Hemingway. To cap matters, Shaw's own novel about the war which was published in October 1948 competed for the top spot on the best seller chart with *The Naked and The Dead* for the rest of the year and well into 1949.

Like Mailer, Shaw was also a Brooklyn Jewish son of East European immigrants. Shaw's father ran a small real estate firm that collapsed during the Depression, leading to the impoverishment of his middle-class family. After completing a B.A. at the tuition-free Brooklyn College in 1934 — Irwin had his sights set on Princeton, but his family could not afford it — Shaw supported himself in a range of jobs including driving a truck. Following strong critical and popular acclaim for his first play, the antiwar drama *Bury the Dead* (1936), Shaw spent the rest of his life as a professional writer, earning a living from short stories published in the *New Yorker*, plays, novels, and film scripts. He left the United States for Europe in 1951, after being placed on the Hollywood blacklist as a Communist supporter. Although his voluminous short stories were critically acclaimed, and his war novel was considered one of the central works of the genre, Shaw became most famous in the 1970s when two of his novels, *Rich Man, Poor Man* (1970) and *Beggerman, Thief* (1977), became popular TV miniseries.

While Shaw's early writings delved into the topic of antisemitism in America and Europe, most notably in his short stories "Weep in Years to Come" (1939) and "Act of Faith" (1946), Shaw's approach was different from Mailer's. For Shaw, the Jewish man was inherently strong and brave: he just was not recognized as such by Anglo Americans.

When America entered World War II, Shaw was a successful script writer, and using his Hollywood connections he could have avoided service. However, he felt strongly that Americans must fight against fascism in Europe (he had donated to the Republican cause during the Spanish Civil War), so in June 1942, at the mature age of thirty, Shaw enlisted, serving until October 1945. Like Norman Mailer, Shaw was on the periphery of battle and experienced no direct fighting: a member of a camera crew photographing the war, Shaw recorded the fight for France after Normandy, and the liberation of Paris, experiences he would write about in his war novel.[11]

The Young Lions is quite different in tone, texture, and content from *The Naked and the Dead*. Unlike *The Naked and the Dead*, which describes the Pacific campaign and has the enemy as the Japanese, in *The Young Lions* the foes are the Nazis. In Mailer's novel, the events take place on a fictional island, whereas in Shaw's work, the story describes real battles including the African campaign, the Normandy invasion, the bombing of London, the fight for Paris, and the Battle of the Bulge. Where Mailer documents the diverse chorus of voices of American soldiers, and Wolfert tells his tale through a single protagonist, here the story revolves around three main characters: the sensitive, recently married, young Jewish father Noah Ackerman, the sophisticated yet restless Hollywood player, Michael Whitacre, and the Nazi, Christian Diestl. The three men represent the three sides of the war story: the Jew, the American GI, and the Nazi. World War II is the connective thread joining Noah, Michael, and Christian, disparate individuals who normally would not have come into contact with one another.

As we see Noah, Michael, and Christian interact with the secondary characters, we gain insights into their moral being, discovering that Noah and Michael are good and loyal men, while Christian is disturbingly evil. The main female characters, Peggy and Hope, are drawn more realistically than the caricatures of women found in Mailer, with Shaw even exploring the terror felt by Peggy when she is nearly raped. The macho posturing so prevalent in Mailer does not exist at all in *The Young Lions*, and the women are as sympathetic and complex as the male characters.

Where in *The Naked and the Dead*, the narrative begins right in the heart of the battle, and we learn the biographies of the characters only through the retroactive "Time Machines," in *The Young Lions* there is a traditional diachronic plot, beginning in the years before the war and leading to the final climactic showdown between Christian (who shoots Noah), Noah (who is killed by Christian), and Michael (who in response kills Christian). Shaw charts the internal development of each character as he undergoes the war, giving a panoramic overview of how Americans and Germans conduct themselves in the lead-up to and during battle. Shaw's prose has an immediacy that imparts the story in an exciting and quick tempo, as for instance in his account of Noah's landing at Normandy: "The barge grated against the smooth beach and a second later the ramp went down. Noah leaped out, feeling his equipment banging heavily against his back and sides, feeling the cold water pouring in over his leggings. He raced for a small dune and flung himself down behind it" (389).

In the novel Noah changes from a lost young man to the bravest and most adept soldier who has a higher moral stance than just about anyone else in the book. By contrast, the Nazi, Christian, becomes increasingly twisted: he emotionlessly witnesses the torture of two Frenchmen he has falsely accused of murder; he kills in an almost arbitrary way a young French boy; and he has his closest friend in the SS shot as a deserter. Shaw devotes about a quarter of the book to Christian, exploring what makes a man become a Nazi and aiming to show how, according to Shaw, he becomes

> bestialized, almost bereft of humanity, almost dead to the instincts of survival even, as the Germans finally were, by believing in one false thing, which spreads and spreads and finally corrupts them entirely. The false thing I had Diestl believing in was the conviction that at that one time and in that one place (Austria) the end justified the means. The belief, in the course of the book, corrupts him to a point of fanaticism at which no horror any longer has the power to move or disgust him.[12]

Christian is a brutal cog in the Nazi machine; a shallow thinker who embodies the "banality of evil," to paraphrase Hannah Arendt, in the cool and unemotional manner in which he kills. Christian and the other Nazi character, Frederick, are perverse and evil men who are absolutely different than the Americans, Noah and Michael, who ruminate deeply over the meaning of war and suffer overwhelming sadness at the destruction and death of battle. Also, Christian is an ideologue who is only able to think and act in extremes and because of this he has lost touch with his humanity. Shaw, a committed liberal, was likely using Christian to warn his postwar readership about the evil dangers of extremism, be it Nazism or anti-Communism.

The outcome of the novel is foreshadowed in the novel's opening quote from the book of Nahum 2.13:

> Behold, I am against thee / saith the Lord of hosts, and / I will burn her chariots / in the smoke, and the sword / shall devour thy young lions / and I will cut off thy / prey from the earth / and the voice of thy messengers / shall no more be heard.[13]

The passage describes God's admonition to the Assyrian kings that he will destroy them for abusing their power, likened to the brutal slaughter of prey by young lions. The struggle between Noah and Christian resonates as a biblical battle between good and evil, in which good will win, and the young lions, the Nazis, will be beaten after much bloodshed.

The opening chapter sets the stage for the primal battle, when it describes the innocent, all-American girl, Peggy Freemantle, spending New Year's Eve at a ski town in Austria in 1938 while awaiting her Jewish boyfriend Joseph. It is a cozy and idyllic small mountain town where the children are singing, the partygoers are waltzing together, and everything is bathed in a serene, snowy calm. Peggy is filled with joy at how "warm these people are, how friendly and childlike, and how good to strangers" (*The Young Lions*, 3). After the celebrations, where she chooses to overlook toasts "to the Fuehrer," the young man, Frederick, who had been so nice to her, shockingly attempts to rape her. She successfully fights him off only to learn that his mother allows him to have his way with all the young women who stay at her inn. Austria, while outwardly beautiful, evidently masks a deep and profound evil. Even the ski instructor to whom Peggy describes the attempted rape, who seems to be sympathetic, is a Nazi in ski clothing who without any emotion declares to her that "if the only way you can get a decent and ordered Europe is by wiping out the Jews, then we must do it. A little injustice for a large justice" (17). During the book, Frederick, Peggy's attempted rapist, will become an important, utterly brutal Nazi sergeant; Peggy will become Michael's girlfriend; and the ski instructor is Christian, the Nazi protagonist who kills Noah.

The other main character, Michael, shows the difficulties of being a sensitive man in an era of the hard-boiled: "I'm a weak, intelligent man, Tommy, and we don't live in the right age for weak, intelligent men. Take my advice, Tommy, grow up stupid. Strong and stupid" (35–36). Michael, the educated Protestant, is a tool to explore the inner world of an American man who seeks to fight for his country, but is terrified of the possibility of death. Throughout the early scenes that describe Michael's life as a Hollywood player, we see him desire to enlist but fearful to do so in case he is killed or wounded. As with Shaw himself, he has the choice, which becomes a burden, to skirt service through his work in Hollywood, and he does so for a time. Eventually he decides to enlist rather than regret spending the war in America. At first in Europe he, like Shaw, is on the sidelines, driving cameramen around to shoot footage. His reignited friendship with Noah, however, brings him to fight on the front lines as Noah teaches him how to be a good and devoted soldier. According to Shaw, Michael represents his "faith in America . . . He's Middle America. He's slow to move. He gets dragged into doing some good things. Reluctantly. But then he comes through. And that's the way I felt about America. And it turned out I was right."[14]

The topic of antisemitism is crucial to the plot that begins in Austria in 1938 and ends in the woods just outside a death camp in 1945, and it drives the actions of the three main characters: Christian's unproblematic Nazism compels his war service and the brutality with which he undertakes it; Michael's core as an American is shaken when he watches Noah terrorized by antisemitic fellow Americans; and Noah changes from a weak, kind soul into a fierce, courageous, and brilliant soldier because of terrible experiences at a training camp where he is brutalized by antisemites. *The Young Lions* is as much an exposition of antisemitism in Europe and America as it is a portrait of war.

We first meet Noah at the deathbed of his father, Jacob. Like many of the characters in the book, Jacob is aptly named. In the biblical original, Jacob steals the birthright of his brother Esau by tricking his blind father Isaac. In the novel, Jacob has escaped the fate of his brother in Europe, and on his deathbed he is deeply remorseful that he has abandoned him to the Nazis. Where in the Bible Jacob eventually is reunited with his brother, in Shaw's version, Jacob dies alone in America and his brother is burned in the crematoria. And although Jacob suggests the biblical patriarch, his personality has many aspects that make him an extremely negative caricature of a first-generation Jewish immigrant. Jacob is a shyster who weaves Jewish commentaries into his discussions, not out of respect for Judaism, but as a way to scam people. A "half rabbi, half river-gambler" (43), Jacob has spent his life crisscrossing the country, sleeping with a vast array of mostly Christian women, doing scams, and "making dirty jokes and quoting Isaiah in the same breath" (55). While looking and acting like an Old World patriarch, Jacob's Jewishness is one tool amongst many with which he manipulates people.

On his deathbed, Jacob has an epiphany, and he implores Noah to rescue his uncle and to become the Jew that Jacob has never been:

> You stand there in your cheap American clothes and you think, "What has he to do with me? He is a stranger to me. I have never seen him and if he dies, in the furnaces in Europe, what of it, people die every minute all over the world." He is not a stranger to you. He is a Jew and the world is hunting him, and you are a Jew and the world is hunting you. (43)

Noah is completely unmoved by Jacob's words, although in the end they will prove true, and Noah will be hunted down by a Nazi. Instead Noah views Jacob as trying to manipulate him. Noah's tears over his father's death only come at the end of the long day in which the funeral home refuses to cremate his father because he is a Jew: "You heard what Georgie said. He don't burn Kikes" (50). The "burning of the Kikes" will be left to the Nazis in Europe, who will do this to Jacob's brother. After his father's death, Noah finds he is utterly alone, both as a son without any remaining family, and as a Jew (although he does not admit this to himself) in a country that according to Shaw's rendition, views him foremost as a "Kike."

In Shaw's portrait, Jacob symbolizes Jewish life in America as sordid and devoid of morality. Judaism has fallen from a sanctified religion to one used by scam artists to manipulate the innocent. If a Christian writer had composed this type of character it would be read as antisemitic. Coming from a Jewish author, it suggests the radical transformation undergone by the children of immigrants in America as they sought to redefine their Jewishness as distinct from the Old World religiosity of their parents. In this case, the son's rebellion is total and absolute: Judaism, as represented by the European father, is corrupt and tawdry. For the son to regain a moral stance, he must find a new way of defining himself as a Jew that is distinct from Judaism, Yiddish, and the cultural past of Europe. It will be an entirely American construct that Shaw will create, as we will see in Noah's evolution from a wishy-washy intellectual into a brave warrior.

Noah wants to enlist, although he adamantly denies to himself that he is doing so because he is a Jew:

> If the war began, he could not hesitate. As an honorable citizen, as a believer in the war, as an enemy of Fascism, as a Jew . . . He shook his head. There it was again. That should have nothing to do with it. Most of these men were not Jews, and yet here they were at six-thirty of a winter's morning, the second day of the war, ready to die. (168)

In his first attempt to volunteer for the army, Noah is rejected for health reasons. By his second try, when the military is more desperate for men, he is accepted. In the meantime he has married Hope, a Protestant girl he met in New York who is originally from a small town in Vermont. Her father only accepts his daughter's marriage to a Jew after silently marching Noah through his town where all the store plaques are labeled with WASP names, and where Noah is made to feel how foreign he is in this quintessentially American locale.

The father eventually decides that the quiet man next to him, the first Jew he has ever met, is not one of the "wild, howling heathens, or congenital felons" (207) and accepts him into the family. The old man confronts, and challenges, his own antisemitism in order to do the best thing by his daughter. His interaction with Noah, as Shaw portrays it, forces the old man to come to terms with whether he is "decent or mean." His kindness wins out, giving the readers an impetus to look at their own proclivity for hate.

Shaw's description of antisemitism in basic training is the most explicit, brutally rendered, and one could add overwrought of any of the postwar Jewish novels; a 1948 review stated that it is "one of the most moving and eloquent pleas for decency and justice in any recent novel this reader has come across."[15] At the beginning of basic training, the antisemitic Captain Colclough (whose name resonates with Father Coughlin) derides Noah in front of the barracks for having a copy of the "filthy, dirty book" James Joyce's *Ulysses*, yelling that "You're not here to read" (286). Moreover, since the barracks haven't been cleaned up, no one will receive leave passes for the weekend. Noah is blamed for this and the antisemitic torrent begins as he is called a "Jew-boy," a "Christ killer," a "herring eater," and is told that as a Jew he could have bought his way out of service. The repeated claim is that "you people got us into the war. Now why can't you behave yourselves like human beings?" (389). Shaw is exposing a form of antisemitism that Mailer was silent about: how American Jews were blamed for "causing" the American entrance into the war. As one of the soldiers declares:

> The Jews have large investments in France and Germany . . .
> They run all the banks and whorehouses in Berlin and Paris,
> and Roosevelt decided we had to go protect their money. So he
> declared war. (290)

Noah feels his battle has begun even though he is still in Florida, and that the "weapons" being leveled against him are the men's words. The antisemitic taunts continue, including the most shocking that "Hitler is probably wrong most of the time, but you've got to hand it to him, he knows what to do about the Jews" (293). The attacks do not let up and are supported by Captain Colclough. Finally, Noah breaks after the precious ten dollar bill he has been saving for a leave with his wife is stolen, and then he and Hope are kicked out of a rooming house because the owner discovers that Noah is a Jew. Antisemitism is everywhere in America, arising from innocent looking old women, California funeral home directors, Southern soldiers, small town men. Noah sends Hope home and decides to take action.

Noah posts a sign in the barracks asking that whoever stole his ten dollars come forward so he can "take the matter into his own hands." The next evening, a small sheet of paper is posted up which reads:

We took it, Jew-Boy. We're waiting for you. Signed, P. Donnelly, J. Wright, L. Jackson, M. Silichner, P. Sanders, B. Cowley, W. Demuth, E. Riker, R. Henkel, T. Brailsford. (308)

The ten who have put themselves forward to fight with Noah are the largest men in the barracks. Noah's response, as with Roth's in *The Naked and the Dead*, is potentially suicidal: he will fight each and every man on the list, even though he weighs only 135 pounds and has no fighting experience, while most of the men are close to 200 pounds, and have vast fighting experience. Over the next weeks, Noah is beaten to a pulp by each of the men. His nose is shattered, his teeth are knocked out, and his bones are broken. After brief hospital recoveries, he returns for the next fight. Finally he reaches the last name on the list, the fat and out-of-shape Brailsford. Overtaken by all the rage he has been suppressing, Noah savagely beats up Brailsford, for once finding himself as the last man standing. When the fellow soldiers see that Brailsford has been beaten, rather than offering Brailsford a hand, they turn their backs and walk away, leaving Noah and Michael to nurse the sobbing Brailsford. Shocked by the profound psychological cruelty of the soldiers to Brailsford, and their reluctance to admit that Noah has finally won a fight, Noah goes AWOL.

Noah successfully pleads to an army psychologist to be reinstated and sent to a different division. Shaw, in an extremely idealistic portrayal, has the psychologist decide not to court martial Noah for desertion and instead gives him the option of returning to his old division. When Hope shows up and Noah realizes that she is pregnant, Noah agrees to return to his old platoon, since his only other choice is prison.

Upon returning to training camp Noah brandishes a switchblade and lets the others know that "if anybody in this Company ever touches me again I'm going to kill him" (337). Much to his surprise, he is treated respectfully, and Brailsford even returns the books that Colclough took from him. Noah is now an accepted member of his company, although to become so he had risked his life by undertaking all the fights. From his brutal months in training, Noah has transformed. Foremost, he has become strong and capable as a fighter, and the American GIs readily accept him once he toughens up. Most of them are inherently good and ready to discard their hatred, much as postwar Americans will do when they welcome back soldiers from a range of ethnic groups.

When we next see Noah waiting in the cold rain on a barge preparing for assault training in England, unlike all the other freezing and wet soldiers, he is "enjoying it" (388). In the practice runs Noah stands out as the most capable, brave, intelligent, and clear-sighted soldier in the platoon. And Noah is finding that the other servicemen are beginning to fulfill the ideal of a pluralistic America:

> The closer they came to battle, the closer they got to the day when each man's life would depend upon every other man in the company, the more all differences fell away, the more connected and friendly they all were. (392)

Raised in a home where Judaism was a tool for manipulation, and where he "had never gone to synagogue" (399), Noah finds spiritual peace in a small Dover church where the priest preaches the gospel of brotherly love and lectures on the moral challenges soldiers face in battle. Where Judaism had offered Noah no guideposts for spiritual certitude, the words of the priest delineate for him the moral complexities of a soldier at war. For Shaw, the primary concern is that Noah finds authentic truth and moral guideposts in religion, be it from Christianity or Judaism. Noah, in this portrait, is no less a Jew for embracing aspects of the gospel. Clearly pandering to his mainstream readers, Shaw gives a rendition of Judaism as a spiritual path that is accepting of Christianity, while also showing his Jewish readers that they need to open to other religious pathways.

Noah becomes the leader of his platoon as they seek to return safely back to the Allied side after fighting harrowing battles for French villages. Noah's leadership, abilities, and bravery contrast starkly with his antisemitic nemesis, Captain Colclough, who has a massive panic attack and has to be carried out of battle. Noah leads the men to safety and then risks his life for one of them, Cowley, who had beaten him up in Florida. After this ordeal, where Noah not only saves Beidecker but also risks his life for Cowley, he delivers a hand-drawn map of where the Germans are hiding a massive arms depot. Yet in response to his remarkable actions Rickett, rather than congratulating him, states "oh, Christ, we still got the Jew" (488).

From this moment on, Noah is but a mere shell of himself, and with his spirit broken, his potential to be a great leader is undermined. He will now only do the minimum that is required of him, since nothing he does will make any difference because for Germans and Americans alike, no matter what Noah's accomplishments are in battle, he is first and foremost a despised Jew. Shaw's description of the blossoming and then shrinking of Noah as a soldier shows antisemitism in America as being both profoundly soul-destroying and destructive to the war effort. Rickett's action not only destroys Noah's potential to be a great soldier for America, it challenges the idealized image of the armed services as a brotherhood that is devoted to a cause greater than itself. This depiction serves as a wake-up call to postwar readers that they must embrace all members of the country equally or they will be like the hateful Rickett.

The book's final scene takes place at the liberation of Dachau after the Nazi, Christian, has escaped to the nearby forest because he is repulsed by the smell of the dead and dying Jews. For Noah, Michael, and their kind and smart new leader, Captain Green, the shock of the camps is profound and the misery they encounter impossibly painful to see. Noah at first suppresses his emotions, only breaking down after Captain Green allows a rabbi to conduct a service for the survivors against the pleas of an Albanian political prisoner who does not want the service to take place. Green's actions show him to be the ideal American, able to do the fair and good thing, to challenge antisemitism, and to stand up for what is right.

Noah's faith in America thus returns. This is an effective resolution to keep readers invested in the story. Previously, the extreme scenes of antisemitism in the military had served to remind them about their need to forgo their old hatreds. Now, Green comforts them by suggesting that America really is not so bad after all and that in the postwar era, all Americans can and will be similar paragons of brotherly love.

Taking a walk with Michael in the woods near the liberated camp, the final scene unfolds:

> "When the war is over," Noah said and his voice was growing loud, "Green is going to run the world, not that damned Albanian . . ." "Sure," said Michael. "The human beings are going to be running the world!"

As Noah yells with unbridled joy that the "human beings!" will run the world and that " 'the world is full of them!' It was then that the shots rang out" (654). At that moment, Christian kills Noah.

Where Green's actions had offered the potential of a better world shorn of antisemitism, where all men would be "human," Noah is still a Jew in Europe, and Christian is a Nazi who kills him. The Nazis have won for the moment by pointlessly destroying an enlightened, kind, intelligent man and by so doing have delineated that the Germans are different than the Americans, and that Shaw really has not intended to cast them in the same light.

Michael responds to Noah's murder by becoming an exemplary soldier, tracking down Christian and shooting him in the head. Christian's final words are "Welcome to Germany," meaning it's the land that kills Jews (which differentiates it from America which is the home of the virtuous Captain Green). The final scene depicts Michael carrying Noah's corpse:

> And he refused to allow any of the other men in the Company
> to help him carry the body, because he knew he had to deliver
> Noah Ackerman, personally, to Captain Green. (662)

Noah has been sacrificed and he must now be brought to the righteous Captain who represents the future of humanity.

In Shaw's rendition, World War II is the stage on which the forces of good and evil fight for supremacy. With Noah's and then Christian's death, the battle is concluded. Like Roth in *The Naked and the Dead*, Noah is a symbolic martyr for the good of humanity. He is an ideal American soldier who is "too good for his time" and his death is the catalyst for a new and better future.[16] Noah is reborn in the form of the aptly named "Captain Green"; a greenhorn going to America to rebuild it according to the lessons learned in Europe about the importance of fighting for a world in which intolerance has no place.

Noah's death not only brings on a new and better age, he also unites the Holocaust and World War II. As James P. Giles notes: "Noah has to die to symbolize the incalculable horror of the Nazis' crimes against the Jewish people and against humanity."[17] Noah therein dies as an emblem of all Jewish victims of the Nazis, and as an American martyr in the fight against Germany.[18]

What, indeed, if anything, is "Jewish" about Noah beyond his death at the hands of the Nazi? First and foremost, he is a representative of the Jew as the ennobled sufferer: through being treated cruelly Noah develops into an ideal soldier and friend. Noah also evokes the second-generation Jewish American immigrant who has assimilated and seeks to redefine himself along cultural rather than religious lines: he practices no Judaism, is intermarried, and is a Jew not because he follows the law, but because he develops his humanity in response to antisemitism. In this case, assimilation is a positive force that makes all Americans united and better, and as with Captain Green, Noah represents an ideal American who seeks a brotherhood of all men. Noah thus overcomes his tawdry Jewish roots by becoming a perfect American soldier, combining compassion with braveness.

In Shaw's portrait, Noah changes from a weak, intellectual, second-generation urban Jew into a strong American man. Unlike Noah in the Ark, he will not live to step onto the new shore after the flood, but will be martyred so that the Protestant Captain Green can do so. Noah's father, a first-generation Jewish American, was corrupt and weak and a symbol of the worst aspects of Jewish shtetl culture. The new Jewish man, Noah, has infused into himself the New World's ideas about masculinity and heroism and has transcended his European shtetl heritage. Shaw, a loyal Zionist, has Noah embody the belief that the pioneer in Palestine must break free of his shtetl heritage in order to become a tough warrior who can fulfill the Zionist dream.[19] Noah, however, in contrast with his Zionist brother in arms, must die so that America can fulfill its potential. The America of the future is one where the old European Jew will be a relic to be discarded.[20]

At the same time that he asks Jews to overcome their Old World heritage, Shaw also uses *The Young Lions* as a pedagogical tool to teach Christian readers how to treat Jews. His lesson is three-pronged. First, antisemitism is detrimental to America generally, and to the war effort specifically. Second, the Americans who represent the best aspects of the country are those like Captain Green who stand up for the rights of minorities and who treat everyone equally. Third, despite the worst antisemitic smears leveled against them, Jews were not the cause of the war nor were they seeking to evade service. The cause was the intrinsic and total evil of the Germans, as personified by Christian. Jewish soldiers such as Noah were loyal and heroic to the American cause once they were given the chance to prove themselves.

Critics were divided about how to view the novel. Two different critics in the *New York Times* lauded *The Young Lions* as a great book: "the best war novel yet written by an American"[21] and one that "deserves to be one of the most widely read books of the year."[22] Critics also praised Shaw's adeptness at manipulating the emotions of his readers in such a way that they felt deeply for the characters. For Jewish critics the book was deeply problematic. Alfred Kazin and Leslie Fiedler, for example, evoked the disgust of the "middlebrow" that I discussed earlier, viewing Shaw as a hack who sold out to a mainstream readership that wanted to feel that they were consuming "high art" when they were really reading "lowbrow" fiction that fed their worst fears and desires about how Jews should be. In Alfred Kazin's scathing 1948 review for *Commentary*, he asserts, in a voice dripping with sarcasm, that the sacrifice of Noah Ackerman shows the terrible insecurity of the postwar Jewish writer as he seeks to be accepted by the American critics:

> Poor Noah, who must bear the brunt not only of being all the Jews confronting all the antisemites, but of Irwin Shaw's life in an irrational world, full of critics.[23]

For Kazin, by killing off Noah, Shaw is pandering to Anglo critics while, at the same time, trying to appeal to a mainstream readership's worst tendencies to view Jews as expendable for their own evolution. Leslie Fiedler's 1956 essay "Irwin Shaw: Adultery, the Last Politics," also attacked Shaw on a wide range of fronts, including the way he created feel-good books that were the "sort of work in which slickness and sentimentality are turned from the service of entertainment and name brands to social awareness and human understanding."[24] Moreover these Jewish critics were deeply uncomfortable with the idealization of the "new Jew," Noah Ackerman, who has few Jewish traits except his victimhood.

The Young Lions is a chronicle of the conflict felt by some Jewish

Americans in the postwar years. Shaw first shocks the readers into taking stock of their own hatreds, and then assures them that they are intrinsically better than the Nazis. And Noah is the perfect foil to do this since he has distanced himself from the more unsavory aspects of the shtetl Jew-as-immigrant, as represented by his father, in order to become a tough, fighting, American man. Noah then is emblematic of Shaw's desire to present an acceptable portrait of "Jewishness": he is a deracinated Jew who has become a positive figure because he has shed his Old World Judaism for Anglo American maleness.

Merle Miller: *That Winter*

Merle Miller (1919–1986) was a prominent war journalist who regularly wrote pieces for *Yank, the Army Weekly,* the hugely popular magazine written by and for U.S. soldiers during World War II. As a reporter covering the war, Miller was on the front lines of the Pacific campaign, experiencing many bloody assaults firsthand.[25] Like Wolfert, he also decided to try his hand at novel writing, and his book *That Winter* was a best seller from February through April 1948.[26] Unlike most of the other writers, Miller did not come from New York. He was from a small Iowa town where his family was extremely hard hit by the Depression, and after attending the University of Iowa, Miller managed to escape his home state by heading to graduate studies at the London School of Economics. Throughout his life, Miller worked as a journalist and also wrote a handful of novels, nonfiction accounts of working for CBS, and biographies of Harry Truman and Lyndon Johnson. He gained notoriety when his 1974 biography of Harry Truman was attacked for having fabricated quotes.

In 1971 Miller composed the groundbreaking essay for the *Sunday New York Times Magazine,* "What It Means to Be a Homosexual."[27] The essay thoughtfully and emotionally charts out how destructive it has been for him to undergo homophobic intolerance, and he challenges liberals to be as disgusted with the mistreatment of homosexuals and lesbians as they ostensibly are with antisemitism and racism. As he writes in his essay, "The late Otto Kahn, I think it was, said, 'A kike is a Jewish gentleman who has just left the room.' Is a fag a homosexual gentleman who has just stepped out? Me?"

The topic of hiding one's true identity was central in *That Winter*, a Jewish reworking of the themes made popular in the 1946 Academy Award-winning film, *The Best Years of Our Lives*, which was also about returning soldiers trying to fit back into America. While *That Winter* also focuses on three protagonists who are struggling with alcoholism, post-traumatic stress (which as yet had no name), and their relationships with women, the perspective is altered to give us a specifically Jewish take on returning servicemen since a central focus is how the three main characters confront the ramifications of antisemitism.

That Winter is a fast paced account — without any chapter breaks — of three men spending their first winter back in New York after their war service: the narrator, Peter (like Miller himself), works at *Time* magazine while trying to achieve success as a novelist and attempting to come to terms with the profound guilt he feels over having accidentally caused the death of his best friend in France; Ted is a "poor rich boy" who found his first real family in the military, lost an arm in the war, and is now an out-of-control alcoholic who commits suicide in the first half of the book; and Lew, a Jewish man who has become so insecure in response to the antisemitism leveled against him while growing up in America and in the U.S. Army that he has legally changed his last name from "Colinsky" to "Cole" in order to marry his antisemitic, Catholic girlfriend, Jane Walker.

The events are told through the voice of Peter as he describes his postwar life in New York and details his daily encounters with the other two men. The style of the prose and oftentimes the content mimic the hard-boiled world of James Cain and Dashiell Hammett, as in the book's opening paragraph:

> We all drank too much that winter, some to forget the neuroses acquired in the war just ended, others in anticipation of those expected from the next, but most of us simply because we liked to drink too much.[28]

World-weary Peter is the filter through which the tale is delivered, enabling the reader to view the other two main characters through his eyes: Ted, whom he sees as a pathetic, sweet, messed-up drunk, and Lew, whom he views as a weak man trying to overcome antisemitism and sort out his messy New York life. The narrative is retroactive, delivered from some unspecified future time, looking at the men's first months back in the United States after service. The terse, third-person prose does not linger on descriptions but instead quickly moves along, evoking the fast pace and loss of footing of the three veterans.

All three of the war weary men are outwardly hardened. They spend their time womanizing, drinking, and fighting. Yet inwardly they are weak and terrified. With Ted this is evident when he kills himself because he cannot find a way to stop drinking and suffering from his post-traumatic stress nightmares. For Peter and Lew, in contrast, their fears are expressed to each other in conversations and in tears. They are a lost generation that feel that there is no certitude about anything. Or, to quote the narrator, "The purpose," I said, "is purposelessness. That is the slogan for our age" (*That Winter*, 12).

The narrative portrays the "reconversion," as the *New York Times* labeled it, of three men trying to regain their footing in postwar America.[29] The day-to-day account of the first winter back is interwoven with memories and stories of events that occurred while they were in Europe. The book forcefully presents the chaos and fear felt by returning soldiers as they seek to build a new life in America while struggling with their terrible memories of combat.

The search for a good life in postwar America ends in dramatically different ways for the three central characters. Ted shoots himself; Lew gives up on his writing career and returns to Los Angeles to run the family jewelry business; and Peter, after the death of his father, quits his job and heads to Mississippi to visit the widow of the friend whose death he believes he is responsible for. Where Lew thus chooses to retrench himself in his Jewish family, although the decision terrifies him, Peter sets out on a quest of soul searching.

That Winter shows how hard it was for returning soldiers to sort out their recent experiences while at the same time building a life in the United States. In nearly every scene a variety of strangers — taxi drivers, bartenders, friends of friends — describe to the protagonists where and when they served. They are all desperate to share their war experiences with anyone who will listen. All the returning servicemen are lost and seek out anything that will bring them solace: alcohol, one-night stands, fistfights. Moreover, each is trying to come to terms with the new realities of their relationships with their wives and girlfriends. The book describes numerous divorces and affairs as relationships fall apart in response to men having undergone the trauma of combat, and women having been on their own, sometimes for years, while their menfolk served.

That Winter gives no easy answers, instead empathetically portraying how difficult things were for everyone when the soldiers returned. While war service brought about often crippling anxiety and sadness, according to Miller it also had the good effect of creating friendships between those who would never have known each other "except for the accident of war" (36). Moreover, combat has taught some non-Jewish men a new form of compassion for minorities. The Protestant narrator thus asserts that in battle he learned "what it's like to be a second-rate citizen; I began faintly to appreciate something of how it feels to be a Negro or a Jew; all enlisted men do. But, of course, I was in the Army less than four years; it takes a lifetime to understand completely" (48).

Merle Miller is reminding his readership that they need to disavow antisemitism and racism so that the war effort will have been a force for equality. The drunk rich boy, Ted, shows this when staying at a New England inn where he encounters a rich friend of his father who describes how the hotel, fortunately, has instituted a policy that excludes Jews. This shocks Ted and it is "the first time since I got back I was mad. Been mad a lot since" (89). Ted responds by telling the man off, packing his bags to leave, and then getting too drunk and "comfortable" to do anything. For him, as for many Americans, inertia and inaction override a clear response to hatred.

The topic of antisemitism in America and Europe, as with the other war novels, is a constant refrain. Miller uses the WASP narrator as a foil to examine how Jews are viewed in America. He thus describes the first encounter between Lew and the narrator:

> Then he added diffidently, as if he wasn't quite sure of my reaction, "I'm Jewish." "Oh," I said. You never know what to say at a time like that. Should you say, "You don't look Jewish"? And Lew doesn't, not as most Protestant-Americans like to think of Jews . . . Or should you reply, "It doesn't really matter to me"? Trite and smug. Or perhaps, "So what? Who cares?" But you knew that a great many people do care and care very much in-

deed, including a girl from Denver named Smith. I simply said again, "Oh." (27)

In Miller's rendition, being a Jew in America is perceived as being shameful and embarrassing. The narrator, a good and decent man who deplores antisemitism, cannot think of any way to respond appropriately to the embarrassment felt by the Jew. Miller, like most of the other authors of the novels of 1948, is using the topic of American antisemitism as a means to signify a larger theme of the need for equality for all Americans in the postwar era.

Lew confronted the Holocaust firsthand when he, like all the Jewish soldiers in the war novels of 1948, was at Dachau after its liberation, and met a Polish boy whose parents and two sisters had been killed in the death camp. The boy kissed Lew's hand when he discovered that Lew was a fellow Jew. As Miller depicts it, the antisemitism of Europe is connected with that of America, much as Shaw described it in *The Young Lions*. In both books, the Jewish soldiers encounter the same terrible smear: "one of the [enlisted men] said there was one thing about the Germans. They had some pretty good ideas about the Jews." When the soldier who asserts this finds Lew crying, he declares "that was the trouble with the Jews. Always feeling sorry for themselves" (220).

After recounting this, Lew describes how a few days previously at work someone made an antisemitic slur and "I didn't say anything. Not a damn word. He didn't know I was Jewish, and it didn't matter. He still liked me. That was the day I became Lew Cole — officially" (221). The cumulative experiences have beaten Lew down and he has given up even trying to fight back. Instead he will simply change his name and hide. Miller wrote that at the time when he was publishing *That Winter*, he chose to marry a woman in order to pretend that he was "as straight as the next man."[30] The character Lew's decision to "hide" his Jewishness by marrying a Catholic mimics Miller's own attempt at the time to "hide" his homosexuality through marriage. (And as with Lew, Miller's sham relationship quickly fell apart.)

Lew's anger only returns after arranging a meeting between his fiancée and his immigrant mother when his mother reminds him that he should feel pride, not shame, in his Jewishness. When Lew telegrams Peter about the meeting he inserts the Yiddish word "schlemiel" (mistakenly spelled "schlameel" by the telegram operator). At that moment, Lew has reasserted his Jewishness, and when his fiancée treats him rudely in front of his mother, after ordering pork chops for herself, he slaps her and the relationship ends.

Miller's *That Winter* describes the struggles of returning soldiers as they seek to find their way in America. Each has a burden to overcome: Ted the neglect of his wealthy parents, Peter his childhood poverty, and Lew antisemitism. The larger message is clear: Americans must be aware that the returning soldiers are not as tough as they may seem; many are struggling to merely get through the day. Moreover, Americans must work to root out their ignorant hatreds toward Jews, blacks, and all minority groups in order to rise to the decency embodied by the Anglo narrator. *That Winter*, another neglected work, aims to make its readership accept that they must give returning soldiers of all creeds and colors the warm and considerate reception that they deserve after having lived through the horrors of war.

Lew undergoes the greatest transformation in the book, from initially hating himself for being a Jew, to finally choosing to return to the bosom of his family. He shakes himself out of his depression and awakens at the moment he slaps his fiancée. This is seen as a positive rather than negative or abusive act because it shows that Lew has reasserted his independence as both a Jew and as a man. His fiancée throughout the book had constantly belittled him and he had responded by being cowardly and submissive. In hitting her he becomes a strong and assertive man who has taken control of his life. Lew had lived through many of the worst campaigns of World War II, but could barely survive living in peacetime America. Only by taking an assertively active male stance can he regain his footing, and by so doing, become a positive image of an American Jewish male: one who is not effete and cowed, but who is tough and strong.

Mimicking Ernest Hemingway's *The Sun Also Rises*, about a "lost generation" of ex-servicemen seeking to find their footing in Paris and Spain, Miller's New Yorkers are being offered all the dizzying enticements of a boom economy. There are a surfeit of choices, a nonstop parade of things to do, women to meet, places to eat. They can easily find a way to keep too busy to look inside themselves, but late at night when things quiet down their souls are tormented and scared.[31] This was the same type of theme as found in Salinger's dark story "A Perfect Day for Bananafish" that ended with the veteran's suicide.

That Winter gives a Jewish take on the motif of the lost soldier by delineating that for Jewish soldiers in particular, the return home was especially hard because of entrenched antisemitism in America. When Lew breaks free by slapping his fiancée, he nevertheless does not have the option of setting out on his own as does Peter; his only choice is to leave New York and rejoin his family. In the immediate years after the war, this novelist was trying to challenge entrenched antisemitism, without yet knowing how to give to his Jewish readers in particular a range of choices about how they could reconstruct themselves, and their lives, after returning home.

Stefan Heym: *The Crusaders*

Stefan Heym (1913–2001), author of the best-selling 1948 novel *The Crusaders*, was a lifelong radical: first fighting against the Nazis in Germany, then in America against censorship, and finally when back in East Germany against the Communist Party.[32] Originally named Helmut Flieg, while still in high school Heym published caustic poems and essays about Germany which raised the ire of the rising Nazi Party. In 1933 at the age of 19, Heym fled Germany after a warrant was issued for his arrest, going on foot to Prague and then to the United States. Heym's daughter as well as many members of his family were killed by the Nazis.

Awarded a scholarship by a Jewish fraternity, Heym wrote an M.A. thesis on Heinrich Heine at the University of Chicago. After graduating, Heym became head editor of the leftist German American newspaper *Deutsches Volksech* and published two novels in English. He was drafted into the U.S. Army in 1943. Heym's fluency in German and his training and previous work in journalism landed him a position with the psychological warfare unit that was part of the counter-intelligence unit called the Ritchie Boys, so named because they were trained at Fort Ritchie in Maryland. The group was composed of thousands of Jewish German émigrés like Heym. The Ritchie Boys participated in the invasion of Normandy and took on an array of roles in the war effort: disseminating propaganda against the Germans, interrogating captured soldiers, inserting false stories in the local German press, and overseeing radio broadcasts into Germany.[33] Even though capture would have likely meant Heym's death because he was a Jew and a previous enemy of the Nazis, Heym bravely served on the front lines, even manning a radio station while under German attack. For this he received the Bronze Star.

In 1945 Heym was discharged from the army because he refused to write a negative story about the Soviet regime for the American zone German paper *Die neue Zeitung*. In 1948 he published *The Crusaders* to extensive critical and popular success. In 1952 he returned permanently to Communist East Germany where he wrote novels in English and German and served as a freelance journalist. By the late 1950s, Heym, ever the "rebel," was on the outs with the East German leadership for his increasing challenges to their repression of individual rights, and by the late 1970s his works were unofficially banned from publication in East Germany.[34] After the fall of Communism in East Germany, Heym served briefly on a socialist platform in the Bundestag. Heym died of a heart attack in 2001 while attending a Heinrich Heine conference in Israel.

The Crusaders is a historical novel — as Heym asserts on the cover page — based on his experiences in the Ritchie Boys (although the unit is not called this in the book). The term "Crusaders" is used in both an ideal manner, as a group devoted to spreading the American belief in helping the world's oppressed and beating tyranny, and ironically since many soldiers "aren't crusaders . . . we're egotists, opportunists, cowards" (*The Crusaders*, 82). Because it evokes the genre of the historical novel, *The Crusaders* is long, detailed, and panoramic in scope beginning with the invasion at Omaha Beach and ending with the postwar de-Nazification of German towns. Heym uses an evocative third-person narrative voice that comfortably shifts between internal accounts of how the men understand the events they are undergoing, and external descriptions of the landscapes of both war and civilian life, as in this brief account of troop movements during the Battle of the Bulge: "The men were slowly advancing over the hillocks, weaving up and down like the little flags of a fisherman's net in the tides" (418).

The two main protagonists are the Jewish-German Sergeant Walter Bing and Lieutenant Yates, a German Studies professor from the States. Bing and Yates combine aspects of Heym himself: Bing is a German Jew returning to Germany with the Americans, while Yates is a scholar of German literature. The book also covers the actions and thoughts of some of the Nazis they are trying to root out, and the French, American, and German women with whom they become involved.

While the fighting is taking place all around them, the members of the unit have private battles, from the corrupt Dondolo trying to set up a black market for French goods, to the virtuous Yates trying to live with himself after cheating on his beloved wife, to Bing attempting to sort out how German he really is in light of the war. Although the American armed services have some corrupt and mean men, such as the bigot Dondolo, nevertheless they generally act from a higher ethical stance than do the Nazis.

The story also covers the liberation of the "Paula camp" — a German concentration camp where experiments were conducted on prisoners. The sadistic treatment and mass murder of the prisoners is described explicitly. When the American soldiers, overwhelmed by the horror that they are witnessing, begin to hunt down and lynch the hiding SS, they are reprimanded and reminded that "there'll be justice, in due time, and by the proper authorities. There'll be no more lynching. We're not Nazis; we're fighting for something better" (543). Yet in Heym's work nothing is black and white, and to counter this idealistic vision of the Americans, he describes General Farrish, who is more intent on having press photos taken of himself with the camp inmates than in organizing food for them.

The final quarter of the book shows the surviving members of the group attempting to clear Nazis out of German towns. As they do their work, there are corrupt actions on both sides, with some Americans more interested in making money than in clearing the land of the Nazi influence. The book ends with a surprising plot twist when Yates discovers that the German woman who has been employed by him (and with whom he is sleeping) is not really a survivor of the camps but a German scam artist. In the final scene, the evil Nazi Erich Pettinger is finally caught, and the Americans give a leadership role to an old German professor who has survived the camps. The book ends optimistically with the Americans kicking some corrupt Germans out of a local estate to make it a home for displaced persons.

The focus on a propaganda unit enables many of the descriptions to involve groups of intellectuals attempting to undermine the Germans by outwitting them. Bing, who is in charge of writing the propaganda leaflets, is asked to compose one to persuade the Germans that it is time to give up their arms. As he notes, "He, Sergeant Walter Bing, a nobody, a boy who had come to America without roots and ties, banished from home and school, was about to state the aims of this war" (27). In other words, American readers should feel proud knowing that their country took a Jewish refugee and transformed him into a true patriot. Moreover, as an outsider to America, Bing is best positioned to see and re-create the larger virtues of the country and he writes a pamphlet describing the values of America as "a nation of free men, equal before the law, and determined to govern themselves . . . Wherever people are oppressed and suffering, we are affected. Because we are that kind of nation" (79–80). Bing is so good at propagating the virtues of America that his pamphlet succeeds in getting twelve German troops to desert.[35]

By showing that America joined the war because it was devoted to spreading good, Heym rebuts the widespread antisemitic belief that European Jews manipulated the United States into entering the war in order to protect their banking interests. However, as a fellow soldier quickly points out to Bing, his pamphlet overlooks or ignores the fact that "millions of men in our country don't even have the right to vote" (81).[36] In other words, while the United States seeks to help the oppressed of the world, it does this hypocritically since it has not yet dealt with its own mistreatment of African Americans. Heym is both comforting and challenging his American readers about their nation.

It is extraordinary that a novel about a German Jew returning to Germany in the final stage of the war mentions almost nothing related to Jewishness. Moreover, when the novel does discuss the horrors of the death camps and the Nazi slaughter of innocents, it focuses on the story of two German political prisoners, rather than on Jewish characters. Where all the other novels of 1948 make antisemitism a central theme, the subject barely appears in Heym's novel. While Bing, the German Jew, would be expected to feel strong emotions upon his return to Europe and his firsthand witnessing of the destruction of the Jews, he has no specifically Jewish response to what he sees. He does not practice any Judaism (one of his favorite foods is pork chops). Furthermore, when he returns to his hometown during the German retreat, Bing discusses his happy childhood without mentioning that he is Jewish or that the Nazis killed his family. His Jewishness only comes up when a neighbor talks about how she worked for his family, and when her husband finds her with Bing and proclaims "And a Jew—too. In my house. The blood has been spoiled" (530). The only other antisemitism that is described in the book is when Pete Dondolo, who spews hatred against everyone, blames the Jews for the war, rather than Hitler "who knew what he was doing" (50). However his words bear no particular weight on the Jewish soldiers.

For Heym, perhaps because of his internationalist ideology, Jewishness was a parochial theme and it was best to make the topic all but disappear.[37] Also, typical of many Jews raised in Germany before the war, he may have believed fully in an assimilationist credo and felt a discomfort about delving into the topic of Jewishness. As Thomas C. Fox notes, Heym's "de-emphasis on Bing's Jewishness" is tied both to Heym's desire to appeal to a mainstream American readership and is a reflection of Heym's Communism and his "unwillingness to recognize forms of otherness that fall outside class distinctions."[38] Or perhaps in Heym's unit, composed mostly of German Jews, he did not experience the antisemitism that others underwent in different branches of the military. Whatever the cause, reading a book about Germany and the liberation of the camps in the final stages of the war with barely a mention of Jewish matters is indeed a strange experience because it erases from view the specific anti-Jewish nature of the Nazi assault.

Heym's novel gives readers the opportunity to see the war in Germany as unfolding on an international stage where the Holocaust was directed against a range of people, including German intellectuals, and where Americans showed themselves to be, overall, good leaders. Moreover Bing, the German Jew, is more American than anyone: he is so knowledgeable about the rhetoric of the United States that he can disseminate its propaganda lessons to the Germans.

Bing, like most of the Jewish soldiers in the 1948 novels, dies prematurely when he is killed by friendly fire in the final stages of the war. It is a moment fraught with irony because although he is fighting on the American side, in the end he is a German being killed (although accidentally) by the Americans. As with *The Young Lions*, when Michael must reckon with the death of Noah, Bing's death is a sacrifice for the greater good and brings the Christian protagonist, the intellectual David Yates, to try and become a more honest and ethical person. The other Jewish character in *The Crusaders* is Abramovici, an Eastern European who has escaped the Nazis, but with both Jewish characters there is no mention that either has any type of personal response to the Holocaust, and we only know Abramovici is Jewish because of a brief mention that "as a child he had seen pogroms" (47). The sole moment in the book when either character acts in a Jewish manner is when Abramovici recites the Jewish prayer for the dead, the Kaddish, over the spot where Bing has been killed. Only through death does Bing become Judaized.

As a German Jewish outsider on the Allied side, Heym more than anything creates a portrait of intelligent men using their brains to beat the enemy. It is a psychological battle and the victors are the smarter and more ethical Americans. The book ends on the optimistic note that the Nazis are being eradicated and that in the future Germany will be a much better place. Although written in English, Heym also published a best-selling German version of the novel, and he is showing his German readers that they need to transform themselves in order to create a better future, while reminding American readers that they still need to overcome their racial prejudices.[39] Heym clearly is not interested in using his book to shine a light on the struggles of Jews even though he makes his central character a Jew. Bing, like Heym, is an internationalist whose broader concern is the good of all humanity. This is a novel intended to show the struggles and pitfalls of Germany in the postwar era, and to warn American readers that they must challenge hypocrisy and bigotry in their own midst so that the United States does not go the same way as did Germany.

Martha Gellhorn: *Point of No Return*

Martha Gellhorn (1908–1998) was one of the most important American journalists of World War II. Gellhorn devoted her entire life to reporting on combat firsthand in a range of wars from Europe during World War II to Vietnam to the Six Day War.[40]

In 1945 Gellhorn managed to get into Dachau right after its liberation even though she had no journalist pass. What she saw there was the basis for *Point of No Return*, which was published with Scribner's in the fall of 1948.[41] Although it did not make it onto the *New York Times* best seller list, it sold enough copies to generate a second printing the following year with Bantam Books.

Gellhorn and her three brothers were raised by upper middle-class, intellectually minded, progressive parents in St. Louis, Missouri. Her father, originally from Germany, was a gynecologist and obstetrician, and her mother was a suffragist activist. Both parents were half Jewish, although the family did not practice any aspects of Judaism, and according to a childhood friend "they were accepted in St. Louis as gentiles."[42] Gellhorn attended Bryn Mawr College for a few years and then dropped out to work as a correspondent for newspapers and journals such as the *New Republic* and *Collier's*. In the late 1930s she made her way to Europe and wrote essays about the terrible treatment of the Jews and other refugees. When the war broke out, Gellhorn traveled all over Europe, often without a press or army pass to assist her safety, writing thirty-six reports on a variety of war campaigns for *Collier's*.[43]

The turning point in Gellhorn's life was her trip to Dachau.[44] She wrote an essay about it for *Collier's*,[45] and her explicit descriptions of the horrors she witnessed there would reappear in the final section of *Point of No Return* when the protagonist witnesses it himself.[46] As Giovanno Dell'Orto has traced, Gellhorn's novelistic account of Dachau mimics her journalistic dispatches, since her main aim was to accurately get across the realities of the camp.[47] This journalistic approach may be why her descriptions of Dachau in the novel are so explicit, lengthy, and horrifying. Gellhorn does not shy away from anything, describing in detail the medical experiments conducted on live prisoners, the full process of how the Germans did the gassings and cremations, the details of the dying skeleton-thin survivors, and the piles of corpses that are everywhere:

> On the right was the pile of prisoners, naked, putrefying, yellow skeletons. There was just enough flesh to melt and make this smell, in the sun. The pile was as high as a small house.[48]

Gellhorn wrote *Point of No Return* "in order to get rid of Dachau. The whole book, for me, was that: to exorcise what I could not live with."[49] The main character, Jacob Levy, an assimilated Jew from St. Louis, becomes her stand-in: "I wanted him to relieve me of the memory of Dachau ... If I gave Dachau to Jacob Levy, I would leave it."[50]

Yet writing the book did not rid Gellhorn of what she had witnessed, and she was never the same again:

But Dachau, and all I afterwards saw: Belsen, etc., changed my life or my personality. Like a water-shed. I have never been the same since. It's exactly like mixing paint. Black, real true solid black, was then introduced, and I have never again come back to some state of hope or innocence or gayety which I had before.[51]

Although half Jewish, Gellhorn's firsthand experiences of Dachau made her re-avow the importance of her Jewishness.[52] Moreover, it made her feel that it was a priority to witness and report on the Final Solution, and she followed her time there with visits to Belsen and Ravensbrück.[53]

She came to believe that Dachau was only the starting point of the true horrors that the world could inflict, and in 1988 she asserted that:

More than forty years on, I know that my fear of Dachau was justified. If men could do that there, men could do it again anywhere, when sanctioned by the State. And they have. Various adaptations of Dachau thrive in some ninety countries now. It has been a splendidly successful model.[54]

Gellhorn remained deeply concerned with the Jewish plight after the Holocaust, and attended and reported on the Nuremberg and the Eichmann trials. She also became a lifelong staunch Zionist, feeling pride in the Jewish state, visiting it multiple times, and writing positive reports about it. Gellhorn believed that the world owed Israel its support in light of the Holocaust. As she said in response to Arab attacks on the country: "When I stand before you here, O judges of Israel, I do not stand alone. With me are six million accusers."[55]

Gellhorn published eleven novels, travel essays, and collections of her journalism. She was famous as well for having been Ernest Hemingway's third wife from 1940 to 1945. She first met him in Florida in 1936, then they lived together in Cuba, after which they went to Spain to report on the Civil War. (Hemingway dedicated his novel about the Spanish Civil War, *For Whom the Bell Tolls*, to Gellhorn.) During World War II both covered the war and wrote accounts of D-Day for the same July 22, 1944, issue of *Collier's*, with Hemingway getting the lead piece even though he had not made it ashore (although he pretended he had) while Gellhorn had actually been there to witness the fighting firsthand (she snuck aboard a Red Cross ship to the front lines).[56] Gellhorn was so good at her job that Hemingway became deeply resentful of her.[57] Although her reporting style had many similarities with his, the subject matter differed greatly, with her aim to show the true evil of the Germans even if it meant "abandoning neutrality" in her reportage.[58]

Gellhorn's books were often read and evaluated through the prism of Hemingway with, for example, the largely positive *New York Times* book review of *Point of No Return* mentioning by the second line that "Miss Gellhorn writes in a vigorous style, suggestive at many points of an ex-husband called Ernest Hemingway."[59]

"Point of No Return" was a term that Gellhorn first heard at a British bomber base to describe "a specific time limit, stated in hours and minutes. When reached, the pilot must head the plane back or it would have insufficient fuel to stay airborne and land in England. Turn or die." When Scribner's published the book in 1948 they pressured her to use a less militaristic title and Gellhorn came up with "The Wine of Astonishment" after spotting the term when thumbing through the *Book of Psalms* in a motel room Bible.[60] Of the title change, Gellhorn wrote that "it simply spoiled the book for me"[61] particularly since "*The Wine of Astonishment* is a ludicrously wrong title. Hitler, not God, had made the earth to tremble."[62] When the University of Nebraska Press reprinted the novel in 1995 they returned to Gellhorn's intended title in part as a feminist form of reclamation of the author's intention. In the book's afterword Gellhorn wrote that "In this new re-issue, I am reclaiming my original, true title, *Point of No Return*, and thus reclaiming the book for myself."[63] Following her lead, I also call her novel *Point of No Return*.

The plot of *Point of No Return* focuses on Private First Class Jacob Levy during the bloody Hürtgen Forest campaign and the Battle of the Bulge, and the fierce close-hand battles between the U.S. Army and the Germans that resulted in exceptionally high death tolls. *Point of No Return* depicts the horrific reality of these operations and the daily life of combatants forced to live in trenches during the freezing winter months. Using a traditional third-person omniscient narrator, Gellhorn probes the inner workings and the psychological trauma of this type of warfare, describing a number of soldiers who have gone insane as a result of the stress suffered in battle. The plot moves along quickly, although from time to time the pace slows down in Gellhorn's beautiful and evocative descriptions, as in her rendering of the detritus of the Battle of the Bulge after the German retreat:

> The snow had fallen over the garbage of battle, covering smoothly tank tracks and shell holes and dirty papers and tin cans and live mines and excrement and all the other by-products of war. The ruin of Hackenthal was softened by the snow. A German self-propelled 88 tilted against a low stone wall; its treads were ripped off. In the disturbed snow, the possessions of the gun's crew were blown about it; a pair of bedroom slippers, a diary, two helmets, a first-aid kit, rations, and a woman's embroidered handkerchief. (*Point of No Return*, 140)

Gellhorn's sketch elegantly renders the uniquely terrible landscapes of war, empty of humans, where snippets of a life once lived are frozen in time in the snowy landscape.

During the novel, Jacob Levy, who has already survived numerous other campaigns and two brushes with death, is convinced that he will shortly be killed. Although he would rather blend into the background in order to be seen as just like everyone else — in other words as a Christian — "because Levy's name is clearly Jewish, his heritage often precedes him."[64] He falls under the protective wing of Lieutenant Colonel John Smithers, who originally views Levy as a "dirty Jew," but comes to respect him because of his work ethic and quiet demeanor. Part of the reason why Levy works so hard, and keeps so quiet, is because he does not want to be castigated as a whiny Jew.[65] At first, when they are encamped just outside the forest, Levy works as Smithers's jeep driver, but shortly thereafter they enter the forest where Levy becomes an ammunitions bearer. Their battalion, like all the others, fight intense and terrifying battles and suffer extremely high casualties.

Eventually Levy, still working for Smithers, makes his way to occupied Luxembourg. There he meets a Catholic waitress named Kathe. She does not speak English, so they converse and fall in love using rudimentary French. He tells Kathe that his name is that of his Commander, John Dawson Smithers, since he does not want her to know that his real name is Jacob Levy, because he believes she will reject him if she knows he is a Jew. After a few dates Kathe loses her virginity to him, and he decides that after the war either he will convert or they will marry and live together in the American countryside since "where they were going to live it would not matter about being a Jew. There would be no one but Kathe and him, alone, with the clear, fast stream and the peaceful days, and their home to build, and their life" (195).

In the final section of the book, after Germany has admitted defeat, Levy tells Smithers that he wishes to go to Dachau to see the camp that he has heard about. He actually has no interest in this, only using it as an excuse to make a side trip to see Kathe. Upon witnessing Dachau, however, Jacob is overtaken with an unstoppable rage at himself for not having fought harder during the war, and against the Germans who did this to the Jews. Gellhorn described this moment as "Jacob's point of no return" and as he drives wildly out of the camp, Jacob spots a group of Germans and is overwhelmed with anger toward them for laughing and enjoying themselves while the Jews were dying. His main rage is against all the bystanders who let this happen, and his indictment includes himself for not having fought harder to stop the Shoah. Levy plows his car through them, killing three. When Levy kills the Germans, according to James Dawes, Gellhorn begins "to lose authorial control: one can feel her barely contained fury in the concluding section."[66] Levy's actions are thus a reflection of what happened to Gellhorn herself at Dachau:

> Between the moment when I walked through the gate of that prison, with its infamous motto, Arbeit Macht Frei, and when I walked out at the end of a day that had no ordinary scale of hours, I was changed, and how I looked at the human condition, the world we live in, changed. I remember what I felt: frantic, insane fear. I had to get away from Germany at once, no matter how; I could not breathe the air or endure the faces of Germans around me.[67]

In the last few chapters of the novel, Levy is in a prison hospital being treated for wounds suffered during the crash. Everyone is doing their best to try and get him off the charges since they assume he killed the Germans by accident. Levy, however, keeps asserting that he murdered them on purpose, and that he wishes that he had killed more of them. It seems likely that in spite of Levy's protestations, he will not serve much prison time. Levy also begins to assert over and over again to anyone who will listen that he is Jewish, and he also writes a letter to Kathe and signs it with his real name in large, capital letters. The book ends with Levy quite feverish with an infected arm from the car crash and looking out the prison window while telling himself that Kathe will still marry him. It is unclear whether he lives in spite of his infected arm and goes on to win his court case and get his girl, or if he dies. In either case, the book concludes with him holding onto his love for Kathe and his belief that she will remain with him even if she knows that he is Jewish.

The forbidden love between a Catholic woman and a Jewish man was the main topic that Bantam Books focused on in their 1949 paperback. Thus the cover shows a sitting woman in a low-cut dress staring up at a GI under the subheading: "He lied to her . . . was driven to violence . . . because of the secret within him!" The image mimics the poster for the winner of the 1947 Oscar for Best Picture, *Gentleman's Agreement*, which was about the inverse case of a Gentile masquerading as a Jew (and was the top-grossing movie that year for 20th Century Fox). In the movie poster, however, it is the man sitting in the chair and the woman in the low-cut dress who is standing behind him. And Jacob's personality supports his leading man rendition: he is handsome and rugged, tough and brave, and knows how to love a woman. There is nothing bookish or intellectual about him, although he does have a sensitive side that shows up in the deep fears he suffers in close combat.

As with nearly every other Jewish soldier from the novels of 1948, Levy's Jewishness is entirely limited to being the recipient of other people's hatred. According to Gellhorn's biographer Carl Rollyson, this was in part because Levy like Gellhorn came from a "vague St. Louis German-Jewishness, a Jewishness never acknowledged or confronted."[68] As Jacob says when considering life in the U.S. Army: "This was the principal difference, to his mind, between being a Jew and being a Gentile. They left the Gentiles alone until the guy proved he was out of line but a Jew had to earn being left alone."[69] He does not practice any aspects of the religion. As he asserts: "I was born a Jew but I'm not religious. I've never even been inside a synagogue" (5). He has no strong cultural ties and for him to be a Jew is to be hated, as he experienced in America when he was excluded from things such as fraternities. Moreover, as with the mother in *An Act of Love* who learns to keep to herself and not stick out, Levy's father has taught him that "if Jews would stay quiet and not get together and make a squawk and mind their own business and pay their taxes, pretty soon people would stop picking on them" (101). In other words, only by keeping their mouths shut and not making a fuss will American Jews deserve to be treated with respect.

Internalizing the self-hatred of his father's generation, Levy had blamed European Jews for what had happened to them at the hands of the Nazis, and like many fellow Americans he was against the entrance of the United States into the war:

> It don't stand to reason that the American government and the whole army and navy and air force would go to war with Hitler because of the Jews . . . I'm sympathetic to these poor Jews over here and if I wasn't American I'd probably be exterminated myself by now, but honestly Kathe, why didn't the Jews get out of Europe a long time ago.

Once Jacob met the dying Jews at Dachau, saw the piles of corpses, and overheard the screaming women who had gone insane because of the experiments conducted on them, Levy realized that he was one of them and that his father's passive stance was wrong: "I never thought about them except it was pretty tough on them and they should of left Europe long ago. I never knew. They had their lives and their friends the same as me" (219). The Holocaust has taught him, Martha Gellhorn, and countless other American Jews that they must rid themselves of the burden of fear typical of first-generation Jewish immigrants in order to become assertive and strong.

Gellhorn dedicated the novel to "James Gavin and to the men he commanded in World War II" and she clearly has no intention of writing a negative portrayal of the armed services, and unlike the other novels of 1948, there is little antisemitism portrayed within the military. Her aim, instead, is to show the American military as the victor over German tyranny. In fact, the sole American character who acts like an antisemite is Officer Smithers, who quickly overcomes all his prejudices and becomes Levy's strongest ally. Gellhorn's limited portrait of antisemitism may also have come about because as a "vaguely Jewish" war correspondent she did not witness nor suffer antisemitism in the military.

Instead, Gellhorn directs her rage toward the Germans who annihilated the Jews of Europe, and Levy's transformation revolves around him also sharing that same anger. The sole, though profound, indictment she directs against America is that it did not bomb the death camps. Thus, Levy notes on seeing Dachau that "the bombers had not troubled this place: it didn't seem as if the war had bothered them anyway" (203). As with the German bystanders in the local town, the American administration is culpable for not having done anything to stop the Holocaust. Jacob is therefore Gellhorn's mouthpiece for her own view that "we," the Americans, "are not entirely guiltless."[70]

Point of No Return attempts to portray the absolute trauma undergone in Jewish life in response to the Holocaust. Levy, who starts the war an innocent assimilated Jew who only wants to be left alone, ends the war murdering Germans even though peace has been declared, and wishing that he could kill even more. All the pleas of his parents not to make waves, to quietly assimilate, have been wrong, because antisemitism is permanent, endemic, and can even reach the safe shores of America. He is a raging warrior, and his murder of the Germans enables Gellhorn's Jewish readers to feel a cathartic pleasure at having gotten even with the citizens who have allowed the destruction of their Jewish brethren in Europe. Perhaps because of Gellhorn's firsthand experience of Dachau, this novel is much more singular in intention than the others: to get the information about the Holocaust out to readers and to show them that this event will forever traumatize all Jews.

The four novels about the European campaign each explicitly render life in the Nazi death camps and show the manner in which coming into contact with it impacts upon the Jewish soldier. The descriptions read like firsthand reportage rather than mediated novelistic discourse since the authors preferred the verisimilitude of a journalistic account to convince a potentially skeptical reading public that yes, this had indeed happened. In all the novels, even those composed by authors who did not enter Dachau after its liberation, the description of the extermination camp serves a number of functions. First, it documents the horrific realities of the Final Solution for a broad American readership. Second, it becomes a "type scene" that delineates the moment when the Jewish soldier must reckon with his particular status.[71] Third, it stresses the liberal mandate that Americans must embrace pluralism and banish racism to differentiate themselves from the German Nazi tyrants. And finally it shows that the Holocaust must be remembered as a central aspect of the war, rather than being divorced from it. A Jewish GI, both a Jew and an American, embodies this merging of the two narratives of the war and the Holocaust.

Even though these are Jewish-authored novels, the events are presented from a paradigmatically American angle. The starting point of the Holocaust is at the moment when the U.S. Army infantry divisions liberate the camps in April 1945. The end point is when the Jewish soldier finds a means to acclimate this moment into his view of himself as a Jew and as an American.

In these novels written so soon after the war, there is, however, as yet no suitable term to describe the extermination of the Jews; no "Final Solution" or "Holocaust" or "Shoah." Instead we have "Dachau" or "concentration camp" as the term to cover this broader event. The shifting labels for the Holocaust are evident as well in the *Jewish Book Annual* where literature about it is categorized under the heading "Literature of Martyrdom" for 1947/1948 and "Accounts of Displaced Persons" for 1949/1950.[72] (After 1950 the annual stopped breaking down the books into specific categories.) In the two novels by journalists, Martha Gellhorn and Merle Miller, perhaps reflecting their training, the Nazi camp is specifically named as Dachau. In the novels of Shaw and Heym the camp remains unnamed.

In this early stage where the exterminations of the Jews had not been broadly described as a unique event of World War II labeled as "the Holocaust," it is still understood as one aspect of the war that the Allied victory has managed to stop. As Jacob describes it in *Point of No Return*:

> He thought that the war was a good thing and he would write and tell Poppa so. They did not make the war because of Dachau; if they had, he would certainly have heard about Dachau long ago. But in the end, they reached it. And the S.S. guards were there, piled up dead in a mound, and their dogs were dead. So the war was a good thing. (230)

In *Point of No Return*, *The Young Lions*, and *That Winter*, the camp as well symbolizes that this is a specifically Jewish tragedy with Jews as the main victims of the Nazis. The exception is Stephan Heym's *The Crusaders* where, perhaps because of his Communist, universalist orientation, the camps are populated by a range of victims.

After the war Gellhorn and Shaw became staunch supporters of Israel and felt deep pride in the Jewish state. For them, both secular Jews, the only positive outcome of the Holocaust was the establishment of Israel. Their Zionism played out in part in their graphic documentation of the death camps as a way of suggesting that Israel is a necessary and positive outcome of the horrors of the Holocaust.[73] Moreover, their fictional protagonists, Levy and Ackerman, represent ideal Jewish warriors who fight for their people, destroy their enemies, and see their Jewishness not as a cultural or religious form of self-definition, but as a tough response to victimization.

These Jewish warriors embody cultural notions of masculinity from both the American and Zionist arenas that contrast with the "weak" figure of the Eastern European Jewish intellectual.[74] As Americans, their toughness resonates with the brave, Hemingwayesque soldier who is always ready to fight for his country and to protect his good name. By becoming a soldier, to use Beth Wenger's terminology, the Jew is "reinvented" and "reinvigorated" as a loyal and assimilated American who is "reclaiming his masculinity."[75]

After the publication of the works that I have discussed, the "Holocaust" novel followed a different trajectory than the Jewish American war novel.[76] In the United States, the Holocaust novel as a distinct genre begins with the 1950 best seller and winner of the National Jewish Book Award, *The Wall*, by John Hersey. It is an account of the Warsaw ghetto, its uprising and destruction. Like Leon Uris's 1961 best-selling *Mila 18*, this is a work of historical fiction aimed to showcase the heroism and martyrdom of the Jews in Poland. The novel uses the device of the found diary to impart historical verisimilitude to the story being told. In this case the diary is about the Warsaw ghetto uprising, suggesting a found artifact from Emmanuel Ringelblum's Oyneg Shabbes archive.

Where the war novelists had turned to a journalistic voice when describing the death camps, Hersey and Uris instead would utilize the literary genre of the historical novel to present a "factual" account of what had happened for American readers. In these novels, while they wear the costumes of "true" accounts, the works undermine this by having most of the central protagonists survive the war. Rather than the typical fate of death for the majority of the diarists of the Ringelblum archive, in Hersey's book the central characters escape to the forests.

By 1960, the American Holocaust novel crests with the English translation of Elie Wiesel's *Night*, which conflates literary devices from the memoir and the novel, and which does not have the same struggle for verisimilitude since it is a survivor's account of what happened.[77] Yet similarly with Hersey's and Uris's novels, the account ends with the survival of the protagonist whose life enables him to get the story of what has happened out to postwar readers. By contrast in the war novels, published earlier and with different intentions, there is no such happy ending: the Jewish Holocaust victims are presented as near death, or as piles of corpses. The job of the Jewish American soldier is to bring this vision of complete destruction back to America as a permanent reminder of the path that hate can take.

The Holocaust novel transformed again in 1961 to the trope of the victim/survivor who is haunted in America by the horrific events he or she had undergone. This was the theme of the "prototypical Holocaust novel," Edward Lewis Wallant's *The Pawnbroker*.[78] Using a straightforward, third-person, novelistic voice, *The Pawnbroker* does not attempt to establish that it is a historical account because its focus is how the survivor in America embodies two temporal and spatial moments, the European Holocaust that is the past, and the American present. He is the inverted counterpart of the Jewish soldier who experiences the Holocaust through his American Jewishness as fighter. In this case, the survivor experiences America through his European Jewishness as victim.

In *The Pawnbroker*, through the survivor, Sol Nazerman's, encounters with a series of Americans — his young Hispanic assistant, Jesus, and Marilyn Birchfield, a social worker — he transforms from a cold, empty shell of a man to someone capable of grieving for his huge losses and having connections with other humans. Sol's return to humanity begins after the gentle character Jesus is killed when protecting him from robbers, and Sol is stunned that such an act of heroism and kindness can still exist. The Americans who help Sol represent the best aspects of a broad, diverse society, and his pawnshop are, of course, situated in Harlem. This positive image of a diverse America is the same lesson of the Jewish war novels of 1948 as embodied by the ideal platoon which is a buttress against the tyrannical hatred of the Nazis. But in this case, it is a European survivor rather than an American soldier who becomes the prop for the message of inclusion. Also, as with the war novels, the work presents the details of the Holocaust's exterminations in an unflinching and graphic way, but here they come through flashbacks.

Having just risked their lives for the larger ideal of "America," returning Jewish soldiers and journalists wrote war novels that presented portraits, good and bad, beautiful and ugly, of what it meant to be an American man. The books showed not only the troubling divisions in the United States, as symbolized by the antisemitism in the platoons, but also the possibility for a new type of brotherhood, as for instance when the Anglo Michael Whitacre risks his life to avenge the death of the Jew Noah Ackerman. Even the officers, the bastion of the WASP world from which the Jews were excluded, could transform, as we saw in the evolution of David Yates in *The Crusaders*. In the stress of war, where divisions among the men could lead to their deaths, they had to find a way to work together. This urge to connect with fellow Americans across ethnic and class lines (although problematically African Americans do not come into the picture) remained after war service, as we saw with the three protagonists of *That Winter* who discover how deeply bound they are to one another. Although in war, as the authors showed, the "brotherhood in arms" was an ideal rather than a reality, upon returning home some began to try to realize that belief by establishing new friendships.[79]

These novels suggest that in the postwar era Jewish men had few options. As the authors present it, either they could hold onto their ethnic backgrounds, as embodied by their weak and crippled parents, or they could shed their past and become new Americans. Like pioneers heading west, the Jewish soldiers returning home were rendered as feeling themselves to be in a new land. To survive, they needed to keep hold of what they had become as soldiers: tough, brave, and willing to fight for what they wanted. The ultimate prize was the Christian wife who accepted the returning Jew as a real American hero. Noah and Harry were able to claim this prize by rejecting their parents' Jewish world. This shared motif of shedding the past to embrace a new model of Jewish manhood asserts to mainstream readers that the Jew is now ready to become a full member of society because through war he has learned a lesson on refashioning himself.

The novels of 1948 heavily stress the preponderance of antisemitism in the armed forces and propose that Jewish soldiers felt their lives and sense of worth to be at extra risk not only from the German or Japanese enemy, but also from their fellow antisemitic Americans. The novels then take this theme and show how it led to a range of responses, the most extreme of which was undertaking suicidal missions to prove oneself as we saw in *The Naked and the Dead, The Young Lions,* and *An Act of Love.* Ironically, in these instances, the Jew becomes a heroic soldier not because he is trying to kill the German or Japanese enemy, but because he is seeking to prove himself to his fellow Americans. Other responses included putting pressure on fellow Jewish soldiers to act "appropriately" in front of Christians, seeking out friendships with non-Jews as a buttress against antisemitism, and downplaying the endemic hatred of Jews. In all cases, it meant that Jewish soldiers were undergoing multiple campaigns to fight the enemy and survive as Jews.

In all of these 1948 novels, in fact, the definition of "Jewish" is almost entirely about being a discriminated member of a minority within a majority culture. In two of the books, *That Winter* and *Point of No Return,* the mistreatment of the Jews has led the soldier protagonists to the radical choice of hiding their Jewishness by changing their names and passing as Christians. These novels may have been influenced by the popularity of the trope of the hiding Jew as found in the movie *Gentleman's Agreement* (where a Christian masquerades as a Jew) or Arthur Miller's 1945 novel *Focus.* This is also part of a larger trend in Jewish American writing in the immediate postwar years of cloaking Jewish characters within the costume of WASPs, as for instance in Arthur Miller's *Death of a Salesman* (1949) or J. D. Salinger's *Catcher in the Rye* (1951).[80] These works showcase the intense pressures that writers encountered as they sought to navigate the postwar literary landscape and felt unable or unwilling to explicitly assert the "Jewishness" of the world they were writing about. Hiding one's Jewishness became, for many, a common and acceptable type of assimilation in the immediate postwar years, and when the literature took on this form, Jewishness went underground. In the case of the war novels, however, the Jewish character eventually "comes out" and proclaims his true identity and by so doing seeks to be accepted fully as a Jew and as an American.

Critics of the time responded in varied ways to these characters who are Jews only because they are victimized. The Jewish American writer Harold Ribalow in his 1949 essay "The Jewish GI in American Fiction" condemns the portraits of Jewish soldiers because they

> never apparently saw the inside of a synagogue — and don't want to. They eat oysters and ham. They have no Jewish education to speak of. They seldom discuss Judaism or Jewishness in any reference other than antisemitism, or how being a Jew instills in them a feeling of alienation . . . In a word, these characters are indistinguishable from other Americans, but because of the label "Jew" are not always accepted by other Americans.[81]

For Ribalow it is extremely problematic that these novels do not describe soldiers who embrace Judaism, since it means the authors are portraying their Jewish characters in the same manner as Christian writers: as merely alienated minorities. He would prefer that the authors instead shared with their readership some of the rich cultural and religious legacy of Jewish life.

Ribalow was not alone in his condemnation of the Jewish war novels of 1948. Other Jewish critics, particularly in *Commentary* magazine, decried the trend that made Jewish protagonists appeal to an Anglo readership by depriving them of any positive Jewish aspects. We saw this in Kazin's and Fiedler's caustic review of the pandering and deracination of Jewishness in Shaw's *The Young Lions* (contrasted with mainstream critics who loved the book). As well we find it in Isa Kapp's review of *An Act of Love* in which he admonishes Ira Wolfert for having made Harry Bruner into "a Jew not so much in experience or aspiration as in the violated spirit; the antisemite makes him . . . Thus, his neurotic life is the only life he has, and it constitutes his Jewishness."[82]

The question of whether or not the novels fairly represented the antisemitism encountered in the U.S. military was also dealt with in varied ways by the mainstream press. This was shown most emblematically in the responses to *The Young Lions*, the novel that portrays the U.S. military as the most riddled with antisemitism. All the major New York papers, the *Herald Tribune*, the *New York Sun*, and the *New York Times*, wrote highly positive reviews.[83] In stark contrast, *Time* magazine described the novel as having "failed" and rips apart Shaw's portrait of antisemitism in the military. While asserting that at first there is "a moving description of Noah's pain at coming across antisemitism in the army," it quickly "collapses into a completely incredible bit of hocus-pocus." The unnamed critic ends by stating that "while there was antisemitism in the Army, it never resembled Shaw's paranoiac version of it."[84] The longest review of *The Young Lions*, by Diana Trilling in *The Nation*, does not even mention the transformative experience of the boot camp antisemitism.[85]

Part of the anger these novels evoked in critics who were dismayed by their "overwrought" presentations of antisemitism stems from their misreading of these books as factual because they were written by men and women who had served or had been journalists during the war and they therefore assumed that they were "realistic" accounts of Jewish war service. The critics do not give the novels permission to function as fiction because they conclude that the stories must be based on the authors' own experience, while if the novels had been about, for instance, the plague in Europe, critics would not have made these types of assumptions. By trying to read the novels as nonfiction, the critics overlook the moralistic and ideological imperatives that underlay the manner in which the authors chose to describe the war. Because all these authors were liberal to the core, they were likely using a heavy-handed approach to presenting anti-Jewish hatred as a means to remind American postwar readers that racial inequity was a thing of the past or the domain of German totalitarianism.

Where some Jewish critics had commented on the lack of positive portraits of Judaism, and bemoaned that the soldiers were more American than Jewish, in stark contrast the well-known Anglo American critic John W. Aldridge in his influential 1951 book *After the Lost Generation: A Critical Study of the Writers of Two Wars*, decried that the Jewish soldiers in these books were far *too* Jewish:

> Yet the Jewish character in three of the new novels of the war and the aftermath — *The Naked and the Dead, The Young Lions*, and *That Winter* — is distinguished by his Jewishness only; and in the

last two novels, that one quality so distorts the authors' perspective that it forces the character to act in a way that is inconsistent with reality and with human nature.[86]

For Aldridge, the troubles of Jews and other minorities (he likens them throughout to "Negros" and "Homosexuals") are "simply minor issues" that are not "central to the meaning of this age."[87] These varied responses shed a light on the real tensions felt in the late 1940s about how to view the Jews in America. For many Jewish critics, an authentic portrait of the Jewish experience should consider the religious and cultural aspects of being a Jew. Alternatively, Aldridge views Jews as similar to African Americans and asserts that in order to present them as more than "cardboard" figures, as he labels it, the writers must downplay discrimination to show their "universal characteristics."[88] For Aldridge it is nevertheless impossible to imagine minority characters existing for any other reason but as literary devices to manipulate readers with false dramas. The idea that writers may use these characters for more than literary reasons, in order, for instance, to shed light on the poor treatment of minorities in America and to give voice to the realities of their daily lives, never enters Aldridge's discussion.

There is, in fact, a remarkable dissonance between how Jewish soldiers experienced the war and how it was written about in the novels of 1948. Deborah Dash Moore's *GI Jews: How World War II Changed a Generation* is the central historical text on the Jewish war experience, and her book documents the manner in which service brought Jews to reconnect with and strengthen their Jewish identity. We also find accounts in Isaac Rontch's edited volume *Jewish Youth at War: Letters from American Soldiers.* For this volume, Rontch chose hundreds of war letters from an assortment of thousands to present "a typical cross section of American Jews in the armed forces of the United States."[89] Rontch's book needs to be viewed cautiously as a historical document for a few reasons. Foremost, Rontch was a committed leftist whose political views would have influenced which letters he chose out of the thousands that he compiled. Also, the soldiers were likely censoring themselves in order to sooth their families about what they were going through, or to avoid trouble with military censors. Nevertheless, the volume gives us some insights into how Jewish soldiers understood the war while undergoing it. What is evident in the letters is that war service brought the "Jewishness," as Rontch defined it, of these men into focus in a new way for a range of reasons. In platoons where they were in the minority, they sought out fellow Jews as friends and also pursued the cultural and religious aspects of being a Jew, with many attending services and returning to the Judaism they had foregone for years: "I went to Jewish Services tonight. I think I can count on the fingers of one hand the times I have gone before. However, I went tonight with a sincere desire."[90] When they wrote home to their parents, they mentioned the things they missed such as Jewish food: "Ma — some marrinated [sic] herring. You have no idea what that would do for my morale. Send me a jar of it, won't you?"[91]

And when the full horror of the Holocaust began to become clear, they responded as Jews suffering empathy and pain for their European brethren, since for many, "Europe's geography was mapped by Jewish associations — birthplaces of aunts, uncles, cousins, grandparents, parents."[92] In Europe, they decided that all Jews were united like an extended family, and that the Yiddish of their parents, which many had not used in years, was their lingua franca, as we read in a letter about attending Jewish services in Liege, Belgium: "After the services the kinfolk congregated around us. My Yiddish is coming in quite handy insomuch as I can converse with these people The first question they asked: 'Where are you from?' New York, I answered. 'Oh, I've relatives in Brooklyn. Do you know a Millman? . . . My uncle's name is Rotherberg. You must know him. He lives in New York City.' And so it went."[93] The letters home also regularly describe Jewish survivors of the Holocaust using their Yiddish to search out Jewish American soldiers in order to share with them their tragic stories.[94]

The blossoming of Jewish identity that occurred during war service was further evident in a writing contest held in 1946 at the central Yiddish library and cultural center, YIVO, where American Jewish soldiers were asked to submit an essay on "My Experiences and Observations as a Jew in World War II." There were fifty-two submissions, and according to the judges of the contest, "The most important statement made by almost all of our contestants is that they all came back from the war with a feeling of pride in their Jewishness, with an awakened interest in Jewish life and with a readiness to carry out actively certain Jewish responsibilities."[95] Granted an essay contest meant that there was self-selection by those seeking to write on the topic, nevertheless this bespeaks that for some there was a cultural shift toward pride in Jewishness in response to their service in the European and Pacific theaters.

Besides the letters home and the YIVO contest, there were other points for exploring how the best-selling novelists described Jews in the military, and how others viewed it. For instance, in 1948, Henry J. Berkowitz's novel *Boot Camp* came out with the Jewish Publication Society. By publishing with a press whose list focused solely on the Jewish experience, Berkowitz was aiming to address his novel to a Jewish readership. His descriptions of Jewish life in the military in general, and specifically in a navy boot camp, contrast quite starkly with their portrayal in all the other novels I discussed. While the novel delineates regular, insistent, and at times frightening antisemitism in the armed services, at the same time, the work emphasizes a whole range of positive Jewish cultural aspects, and the manner in which soldiers find deep meaning in continuing to be practicing Jews. For instance, *Boot Camp* describes the profound emotions felt by Jewish soldiers when attending religious services in the military, the ways that they go about attempting to be kosher, how they continue to pray regularly, and the love they feel for their traditional parents. The novel ends with an idealistic portrait of Christian soldiers attending a Jewish service because in boot camp they have come to discover the positive aspects of Jewish culture and religion. The larger message of the novel, aimed at a postwar audience, is that Jews should stay true to their culture since by so doing the larger American public will come to respect their proud traditions. Moreover, by having the Christian soldiers attend a Jewish service, and earlier in the novel a Jewish chaplain perform the last rites on a Catholic soldier who commits suicide, the novel positions Jews as part of a larger American Judeo-Christian tradition rather than as a religion in opposition to Christianity.

Nevertheless, turning Jews merely into victims of hatred as was evident in the best-selling Jewish war novels was a widespread trend generally as Americans sought to understand the relationship between the Holocaust and postwar life.[96] In the immediate postwar years there was a vast public discourse on the topic, coming from the movies, the arts, congressional debates, and Jewish organizations, to name a few. It was also evident in publications on the topic, such as Jean-Paul Sartre's *Anti-Semite and Jew* that was translated into English in 1948, and Ernest Simmel's edited volume *Anti-Semitism: A Social Disease*.

The issue of antisemitism was on center stage for Jewish writers as well. As Joshua Bloch noted in his "Survey of American Jewish Books in English for 1947–1948" about the vast number of books devoted to the topic: "The Jews are incessantly pre-occupied with anti-Semitism and with the abnormality of their existence."[97] Three novels about anti-semitism by American Jewish authors were published right after the war: Arthur Miller's *Focus* (1945), Jo Sinclair's *Wasteland* (1946), and Saul Bellow's *The Victim* (1947). All three novels have male protagonists who struggle profoundly to understand their Jewishness when antisemitism has made them feel a sense of shame about it. While these books are not about World War II or the Holocaust, their focus on the debilitating effects of antisemitism on American Jews can be read as an attempt by the authors to come to terms with how Jewish hatred (and the Holocaust) has had an impact on Jewish Americans. In other words, while these books are not overtly about the Holocaust, they are nevertheless post-Holocaust literary productions.

In the case of war novels, there are many reasons why Jewishness became defined foremost as being a victim: perhaps the newfound confidence in being a victorious soldier for America impelled the authors to feel secure enough to finally lay bare in explicit terms the legacy of antisemitism in the military; perhaps they were seeking to shed light generally on racial injustice in America and they wanted to show the destructiveness of all types of hatred; perhaps the authors sensed that they would sell a lot more books if they focused on the hot and sensational topic of Jews being victimized; perhaps for the authors the aspect of their own service that made the largest mark on them was experiencing antisemitism and this became the topic they most wanted to explore; or perhaps they wanted to remind Americans that the legacy of antisemitism was not confined merely to the death camps and that the United States had its own sinister history that needed to be reckoned with.

The authors of the novels of 1948 found a means to fight back against antisemitism by portraying their Jewish soldiers not as weak, cowardly, and disloyal, as the Jew-haters would have drawn them, but instead as heroic, strong, and loyal. These novels were thus a means to reform Americans, to show them that their mistreatment of the Jews was misguided because in fact Jewish soldiers were some of the bravest members of the armed forces.

The extreme focus on antisemitism in the armed forces as portrayed in the novels should also be seen, as I have noted earlier, as another prop for the authors to get their liberal ideas across to mainstream American readers. Each time the Jew is abused he becomes a stand-in for all victims of American hatred. These novels use the topic of antisemitism to suggest that racism and hatred are underlying doctrines of fascism and totalitarianism, which is the antithesis of America's democratic ideals that assert equality for all. Therefore the Jewish victim in the novels is a propaganda symbol that calls out to the readers to embrace the liberal notion of civil equality for all Americans. And this message becomes particularly important as the McCarthy reign broadened.

The decrease in antisemitism in the postwar years and the establishment of the State of Israel in 1948 put these returning warriors on center stage and allowed their voices not only to be heard, but to be immensely popular. The Jewish soldiers were, however, presented in such a way as to make them palatable to readers: they did not have the "negative" traits of their parents' shtetl Judaism. So while these novels seem to evince a comfort with presenting antisemitism in the military, at the same time the authors' lack of ease is manifested by the very limited type of Jew that he or she is willing to draw as the paradigm of the Jewish American soldier.

For a readership still trying to recover from having served in the war, or having watched their loved ones do so, Jewish authors tapped into those fears and anxieties and the need for a form of literary catharsis. Moreover, authoring these novels enabled their writers to rewrite their own combat experiences, or lack thereof in the cases of Mailer and Shaw, and inject heroism into them. As John Berryman astutely noted, "Few men of reflection can be satisfied now with their actions and attitudes during the recent war."[98] Novels, therefore, became a place to rewrite one's own history.

The novels of 1948 also became a means to rework gender themes. In battle, with death always looming, the soldier directed his efforts "toward momentary gratifications" such as sex, booze, and having fun.[99] Where the soldier embodies manliness, the women he encounters became personified as hyper-feminine. As Morris Dickstein notes, in the postwar years, the widespread trope of the fighter thus edged Rosie the Riveter and other icons of strong working women out of popular consciousness, leading to the dominance of masculine writing with very conservative gender notions.[100] Yet in these novels, from Mailer's mixture of idealization and discomfort toward the brutal warrior Croft, to Noah Ackerman, sensitive, thoughtful, and heroic, Jewish authors were responding to patterns of American masculinity, and in some cases, renegotiating them by imbuing them with more sensitivity and intelligence. The only flesh-and-blood Jewish woman who appears in any of the novels of 1948 is Lew's immigrant mother; the other Jewish mothers and wives exist only in the memories of the Jewish soldiers. However, all the novels present a series of Christian women, most of whom are the Jewish soldier's objects of desire, with the ultimate prize being to marry one of them. This is part of a trend in postwar Jewish American literature that showed intermarriage between Jewish men and Christian women as a positive form of Americanization.[101] The Jewish man does not have a female Jewish counterpart since there is no space for her in this postwar configuration. While numerous Jewish women served as nurses and support staff during the war, in these novels the Jewish soldiers only come into contact with Christian women.

As I have pointed out, in *The Naked and the Dead*, *An Act of Love*, and *The Crusaders* the Jewish soldier had to die, often pointlessly and outside the theater of war, in order to teach the Christians how to become better men. A Christlike figure, his death purified the landscape and brought humanity back. Alfred Kazin noticed this trend in Jewish war novels and asserted that

> the Jew as the scapegoat and outsider is a perennial theme in our history; but the Jew as militant sacrifice, as the hero of death, impatient of complexity, is a new feature.[102]

For Kazin, the Jew's inevitable death is even more tragic because it symbolizes the universal hatred of the Jews. Kazin also astutely suggests that the transformation of characters such as Noah Ackerman from "the Jew as sensitif, as intellectual" into a hyper-tough hero may be a "kind of fantasy revenge for all the Jews who have been flayed, herded, burned in our time. He turns the tables on his enemies; he wins their grudging respect;

he shows himself the best damned soldier in the Army."[103] The collective fantasizing by traumatized Jews in the wake of the Holocaust therefore helped bring on the trend of Jewish soldiers who were not "herded" but who fought back and were victorious.[104] By having these war novels bring in the story of the Jewish exterminations, the authors were subverting the idea that the war had a clear "end" with the Allied victory. Instead, as they show, the Holocaust is an "unremitting" tragedy, and even the victory against the Germans has not stopped it from darkening all of postwar life.[105]

We can also consider this trend as an attempt on the part of the authors to transform the dehumanized portraits of piles of corpses of Holocaust victims into the single, very human, and beloved protagonist, whose death alters the world around him. From a countless slaughter, unnoticed and evocative of nothing, the Jewish American soldier's death brings a range of important results in these narratives. However one views it, the death of the Jewish American soldier shows the complex and difficult relationship between Jews and broader America in the years right after the war.

How to account for the great popularity of the books of 1948? Foremost, they offered a general readership a detailed account of the daily life of American combatants. After all, the United States, unlike every other country at war, did not fight any battles on its contiguous territory, and the realities of combat therefore primarily became known through letters home (where soldiers often self-censored the true horrors) and the media, which kept out explicit renditions of warfare.[106] There was also no widespread cultural memory of direct warfare as World War I had also been fought on a distant shore. It may be that the large number of Jewish war novels came about simply because it was Jewish soldiers who felt the impulse to write about their war experiences in novelistic form. Even in America, many Jews placed extraordinary cultural capital on books, so it was natural for returning servicemen to write novels about their recent experiences. However, these works may have been widely read specifically because they were by and about Jews reflecting the intense postwar American interest in antisemitism.

The novels read like a postwar take on Horatio Alger's tale of American transformation, where the crippled character — in this case he is spiritually and physically weak — overcomes myriad obstacles, including widespread antisemitism, in order to fully come into his own as a true blue American. No wonder these books appealed to a broad readership: they reiterate the old, popular tale of America (symbolized by the U.S. Army platoon) as the setting where the scarred immigrant can be reborn.

The founding of Israel that year may also have piqued American interest in learning about Jewish soldiers. The conflation of the Jewish fighter in Palestine with the American Jewish soldier was epitomized a few years earlier in the article entitled "The Jew as a Soldier" in the major American weekly *Collier's*.[107] The entire thrust of the essay was to show that Jews are heroic fighters rather than passive victims of the Holocaust slaughter. The essay begins by recounting six Jewish soldiers who performed extremely heroically during the war, with the aim to show that the Nazis were shortsighted to kill German Jews because they could have been great fighters for the Axis. The second part of the essay switches to a discussion of the Jews who are building Palestine and infusing into the country American notions of democracy, rather than allowing it to be like the autocratic states of their Arab neighbors.

The essay ends by declaring that "Jews have shown in Palestine that the forces of nationalism can be turned inwardly to benefit nations rather than outwardly in wars. Jews fight, too." In other words, the Jew of Palestine, like the Jewish American soldier, is a brave and sturdy fighter for American principles of democracy. In essence he is vastly different from the Jew of Europe, as is declared in this stunning paragraph near the end of the essay about the Jewish settlements in Palestine: "One of the most striking facts about the settlements is that they are producing a new race. The parents of dark, Levantine coloring raise inexplicably blond blue-eyed children. Nobody has found an answer to this riddle. The Jews on settlements grow into fair or redheaded sturdy people totally unlike the pallid, harassed Jews of terrorized Europe." By employing the worst racial stereotypes with the best of intentions, the essay seeks to show that the American Jewish soldier and Jew of Palestine are new heroic warriors and are of a completely different stock than the weak Holocaust victim. Both America and Palestine have rejuvenated and transformed the Jew, and this is evident in the new Jewish soldier.

All of the problematic trends in the *Collier's* essay show up in the Jewish war novels of 1948, in the counter-image they offer to the negative Jewish victim of the Holocaust. American readers likely found it inspiring and refreshing to read tales of Jewish soldiers who kill Germans, rather than being exterminated en masse by them. As Martha Gellhorn noted in *Point of No Return*, "It was like spitting in the krauts' faces for [the only Jewish soldier in the battalion] Levy to survive."[108] The ability of the Jewish soldier to kill Germans, rather than to be killed by them, symbolized the great superiority of America over Germany.

Finally, these books may have been fashionable because they offered readers a new vision of heroism where the protagonist could fight bravely while at the same time he suffer fears. It may have been easier to accept and be interested in representations of combatants with complex inner worlds if they could readily be characterized as Americans who are not quite Americans, and who are not delegitimizing the trope of the fearless soldier. Parts of the American reading public may have felt far more comfortable with an emotional Jewish soldier than they would have been with an emotional Christian one.

It is important to point out again how unique it was that all of the Jewish war novelists stood out as being the victims of or opponents to the anti-Communist forces as represented by the HUAC hearings. This suggests that these authors also used the genre of the war novel as a way to present their liberalism to mainstream American readers. While I have no historical proof, it is nevertheless possible to speculate that part of the reason these books may have been so popular in 1948 was because they spoke to readers who still had faith in the core values of liberalism. And since the Marshall Plan was just under way in Europe, portraying the military as a liberalizing force was a reminder to readers about the trajectory postwar diplomacy could take.

With the exception of *The Naked and the Dead*, most of the novels of 1948 employed a straightforward, standard third-person omniscient narrative to get these ideas across to the mainstream American readership. Since the story of the war had to be mediated in such a way that it would appeal to a broad readership, using the traditional novel form popular in the book clubs of mainstream America was a way to do this. Mailer's novel diverges from the others because he reaches back to the naturalist style of the 1930s that documented the range of American voices through a polyphonic narrative style. The realistic impulse of 1930s naturalism was political in intent, presenting injustice in the United States and working for the overhaul of capitalism. Mailer's aim was similarly liberal: to showcase, through the private voices of a range of Americans, the inequities in the country and the need for change. The war novel was the ideal mode for Mailer to put forth his moral beliefs, because American soldiers were the new heroes of the country and therefore their gripes had to be taken seriously.

Also alone among all the novels, *The Naked and the Dead* offers a portrait of a man, Goldstein, whose Jewishness is defined as more than being the victim of hatred. Since Mailer made the unprecedented move to have *two* central Jewish characters, it meant that a lone character did not have to carry all the burden of Jewishness.[109] Where the other Jew of the novel, Roth, is the same type as found in all the other novels by only being "Jewish" in terms of being a victim, Goldstein maintains a deep connection with his religiosity and culture. Although at times the portrayal can be negative, showing Goldstein as whiny and weak, Mailer also gives him a number of positive characteristics. Yet in the end what Goldstein learns from his time in the war is that although he is ethnically and religiously different, he can build strong bonds with non-Jews. He is the sole character of all the novels that will approach his postwar life comfortable being both a Jew and an American.

CHAPTER 4

1952 and the New Conservatism: *The Caine Mutiny* and *Battle Cry*

You know kid, if some S.O.B. ever writes a book about
escaping from the evils of modern civilization and going to
some South Sea tropical "Paradise" I think I'll cut his gizzards
out. That or ship him out here.

—JANUARY 23, 1943, LETTER FROM LEON URIS IN GUADALCANAL TO
HIS SISTER

In 1952 the *Partisan Review* hosted a large symposium entitled "Our Country and Our Culture"[1] where twenty-four major American male intellectuals and writers were asked to respond to a set of four questions put forth by the editors. The journal had "flourished as the most sophisticated voice of those intellectuals who sought an alternative to both Stalinism and conventional liberalism."[2] While the previous 1948 *Partisan Review* forum focused on the bleak period, as most saw it, of postwar writing and the rise of "middlebrow" culture, the 1952 symposium took a very different perspective. No longer brooding about the dismal writing of postwar America, the majority of the respondents asserted that American literary and intellectual life had finally come into its own, and that they were now embracing this "new Americanism."[3] According to the editorial statement, this was a time when "most writers no longer accept alienation as the artist's fate in America; on the contrary, they want very much to be a part of American life."[4] United in their distaste for Stalinism, intellectuals were transforming themselves from disaffected outsiders to insiders who sought to promulgate American values. A secondary concern was how writers and artists could support anti-Communist endeavors and the larger needs of the country, while continuing to serve as critics of it.[5] The forum took place when McCarthyism was dominating public life, and the strongly patriotic tone of the respondents marks that this major journal of "highbrow" intellectual Jewish life in America was continuing to distance itself from leftist and radical ideologies.[6] The responses also showed the complex nature of liberalism in the 1950s in that one could assert a belief in egalitarianism in the domestic arena while disavowing Stalinism on the international stage. The real struggle was thus how to enable liberalism to be anti-Communist while also supporting artistic individualism.[7]

The one strong voice of opposition to the "new Americanism" was Norman Mailer, who stated outright that he was "in almost total disagreement with the assumptions of the symposium." For him, the true artist was not integrated into society, as the other forum participants were asserting, but was instead more alienated than ever and was suffering under the constant pressure to prove his loyalty to American institutions.[8] Mailer's call for artistic rebellion, for challenging the conformist ethos, was a cry in the dark at a time when conservatism was a strong pull in intellectual Jewish life.

The shift rightward was seen emblematically in the Jewish war novels that were becoming best sellers at the time: Herman Wouk's *The Caine Mutiny* and Leon Uris's *Battle Cry*. These works represented everything that Mailer despised about the "new Americanism," which advocated a type of Cold War consensus with the conservative right: the assertion of loyalty to the United States, its institutions, and its way of life as a necessary corollary to American anti-Communism. Rather than demarcating opposition to the system, the new war novels were instead calls for conformity. Yet at the same time both novels challenged racial and social injustice in the United States. *The Caine Mutiny* and *Battle Cry* therefore offered a complicated portrait of conservative and liberal tenets. While evoking conformist and patriotic agendas, they also challenged American racism and asserted a renewed call for pluralism. This manner of being inclusive of both liberal and conservative platforms tapped right into the Zeitgeist of the time, making them huge best sellers.

Wouk and Uris, authors of popular "middlebrow" works, were now on the same side as the intellectual elite of the *Partisan Review*.[9] In an insecure time, when many Jews feared being associated with Communism, a broad range of Jewish figures and institutions that in the past would have viewed themselves as being on opposite sides of the political and cultural spectrum were aiming to show that they were patriotic Americans. The desire to affirm one's loyalty to the United States was coupled with the attempt to deride those who were challenging American institutions. We see this when, for instance, Wouk in *The Caine Mutiny* obliquely attacks Mailer and *The Naked and the Dead* as unpatriotic and destructive to America. In the following quote a Jewish lawyer, Barney Greenwald, rails against a novel written by the Mailer-like character, Thomas Keefer:

> I'd like to read it. I'm sure that it exposes this war in all its grim futility and waste, and shows up the military men for the stupid, Fascist minded sadists they are. Bitching up all the campaigns and throwing away the lives of fatalistic, humorous, lovable citizen-soldiers. (*The Caine Mutiny*, 386)

Keefer, like Mailer, is Ivy League educated, intellectual, and views war service as a means to write the great American novel. Keefer is also the novel's most negative character because he is selfish, manipulative, and cowardly. Wouk and Uris were writing their novels under the shadow of *The Naked and the Dead*, and as conservative-minded patriots for the United States, they sought to convince readers that their take on the war and American culture was the opposite of ungrateful rebels such as Mailer.[10] In Wouk's novel the "young emerged as neither rebels nor reformers, but as embryonic bureaucrats and organization men."[11] Where Mailer's novel critiqued the military and sought to showcase the desires of individual men, the tenor of Wouk's and Uris's novels was overwhelmingly in support of the military and against individual acts of rebellion.

The "new Americanism" expressed in the *Partisan Review* forum and Wouk's and Uris's novels was tied in with the economic boom that brought on the dominance of middle-class suburban norms and the ascendancy of corporate culture.[12] Three landmark books of the 1950s demarcated (and criticized) these new trends: C. Wright Mills's *White Collar: The American Middle Classes* (1951), Sloan Wilson's novel *The Man in the Gray Flannel Suit* (1955), and William H. Whyte's *The Organization Man* (1956). Wilson's *The Man in the Gray Flannel Suit* described the attempts of the protagonist, Tim Rath, to create a life not completely dominated by work and the needs of his job. The novel, to quote its author, was "a protest against conformity and the rigors of suburban life."[13] In *White Collar*, the sociologist C. Wright Mills dissected the alienation prevalent in the new middle-class work world, while in *The Organization Man*, Whyte presented the postwar rise of the corporation as creating "the organization man" who sublimated his individuality in order to follow the rules and obediently blend into the ethos of the corporation.[14]

In *The Organization Man*, Whyte makes a direct link between the increasing power of corporations and Wouk's novel by asserting that *The Caine Mutiny* demarcates "something of a landmark in the shift of American values."[15] Whyte saw Wouk's portrayal of the navy as symbolic of the repressive climate of life in America, with Wouk stressing that men should make it their priority to fit into the rules of the organization. Whyte, who was critical of this type of conformist "organization man" was, moreover. quite disturbed to find that when asking a group of high school students to write an essay about *The Caine Mutiny*, all but one agreed with Wouk's underlying thesis that "one should obey orders no matter what the circumstances" and "a subordinate should not have the power to question authority."[16] *The Caine Mutiny* therefore fed into the public's belief in the "corporate" virtues of conformism over individualism, intellectualism, and rebellion by showing that "the 'smart' people who question things, who upset people — they are the wrong ones."[17]

The rise of this "new Americanism" was also in part a response to America being again at war: the Korean War would lead to at least forty thousand American deaths. It was a battle of the forces of democracy against the evils of Communism, a fight that would prove to be unwinnable. This meant that both major Jewish war novels of the 1950s were written and published while a new conflict was under way, in contrast with the novels of 1948, which looked back on one that had just ended. In 1955 Malcolm Cowley noted the relationship between the war and the conservative ethos of the current war novels when he wrote that

> many of the novels — especially those written after 1950, under
> the shadow of another world conflict — are not rebellious at all;

instead they are celebrations of squad-room comradeship, Navy traditions, or the fighting Marines.[18]

Both Wouk and Uris were most likely uncomfortable critiquing men in uniform since so many were again serving, and they painted the American military as an entirely positive force. In the Uris novel, events are narrated by a commander currently serving in Korea who remembers a time when his platoon went through the previous war. Wouk's and Uris's ultra-patriotic take on war paid off personally when their novels were the second and third most popular books at U.S. Army base libraries during the Korean War.[19]

Uris and Wouk, moreover, offered a new take on the Jewish experience, speaking of the Jews not as *others* but as the *same* as mainstream Americans. In the previous wave of war novels Jewish characters had stuck out by being different from other members of their platoon, but in these works the Jewish characters are fully assimilated and accepted into military life. There is little hint of antisemitism in the armed services. Uris and Wouk were showing mainstream Americans that Jews were patriotic and assimilated and that they did not see themselves as victimized outsiders but as stalwart citizens. Moreover, by appropriating in a masterful way the "middlebrow" narrative voice — sentimental, action-packed, nostalgic, melodramatic — they were speaking in a populist voice to the masses rather than presenting war in a self-consciously artistic, individualistic way. Yet, as I will show, both writers nevertheless employed complex and innovative narrative structures that made them highly readable.

The novels of Wouk and Uris were not subtle in any sense. Instead, their novels clearly asserted the patriotism of American Jews, while at the same time satirizing radical values. They were proclaiming, and their book sales were validating, that this was *their* time, while angry, rebellious voices like Mailer were in the minority.

Herman Wouk: *The Caine Mutiny*

Herman Wouk's *The Caine Mutiny* made him such a well-known figure that he made the cover of *Time* magazine the same year he appeared on the popular television show *What's My Line*, where he was called "the famous writer."[20]

Wouk (1915–) was the New York-born son of Orthodox East European Jewish immigrants who ran laundries while raising Herman and his two siblings in the Bronx and later in Manhattan.[21] Attending after-school Hebrew programs, Wouk grew up deeply embedded in, and proud of, his Orthodox heritage. He went to Columbia University in 1930, majoring in philosophy and comparative literature. The two people who had the greatest influence upon him were his grandfather, Rabbi Mendel Leib Levine, who emigrated from Minsk to live with the family in 1928, and his Columbia University philosophy professor, the outspoken cultural conservative, Irwin Edman.[22] Even after his family had moved from the Bronx to Manhattan, Wouk continued weekly visits to his grandfather to learn the Talmud. His 1959 book *This Is My God: The Jewish Way of Life*, which explains the virtues of Judaism to a mainstream reading public, is dedicated to his grandfather.[23]

At Columbia, Wouk was the editor of the *Columbia Jester* and wrote two varsity shows for the university. In 1930, in large part as a response to attending a secular college, Wouk stopped being a practicing Orthodox Jew, although ten years later he would return fully to the faith. The only major Jewish World War II writer who was Orthodox, Wouk's conservatism was tied in part to his religious belief in subordinating "self-interest to larger causes."[24] After college, Wouk worked for five years as a gag and script writer for well-known radio comics such as Fred Allen, while at the same time trying to become a Broadway dramatist. Wouk's job required that he write for a broad audience and this training would serve him well when years later he would author page-turning novels for a mainstream audience.

Following Pearl Harbor, Wouk joined the U.S. Navy and attended Officer Candidate School at Columbia University, graduating in the top twenty of his five-hundred-member class. In February 1943, Wouk began a three-year stint as an officer on a minesweeper "like the *Caine*" in the South Pacific that engaged in important battles in the Marshall Islands and in the Marianas.[25] In a March 19, 1947, letter he wrote that "my Naval career was completely undistinguished."[26] Wouk served a number of different roles as an officer in the navy, rising in the ranks until his final promotion to executive officer of the USS *Southard* (although the ship was destroyed in a typhoon before he could take command of it). Wouk loved navy life, asserting that it was the greatest experience of my life. I had known two worlds, the wise guys of Broadway and the wise guys of Columbia — two small worlds that sometimes take themselves for the whole world. In the Navy, I found out more than I ever had about people and about the United States.[27]

While on shore leave in California, he fell in love with an educated Protestant navy personnel specialist, Betty Brown. They married a few months later, and she converted to Judaism the following year. They had three sons, one of whom drowned in a pool in 1950 at the age of five. Betty was Herman's most important reader, editor, and critic (and also served as his literary agent),[28] and they remained married until she died at the age of ninety in 2011.

After returning from war service, Wouk published a book that he wrote primarily while at sea, *Aurora Dawn*. It was popular with readers and a book-of-the-month selection, and it enabled him to become a full-time novelist and stage writer. Wouk began writing *The Caine Mutiny* in 1949 and it was published in 1951. The novel topped the best sellers list for all of 1951 and 1952 (competing head-to-head with, and then beating, James Jones's *From Here to Eternity*). *The Caine Mutiny* was the highest-selling novel of the postwar era: within a year it had four printings, was the selection of all the major book clubs, was serialized in scores of newspapers, and sold more than three million copies.[29] The novel was also turned into a popular play, and the 1954 movie starring Humphrey Bogart became an American classic, receiving multiple Academy Award nominations. The film version largely follows the main thread of the novel, and Bogart's rendition of Queeg brilliantly captures his neuroses and obsessions. Wouk also received the 1952 Pulitzer Prize (and along with it thousands of dollars).[30] Wouk's second novel, *Marjorie Morningstar* (1955), was another massive best seller. Where *The Caine Mutiny* had tapped into the cultural interest in World War II, his next work ends with a consideration of suburban life, matching the two poles of postwar gender icons: the soldier and the suburbanite. Wouk's fame soared anew in the 1970s with the release of another huge best seller that was turned into a popular miniseries, *The Winds of War*. Even with his celebrity status, Wouk remained grounded and continued to make a point of personally answering every single letter from a fan.[31] Currently Wouk lives in Palm Springs and has a chair of Jewish Studies named after him at the University of San Diego. Throughout the long span of his career, Wouk's books reiterated that "his vision of society is essentially conservative."[32]

The Caine Mutiny opens with a description of articles 184,185, and 186 of the Navy Regulations Manual. These were the protocols that Wouk discovered while serving aboard a minesweeper, and which had inspired him to write the novel.[33] They delineate the "extraordinary circumstances" that may impel a subordinate officer to place a captain either "under arrest or on a sick list." The list of regulations is followed by the author's assertion that the book will document the events of 1944 that became commonly known as the "Caine Mutiny." Then the reader finds a map that shows the path taken by the ship on which the mutiny occurred, with the notes and dates of the major events. Before reading a word of the novel, the illusion has been established that this is a nonfictional account of a major event of World War II. This enables Wouk to speak about the events with the authority of a historian whose main aim is to uncover and share with his readers the causes that led to the mutiny.

The third-person omniscient narrator conveys the events through internal and external descriptions of the main characters, the actions they undergo, and how they view what has occurred. A long novel, the story is divided into seven sections that focus on different aspects and characters central in the mutiny. The first, "Willie Keith," is devoted to the protagonist's prewar life, his enlistment, and his first call to report to the *Caine* minesweeper. "The Caine" focuses on Willie's first impressions of the minesweeper and its Captain de Vriess. "Captain Queeg" discusses the arrival of the tormented and crazy Queeg to oversee the ship. "Shore Leave" describes Willie's time in California before the mutiny. "The Mutiny" tells of the events leading up to, during, and after the mutiny on the ship, and "The Court Martial" describes the court case against the mutineers and how their lawyer effectively wins their case. "The Last Captain of the Caine" is the wrap-up that tells of the ship's final days. The plot moves along quickly, with Wouk adeptly juggling a range of characters and locations as he portrays the domestic life of the hero, life on the ship, the machinations that lead to the mutiny, and the court case. As the events unfold, Willie matures and distances himself from his privileged past to become a good and trustworthy leader.

Willie is a wealthy young man from Long Island, recently graduated in comparative literature from Princeton University, who has fallen for an Italian American working-class singer named May Wynn. She is outspoken, forthright, and extremely clever, but her working-class roots repel him. During the first years of the war, Willie has no intention of volunteering for the military, instead spending his days playing piano at bars. Or as Wouk puts it in a judgmental manner:

> So it was that Willie Keith sang and played for the customers of the Club Tahiti from December 1941 to April 1942 while the Japanese conquered the Philippines, and the *Prince of Wales* and the *Repulse* sank, and Singapore fell, and the cremation ovens of the Germans consumed men, women, and children at full blast, thousands every day. (12)

For Wouk, men who avoided military service abdicated their responsibilities to Americans generally and to the Jews of Europe specifically. Eventually Willie decides to enlist in the navy, not for any larger moral reasons, but merely as a means to avoid being drafted as an infantryman into the U.S. Army. Through the course of the novel, however, Willie transforms from a selfish, spoiled rich boy to an exemplary officer. This is a bildungsroman where Willie's school is the navy.

Willie succeeds in his officer training by memorizing the rule book and becoming "the oracle of the tenth floor in matters of Navy ordnance" (27). Willie is placed on the old minesweeper the *Caine*. Soon after reporting to this "pile of junk in the last hours of decay, manned by hoodlums" (76), the slovenly but competent Captain De Vriess steps down and the new captain, Queeg, arrives. Queeg's obsession with "chickenshit" rules is quickly apparent when he tyrannically bears down on the servicemen for small errors such as not fully tucking in their shirts or taking a couple of extra strawberries, and moreover, has the officers bear the brunt of the punishment by making them write reports on each and every infraction. It also becomes apparent that Queeg is a coward, doing all he can to avoid battle, and reacting to dangerous situations by panicking and freezing. A fellow officer, Keefer, who is a novelist and intellectual, bears a grudge against Queeg for being denied permission to go ashore to see his brother. He manipulates the second in command, Maryk, to view Queeg as insane. When a typhoon hits, and Queeg panics and is unable to take the action needed to keep the ship from sinking, Maryk, with the agreement of Willie Smith, uses article 184 of the navy regulations to take over the ship. (The idea of using this article had earlier been suggested by the manipulative Keefer.)

In the last section of the book, Maryk and Willie Smith are on trial for conspiracy and a new character is introduced who shakes everything up, the lawyer who is to represent them, Barney Greenwald. Greenwald was a fighter pilot but is now on combat leave due to injuries. Until Greenwald's entrance, the historical tone of the narration seems to be building a case against Queeg as a psychopathic despot, and to support the actions of the officers in overthrowing him. Greenwald, even though hired to defend the men, shows that Keefer (who is not being tried) caused the mutiny for his own petty reasons and that Queeg, while a bit crazy, nevertheless should never have been removed from his post.

Queeg's name suggests his double role as a hero and psychopath, as it is overtly a play on Herman Melville's character Queequeg from the most important American ship novel, *Moby-Dick*. Queequeg is a noble savage, covered with tattoos, who looks dangerous and "primitive" and who seems "crazy" because he follows a religion that the others do not understand. He is, as well, a dedicated harpooner and good and loyal friend to the protagonist of the novel, Ishmael. By giving Queeg a shortened version of his name, Wouk suggests that Queeg, like Queequeg, may have heroic aspects that are not readily apparent.

When Keefer is called to testify, in order to not jeopardize his military career, he blames everyone else for the events that he caused. After Greenwald gets the men acquitted by using his brilliant verbal prowess, he gate-crashes their celebrations, paid for by Keefer's large advance for a new novel, to deliver a stinging, incisive and powerful attack on them, particularly Keefer.

In the final chapters, Keefer has become the *Caine* ship captain and Willie his first mate. During a kamikaze attack, Keefer abandons ship in order to save himself (carrying his book manuscript with him), leaving the ship to founder while Willie stays aboard and acts heroically and saves the ship.[34] In the end, Keefer shows himself to be just as cowardly, if not more so, than Queeg ever was, and Willie Smith becomes a heroic man, asking May to marry him. He has evolved, allowing himself to be comfortable with her working-class background.

The Caine Mutiny seeks to be a new type of war novel that is adamantly pro-military and which criticizes as cowardly and selfish those who censure the armed services. Those on the side of good are the men who obey the rules, follow authority, and fight bravely for their country, while those on the other side are the intellectuals and liberals who ask questions and challenge the status quo. As Joseph Waldmeir put it, Wouk aimed to align "himself with the forces of anti-intellectualism and anti-liberalism" and this was in direct opposition to the ideologies of the previous war novelists.[35] This is evident in the most eloquent speech of the book when Greenwald explains to the men whose acquittal he has just gained, that although he was their lawyer, he was really on the side of Queeg, contemptuously called "Old Yellowstain" for being cowardly, but whom he views as a hero:

> The reason I'd make Old Yellowstain a hero is on account of my mother, little gray-headed Jewish lady . . . Well, sure, you guys all have mothers, but they wouldn't be in the same bad shape mine would if we'd of lost this war, which of course we aren't, we've won the damn thing by now. See, the Germans aren't kidding about the Jews. They're cooking us down to soap over there. They think we're vermin and should be 'sterminated and our corpses turned into something useful . . . Of course we figured in those days, only fools go into armed service. Bad pay, no millionaire future, and you can't call your mind or body your own. Not for sensitive intellectuals. So when all hell broke loose and the Germans started running out of soap and figured, well it's time to come over and melt down old Mrs. Greenwald — who's gonna stop them? . . . Meantime, and it took a year and a half before I was any good, who was keeping Mama out of the soap dish? Captain Queeg. (482)

In the years right after the war, young upstart intellectuals had derided the military in their novels, and Wouk's aim was to counter this by having Greenwald assert, in his vulgar and explicit way, that all Americans, and particularly Jews, must remember that the American soldiers were their saviors. Greenwald's memorable and impassioned speech is a plea to a postwar readership to remember how much they owe to the men who served. (And perhaps at a time when the Korean War was under way a call for Americans to support the men going off to this new war.) It is also a veiled attack on the selfish individualism of the "sensitive intellectual" who retreats rather than fighting for his country.

Greenwald's speech can also be viewed as emblematic of the gratitude that many Jews felt toward the military for its stance of encouraging Jewish GIs to have the opportunity to practice their Judaism while in the service by, for instance, allowing when possible leaves for religious observance, employing a large number of Jewish chaplains, enabling Jewish foods such as matzoh to be distributed, and so on. The armed services recognized Jewishness as part of the Judeo-Christian tradition and officially treated it as a religion on a par with Christianity. Wouk, an Orthodox Jew, must have felt a personal sense of appreciation for this which may have been translated into Greenwald's call for gratitude to the U.S. military.

Greenwald, as a Jew, has a particular responsibility to protect Queeg since he "deserved better at my hands. I owed him a favor, don't you see? He stopped Hermann Goering from washing his fat behind with my mother" (483). In this novel the details of the Holocaust and what occurred to the Jews are fully known. Unlike the earlier war novels that aimed to get the news out, by Wouk's publication, the information is common knowledge and the author's job is to show his readers how grateful they should be to the United States military. Greenwald's speech to the men starts the process that will also eventually expose Keefer as a coward in battle. In Wouk's novel, the WASP intellectual is defeated by the ultra-patriotic Jewish American lawyer who uses his brains to outsmart and out-verbalize him. (Yet, the truth remains that if Maryk had not rebelled against Queeg, then the ship would have sunk in the typhoon and they all would have died.)

Contrasted with the novels of 1948 which demonstrated how service in war could transform the Jew for the better, Wouk's novel shows instead how the military transforms everyone in a positive way, including the WASP protagonist, Willie. Where the earlier war novels had depicted the military as the embodiment of many of the worst aspects of America, in Wouk's version it symbolizes the best: it gives everyone equal opportunities while bringing its members to unite in a shared cause. As Willie's father writes to him, Willie needs to embrace navy life since it denotes this new, better America:

It seems to me that you're very much like our whole country—young, naïve, spoiled and softened by abundance and good luck, but with an interior hardness that comes from your sound stock. This country of ours consists of pioneers, after all, these new Poles and Italians and Jews as well as the older stock, people who had the gumption to get up and go and make themselves better lives in a new world. You're going to run into a lot of strange young men in the Navy, most of them pretty low by your standards, I daresay, but I'll bet—though I won't live to see it—that they are going to make the greatest Navy the world has ever seen. (65)

Wouk is reminding his readers that the armed services during World War II were populated by a wide range of immigrants who would be the ones to lead America into a good future. Moreover, Willie, as a representative of the new officer corps, needs to embrace America's diversity more than had the WASP leadership of the past. We see here a similar motif as in the novels of 1948, which suggested that war service could transform Jewish men into positive and strong heroes, although in Wouk's rendition, this idea has been extended to include all soldiers, including Protestants. The novel goes out of its way to avoid mentioning any of the usual traumas that are part of being in the armed forces. Moreover, where in the earlier works the platoon was a mini-America that could evoke the best or worst aspects of the country, in Wouk's (and Uris's) rendition, the military from the start is America at its best.

The Caine Mutiny also stands out by being the opposite in many ways of Thomas Heggen's earlier best-selling war novel also set on a U.S. Navy ship, Mister Roberts. Where Heggen's work was comic, only showing the true dangers of war in the final pages, Wouk's novel is deadly serious, with no narrative room for levity of any type. And where Heggen's novel makes the main "enemy" Captain Morton, who shows no positive characteristics whatsoever, Wouk in the end consciously redeems the similarly narrow-minded, petty Captain Queeg, and shows that the real enemy is the Germans. Clearly intended to give a serious take on war that shows readers the gratitude felt by American Jews toward the military, Wouk, intentionally or not, takes Heggen's novel and turns its precepts on its head. And speaking to the times when it was published, by doing so, Wouk's novel became a similarly huge best seller.

Wouk also uses his protagonist Willie Smith as a tool with which to delve into upper-class non-Jewish America. Wouk's descriptions of Smith's Long Island home and family sound like they were lifted straight out of *Town and Country*:

> The Keith home in Manhasset was a twelve-room Dutch colonial house with heavy white pillars, high-arching black wood-shingled roof, and multitudes of large windows. It stood on a knoll in the middle of two acres of lawns set with soaring old beech, maple, and oak trees and bordered by flower beds and a thick high hedge. (31)

Smith's mother is a conservative older-generation WASP who pushes her son to ditch his ethnic, poor girlfriend May and avoid the draft. Even with all the pressure put on him by his mother, Willie manages to break free, to pursue love with someone his mother considers inferior, and to do his war duty. He shows Wouk's mainstream readers that they can transcend the old ways of their parents to become honest, decent, and egalitarian. They represent the new generation that has rejected the worst xenophobic and racist tendencies of the past.

Willie is a positive character who is able to grow and meet the changing world, in contrast to Keefer, who uses his status to manipulate, to avoid combat, and to bring on another's downfall. Yet at the very end of the novel Keefer also awakens and realizes that he had been misguided and cowardly in his actions. It is a happy ending as the main characters all become cognizant of themselves and actively change for the better.[36] Wouk is showing his readership that the experience of war has been entirely positive in terms of transforming the previous American elite, the wealthy WASPs, into heroic and honest men. In the traditional bildungsroman the protagonist undertakes an inward journey, discovering at the end of the novel that self-knowledge is tinged with sadness and disappointment. Wouk's populism could never allow for such a complex portrait of growth, and instead his characters make the journey into their own psyches and come out as bright, shiny, new 1950s Americans.

Unlike the novels of 1948 where the ultimate prize for the Jewish soldier was marriage to a Christian woman, Wouk turns this upside down. Willie becomes a good man and fighter once he suppresses his prejudice against ethnic Americans and decides to marry May. Yet May is so independent that the novel ends *without* her accepting his proposal, because she is worried about the dull life of an academic's wife. This ethnic, smart, and feisty female is a new type of heroine who is reluctant to become the domestic helpmate of her man. However, there is a sense that eventually Willie will win her over and she will marry him, but perhaps she will manage to continue her music career.

Throughout the novel Wouk drops hints that although May is Italian American, she is nearly indistinguishable from a second-generation Jewish American: her parents are immigrants who can barely speak English and they live in the Bronx, where they run a small store. May, in fact, recognizes this about herself and confronts Willie about it after his first encounter with her Jewish agent Marty: "Possibly you don't like Jews. Or Italians, either. They have a lot in common" (35). Similar to the novels of 1948 that do not have a female Jewish love interest, here Wouk also makes May a Christian, but he gives her "Jewish" traits. Wouk is trying to have it all by suggesting that she is a Jew without fully acknowledging it. (Wouk's next novel, the best-selling *Marjorie Morningstar*, would make a young Jewish female the central protagonist.) The framing device of having two central tales — a domestic love story of Willie's up-and-down relationship with May, and a war story of male-dominated life on a ship — enables Wouk, who had learned populist writing in his radio work, to appeal to a very broad range of male and female readers.

The topic of antisemitism, so prevalent in the novels of 1948, is fairly muted in Wouk's idealized rendition of a navy setting. This in part may have been because — according to Wouk himself — he did not experience antisemitism in the U.S. Navy. In a letter to me he wrote, "In the U.S. Navy I encountered no incidents of antisemitism, and only occasionally a word or tone I'd hear and ignore as hostile."[37] An example of Wouk's Jewishness being accepted rather than derided was when he posted a joke about a pig on the ship's bulletin board (as a way to explain why he did not eat pork even if it meant he went hungry) and a sympathetic officer responded "Give this man something he can eat."[38] The ship's company in Wouk's novel is not the multiethnic, frequently divided America of Mailer and others. Rather, it is primarily a "white" enclave where the concept of diversity rarely comes up, and when it does, is dealt with positively. The only explicitly Jewish character in the book besides Barney is

May's agent and coach, Marty Rubin, who is a very nice guy who always has May's best interests at heart.

It is Barney Greenwald, however, who exemplifies the Jewish soldier. Unlike Noah Ackerman in *The Young Lions* who evolved from an intellectual weakling into a heroic, physical, fighter, Barney is this new type of American Jewish hero from the start. Combining brains and brawn, intellectualism and assertiveness, Greenwald is a Jew respected for his war service who has spent the previous year fighting for the rights of Cherokee Indians. Although one of the commanders jokes that Greenwald may be a "pinko" because of his work for the oppressed, Wouk makes it clear that Greenwald is the most patriotic of Americans and that he is able to combine strength with compassion. Barney is an ideal Jewish soldier who has returned from successful combat and embraces America as the land that beat the Nazis and saved his mother from "being turned into soap." His Jewishness in *The Caine Mutiny* is manifested in his pride in being American, his support for the armed services, and in his opposition to corrupt intellectual WASPs such as Keefer. On the American shore, Greenwald does not need to die to save the others as in the novels of 1948. Instead, he uses his brilliant courtroom tactics to get the men acquitted. Yet, as with the other novels of 1948, the Jewish soldier is the force pushing Americans to take stock of themselves and to seek out the right path.

Wouk also seeks to infuse humanity into the Japanese enemy. But in this case, he does it from a postwar stance which looks back on American defeats in the Pacific and sees them as being based in part on a racist inability to see the Japanese as fully human:

> He seemed to regard the enemy as a species of animal pest. From the grim and desperate taciturnity with which the Japanese died, they seemed on their side to believe they were contending with an invasion of large armed ants. This obliviousness on both sides to the fact that the opponents were human beings may perhaps be cited as the key to the many massacres of the Pacific war. (257)

As Willie Keith grows into a mature adult and breaks free from the xenophobia of his mother, he begins to be able to see the "other" as being as human as he is: "Willie felt a tiny flash of sympathy for the Japanese. He sensed what it might be like to be short and yellow-skinned and devoted to a picture-book emperor, and to face extermination by hordes of big white men swarming from everywhere in flaming machines" (294). And as with *An Act of Love*, homophobic mistreatment in the military also arises. In this case, Keefer tries to manipulate the others by implying that Queeg is brutal because he is a repressed homosexual (289). Queeg as well will use homophobia to cast aspersions on the men who initiated the mutiny by hinting that they may be homosexual (465).

The Caine Mutiny is a psychological drama about the choices that a group of men make on the confined space of a ship, and how they validate their actions. Like Cain in the Bible, with whom the minesweeper shares a name, they have slain their innocent brother in arms, Queeg. Unlike all the war novels of 1948, there are few scenes of direct combat since the cowardly Queeg turns tail during battles. As Wouk portrays it, the ship is an all-male world where men revert to their basic animal and primitive natures when not guided by the naval codes. The real topic is not how men react to the strains of war, but instead, how men respond to leaders who are more concerned with regulations than with combat. Is the greater good of American war success served when men are loyal to the rules of service, even if they seem arbitrary and petty, or is it better to rebel against them since they are a distraction from the serious requirements of combat?

The novel's focus on laws as a proscriptive for behavior grew out of Wouk's Jewish Orthodoxy. For religious Jews a major positive aspect of Judaism is the 613 laws of behavior, or Halakhah. Following the law, be it Jewish or naval, enables the individual to have a structured and meaningful life that keeps at bay the inherent chaos of the world. However, a Jewish mandate is not simply to follow the law passively, but to think about, challenge, and intellectualize the process. The central text of rabbinic Judaism, the Talmud, does just that, taking the Jewish oral law, as presented in the Mishnah, and then gathering together the opinions, arguments, and questions about the law generated from numerous rabbis over time. Wouk's novel mimics this by starting with the Mishnah of naval "law," the articles from the U.S. Navy regulations, and then delving into their fairness (or lack thereof) from a wide range of perspectives.[39] In the end, it is the Jewish lawyer who offers the best argument and shows that the laws are valid and that they serve a greater good.

A central question around which the novel turns is which type of discourse is most useful for a time of war: the administrative, cut-and-dried language of the rules and regulations of the war machine; the straightforward "historical" voice of the narrator; or the personalized and opinionated discourse of the war novelist, Keefer. *The Caine Mutiny* is about war and love and also a rumination on the role that the written word should have in the modern world. Each character has a different method for dealing with texts and discourse, and their varied approaches symbolize elements of their inner psyche. Captain Queeg is despised by Keefer because Queeg stresses that "we do things on this ship by the book" (140). Queeg's problem is that he is not a creative reader and is too rigid to realize that one need not read everything literally. When Queeg states that "I'm a book man, as anyone who knows me will tell you. I believe the book is there for a purpose, and everything in it has been put in it for a purpose" (141), he is the wrong type of book man because it has made him doctrinaire. Keefer, by contrast, uses literature as a weapon with which to manipulate others and show how elevated he is. His greatest crime, however, is using the navy regulations to justify his selfish desire to start a mutiny against a man he dislikes. Greenwald sees this and despises Keefer (and others like him): "These fools find a paragraph in Navy Regs that gives them ideas, and they gang up on a skipper who's mean and stupid — as a lot of skippers are — and make jackasses of themselves, and put a ship out of action" (380). May is working her way through an English literature college degree and appreciates books for the best of reasons: as repositories of truth and creativity. The final approach to the book is that of a Jewish reading, Talmudic in nature, of Barney Greenwald, who believes the laws must be followed but that one can be creative in trying to understand them.

Through most of the novel it will seem that Queeg's misuse of the administrative discourse of the regulation manuals is problematic. However, in the final section of the book Greenwald will teach us that these rules are in fact serving a greater good, and that the real enemy is the novelistic, personalized interpretation of the war made by the novelist(s). In Wouk's worldview, the "enemy within" is not the antisemitic American servicemen who were so prevalent in the Jewish war novels of 1948; rather, it is the intellectual WASPs who believe that their own needs should be more important than the rules that are there to keep things running smoothly. The officers in charge know what they are doing, and the foot soldiers need to obey them.[40] Wouk's novel is thus also a strident attack on the young men who at the start of the 1950s were seeking their own artistic path of rebellion against the authority represented by those who wielded the power. With Wouk, it takes a Jewish soldier to point this out and to remind the readers to be patriotic (and servile) and to accept that things are done for a good reason by those in power. Wouk is therefore showing his readers that American Jews are the most patriotic rule-followers in the land.

Wouk's novel is thus two-tiered in its attack: against the rebellious actions of the young who seek to undermine the status quo for their own selfish needs, and against the previous novelists of the war who did a disservice to the American military when they encouraged their readers to disrespect the officers. Edward S. Shapiro notes that "undoubtedly the most important fictional portrayal of the World War II symbiosis of Jewish and American identity is Herman Wouk's *The Caine Mutiny*." He sees this "symbiosis" in particular in Lt. Barney Greenwald's speech which turns World War II into a battle against the Holocaust.[41] *The Caine Mutiny* reflects a postwar form of intense Jewish patriotism that aims to distance the Jewish community from rebellious trends while reiterating a conservative status quo. At the same time, however, it is pushing for an America that is diverse and open to all its members, rather than being a stronghold of wealthy WASPs. It exemplifies the path of much of early and mid-1950s Jewish liberalism, which was avowedly patriotic and anti-Communist while at the same time pushing for a more pluralistic society.

Although the novel and its conformist ethos appealed to a huge number of American readers, the critical responses were fairly negative. For as Lawrence Mazzeno put it, "Wouk seems to come down on the side of those who argue for blind obedience to command. Few Americans — especially American literary critics — can swallow such conservative medicine without gagging."[42] The critical reactions to the novel shed a light on the culture wars of the early 1950s and reflect two opposing stances toward how society should constitute itself: supporting the rights and needs of the individual over the community, or vice versa. On one side were those who cheered Wouk's attack on the forces of rebellion. Or as it was characterized in the 1955 edition of *Time*, which gave Wouk the cover in its essay entitled "The Wouk Mutiny": Wouk's "chief significance is that he spearheads a mutiny against the literary stereotypes of rebellion — against three decades of U.S. fiction dominated by skeptical criticism, sexual emancipation, social protest and psychoanalytic sermonizing."[43] On the other side were those who derided the novel's McCarthyist tones of blind obedience to authority and its strain of anti-intellectualism.[44]

The most stringent attack came from the *Partisan Review* in 1953, the year after its forum, when some of its writers were beginning to evince a discomfort with the previous year's conformist, conservative ethos. The essay by Harvey Swados, a well-known left-wing Jewish novelist and essayist, sought to account for the huge popularity of *The Caine Mutiny*.[45] What, he asked, was so appealing about a book that pushed an anti-intellectual agenda in its attack on Keefer, while stressing the need for Americans to conform to the authorities? The essay, written in the months leading up to the execution of Julius and Ethel Rosenberg, challenges Americans to question their blind acceptance of anti-intellectual, conformist tendencies. For Swados, *The Caine Mutiny* was such a massive "phenomenon" in sales because it pandered to the fears and desires of the new postwar middle class. Wouk, Swados believed, shrewdly used the liberal Jew Greenwald (who after all works for exploited Native American communities) to level his attack on intellectualism since Barney is seemingly an insider intellectual liberal rather than an outsider. It thus gives him far more credibility. Moreover, according to Swados, Wouk used his skills as a populist writer to make his middle-class readers believe that they were "participating in a thoughtful intellectual experience."[46] In other words, in Swados's view, Wouk cloaked his pro-authority, anti-rebel attack in a seemingly highbrow novel that was really "middlebrow" and pandered to the desire of the middle class to see itself as intellectual: Wouk allows us "to have our cake and eat it, to stimulate us without unduly provoking us, to make us feel that we are thinking without really forcing us to think."[47]

In Swados's 1953 essay we see the battle lines of postwar Jewish American culture clearly drawn: members of the intellectual left who feel under attack by the conservatives who assert that in the postwar era Jews must clearly show their patriotism to a country that saved them. As Swados quite succinctly describes it:

> What the new middle class wanted — and found in *The Caine Mutiny* — was an assurance that its years of discomfort and hard-

ship in the Second World War were not in vain, and that its sacrifices in a permanent war economy and its gradual accommodation to the emergence of the military as a dominant element in civil life have been not only necessary but praiseworthy.

Swados, like other intellectuals who were outraged by Wouk's novel and its huge success, saw this as proof, moreover, that Americans in general were desperate to justify that World War II meant that a new conservative society was not only necessary but good.

Another way to look at the "liberal" Barney Greenwald is that he, in fact, does represent a 1950s Jewish American prototype of liberalism. On the domestic arena, he fights for the rights of Native Americans and others who are discriminated against. On the international stage, he calls for conformism to American military policy. He is a liberal at home and an anti-Communist on the street. Greenwald's (and others) liberalism is not contradicted by their call for conformism which is a product of the Cold War anti-Communist platform.

The criticism of the novel was not only ideological but also artistic: the abrupt shift in how readers are expected to view Queeg was seen as being unexpected and poorly contextualized. Wouk's contradictory portrait of Queeg was aiming to have it all: by depicting Queeg first as inept and nearly insane, and later as a man who did the best he could, Wouk both indicts and excuses the poor leadership. Typical was Joseph Waldmeir's assertion that with Greenwald's speech "formally and ideologically, *The Caine Mutiny* collapses here, at the denouement, at the point where it should peak . . . thus [Wouk] attempts to whitewash one of the most believable villains in all World War II literature in this fantastic, unprepared for, grossly sentimentalized scene."[48] Norman Mailer attacked the ending as well in a letter to his war buddy Francis Irby Gwaltney, writing "*The Caine Mutiny* which I thought was about the best slick novel I ever read until I got to the last fifty pages which were pretty god-awful."[49]

Throughout 1952 *The Caine Mutiny* fought for the top spot on the best seller's list with the iconic American novel of individuality and rebellion, *The Catcher in the Rye*. Moreover, perhaps reflecting the upswing of conservative ideology of 1952, *Caine* beat out *Catcher* on the short list for the Pulitzer Prize.[50] Both *Caine* and *Catcher* addressed a postwar generation seeking to understand its place in the new, confident, wealthy, and increasingly conformist culture. Their contradictory approaches and ideologies would have appealed to two different type of readers, or two aspects of the same reader. Those who bought *Catcher in the Rye* were likely attracted to the portrait of a rebellious youth who is deeply disaffected with the values of his parents, while the readers of *The Caine Mutiny* found a validation of the status quo and a justification that the war had been a force for good. Where *Catcher's* protagonist is a disaffected intellectual who stands up against the ignorant jock culture of WASP America, in *Caine*, the intellectual rebel, Keefer, is negative and selfish. These two novels of 1952 delineate the tension between two cultural movements, with those who felt the need to rebel against middle-class norms able to find a brother in Holden Caulfield, and others who sought to be reassured that the conservative order was good, and who found in Keefer a proof that rebels were in reality cads and cowards without ethics or virtues.

Leon Uris: *Battle Cry*

Leon Uris (1924–2003) was the paragon of the Jewish tough guy author. Of all the Jewish war novelists, Uris saw the most combat and directly experienced the war in a way that none of the other authors had. Serving on the front line of the U.S. Marines in many of the most brutal campaigns in the Pacific, he loved war, the military, and battle. In Uris's letters home from the front lines, he positively revels in fighting and killing the enemy, even sending his father a bloody Japanese flag from a soldier he had killed. As he described his experiences at Guadalcanal in a letter home:

> Yes, Dad, Guadalcanal was hell. Sleeping in fox holes, eating canned rations, and sometimes not even that. Bugs, mud to your waist, and sun so hot you nearly burned. Then there were snipers, planes, machine guns and artillery always trying to get you. It was pretty awful — but we'd do it again and again until we can come home and know that we'll never have to leave again. Yes, the next job will be bigger — more of us will fall, we'll go through more hell, but we'll never stop till we win. The Japs got a dose they'll never forget — there's more coming.[51]

While military service was extremely difficult, it was also a great adventure that allowed enlisted men like Uris to participate in something bigger than themselves.[52] As he wrote in a January 23, 1943, letter home to his sister after the battle for Guadalcanal:

> The marines teach a guy to love and appreciate little things. It's tough to see your buddies die and to live in foxholes. A guy gets tired of air raids, snipers, mortars, and artillery, of the heat and being so exhausted he can barely stand up. But I'd do it over and no matter how long it takes I'll keep trying to do my best until I know that we all can see and mold dreams.[53]

His father was so impressed by his son's military prowess that he posed with the bloodied flag Uris had sent him for the Yiddish paper *Der Morgn Freiheit* under the headline "Heroic Jewish marine took Japanese flag at Guadalcanal."[54] As Uris asserted, even though the campaigns were hell and he was suffering physically, "as long as I am on my two feet I want to stay out here."[55] And although Uris partook in many of the most brutal campaigns of the Pacific theater, his platoon also enjoyed lengthy breaks in Wellington, New Zealand, where he dated local girls, was involved in boxing matches, and even put on a production of one of his plays at the local theater. In the U.S. Marines, Uris found a home, and his love and loyalty for the division were so central to his life that the epitaph on his tomb is: "American Marine/Jewish writer."

In May 1953, while *The Caine Mutiny* still remained high on the best sellers charts, Leon Uris published his first novel, *Battle Cry*. Like Wouk's work, it was a huge best seller for Bantam Books, and it remained on the best seller list for more than a year. (It was also made into a 1955 movie by Warner Brothers that Uris wrote the screenplay for, after taking over the job from William Faulkner. The movie received tepid reviews.)[56] *Battle Cry* harkens back to the best sellers of 1948 that focus on a platoon in battle from basic training to close combat. Different than any of the other Jewish war novels, and the majority of war novels generally, *Battle Cry* is about the U.S. Marines, that "exotic branch of the service"[57] which Jews rarely joined. During World War II, U.S. Marines were sent to the Pacific because they were trained in amphibious battle techniques and close fighting. The marines were generally considered to have some of the toughest and best-trained fighters in the service corps, and they were thus often sent to the forefront of the most brutal conflicts. Uris was extremely proud of being a member of the U.S. Marine Corps, viewing it as superior to the army: "I'm expected to fight full grown men and we marines are the front guard, the suicide outfits. And I'm to be in the most highly trained outfit in warfare."[58] Uris was impelled to write his novel because he felt that "the real Marine story had not been told. We were a different breed of men who looked at war in a different way."[59] One of his aims was to explain the specific qualities of the U.S. Marines and to show that they were the bravest branch of the military.

Uris grew up in Baltimore, the son of Russian Jews. His father, Wolf, was a Communist Party organizer who worked as a paperhanger. According to Ira B. Nadel's biography, *Leon Uris: Life of a Best Seller*, Uris viewed his father as a frustrated failure as a man and as a husband.[60] After his parents separated when he was six, Uris lived with his mother and maintained only intermittent contact with his father until he was fifteen, when he became restless and decided to move in with him and his new wife. Uris dropped out of high school at the age of seventeen to join the U.S. Marines, with whom he would serve in a radio squad in campaigns throughout the Pacific, including at Guadalcanal and in the fierce battle for the Atawa atoll that would be described in *Battle Cry*.

After the war Uris worked briefly as a journalist while writing *Battle Cry*, which was initially rejected by a number of publishers. Once published, the reviews of the novel were mixed, with general agreement that the strongest aspects were the sections detailing the intense manner of Marine Corps training and fighting.[61] Nevertheless in 1953 it came in second place for the top novel of the year by balloted book critics, and it also garnered a medal and citation from the Marine Corps for having "contributed the most" to "the public appreciation of the spirit and ideas of the U.S. Marine Corps."[62]

Uris, like Irwin Shaw, was a hard man who liked boxing, gambling, and chasing women, and he even requested a pistol for his nineteenth birthday (which his father sent to him in the Pacific where he was serving).[63] Uris's extreme conservative patriotism stood in stark contrast to his father's Communism. Uris was best known for his 1958 novelistic account of the founding of Israel, *Exodus*, which was a huge best seller and the first postwar novel to outsell *The Caine Mutiny*. The novel was Zionist in ideology, with portrayals of the Jews as the positive heroes and the Arabs for the most part as the negative enemies.[64] Because of the success of *Exodus*, Uris became one of the wealthiest American novelists of his day. Throughout his life, Uris published nine more historical novels, most of which dealt with some aspect of World War II and the Holocaust, and his popularity may have been due to the fact that as Ira Nadel correctly noted, "History for Uris was never gray; it exhibited an exhilarating moral clarity that appealed to his readers."[65] Despite his huge sales Uris, until recently, has been largely excluded from critical assessment because he was considered to be a "middlebrow" writer of mixed literary ability.[66] Uris had a central role in shaping America's understanding of Jews and his novels need to be considered in terms of their cultural impact.

On May 14, 1944, Uris wrote a letter home to his father from the Naval Hospital in Oakland, California, where he was recovering:

> America, my country, is my love. I've fought beside Catholics, Protestants and Mormons, Indians, Irish, Italians, Poles. They liked me because I was a good man and a regular fellow. And I've seen 750 out of 900 of us who left the States die or be shot up at Guadalcanal and Tarawa. There was a Jewish boy in my platoon — who was well hated. He was a coward, a general no good. We made his life miserable, not because he was a Jew, but because he was a rat. And another Jew, Captain Bill Scherewin — I worked for him. He has won three Navy Crosses. He led a glorious assault which I was in. We loved him and would follow him to hell. It's not the religion we look at, but the man himself.[67]

Nearly ten years later *Battle Cry* would flesh out the same themes discussed in this letter home. As he writes in the letter and as the novel would delineate, in the military everyone, regardless of their ethnic or religious background, had an equal ability to succeed or fail. The military, like America, was therefore the ideal meritocracy and for Jews what mattered was not their religion or ethnicity, but how they performed. In war, Uris was able to succeed because he was a good fighter, and by fighting well he became a part of the U.S. Marine community (evident by his use of the "we" when referring to the Marine Corps). The two Jewish soldiers that Uris mentions in his letter would become central characters in his novel, Jake Levin and Captain Max Shapiro, although through military service Levin would transform from a coward into a brave hero.

Like Wouk, Uris would use his novel to subvert the dark intentions of the previous generation of war novelists: "I am proud to be here because so many of the writers of the second world war wrote bitter novels, damning their branch of the service, damming America, and damning the officers and men they fought with. Well, I hated war as much as any of these authors, but I love my fellow Marines as brothers and I respected and trusted my officers."[68] *Battle Cry* asserts this positive stance on the opening page with its dedication: to the "United States Marines, and to one in particular — Staff Sergeant Betty Beck Uris [his wife]." Unlike novelists such as Norman Mailer, Leon Uris gives extremely upbeat descriptions of the military. In fact his book at times reads like pro-war, pro-Marines propaganda, delivered in a straightforward tone, that insistently avows the positive aspects of the American war effort. In part, this was because for Uris, even when in the heat of horrific battles, the larger war aims and male comradeship made all the daily suffering of life in the military worth it. In the war, soldiers served the greater good of America while at the same time improving themselves as individuals.

The adventures of the *Battle Cry* platoon are told from two distinct voices: a first-person retrospective account from the tough, hardened, but humane soldier in charge of his group of men, Sergeant Mac, and third-person descriptions of the daily lives of the enlistees.[69] As Mac describes it: "This is the story of a battalion of invincible boys. And of my kids, the radio squad" (*Battle Cry*, 3). Mac is telling his tale from the present (1953) where he is currently overseeing forces in Korea. Mac is an extremely positive figure. Moreover, Mac's current role as an officer in Korea suggests to Uris's readers that the men leading the war effort in Korea are similarly positive figures. It is no wonder the novel was extremely popular with enlisted men in Korea: it describes soldiers throughout as brave and decent and worthy of deep respect from fellow Americans. To get his message across, Uris masterfully employs a very quick pace, spare on descriptions except when necessary, and heavy on action.

Nearly the first half of the novel covers the buildup to battle. Initially we have accounts of the men's lives before they enlisted, followed by descriptions of the toughening they underwent in boot camp. The second part of the book is about the Sixth Regiment of the Second Marine Division's sojourn at a base in Wellington, New Zealand, as they await deployment orders. In New Zealand a new soldier joins the squad, the Jewish draftee from Brooklyn, Jake Levin, who is replacing a beloved comrade who has recently been killed in battle. The final section of *Battle Cry* describes the Sixth Marine Regiment as it undertakes the battles at Guadalcanal, Tarawa, and Saipan. These were all brutal and bloody campaigns with very high casualty rates. The men had to participate in close combat in difficult terrain and malaria was rampant. (Uris himself caught malaria while serving.)

The most extensive battle descriptions cover the fight for Tarawa (in which Uris himself had participated) in November 1943. It was largely fought over three days and there were more than six thousand casualties. In the novel the fight for Tarawa is led by Captain Max Shapiro, and it results in the deaths of many platoon members, including Levin. The novel ends with Mac going around the United States to visit with the families of the dead. Woven throughout the descriptions of military life are accounts of the relationships the men have with women: sweethearts they have left behind, women they have fallen in love with at base camp, and romances with women in New Zealand. The novel thus covers all its bases in its aim to appeal to a wide array of male and female readers.

Similar to the novels of 1948, the platoon is a mini-America in exile where men must learn to work together and discard their old prejudices in order to be effective soldiers. Thus the novel describes the transformation of the redneck racist Speedy as he learns to shed his prejudices through his friendships with the Jewish and Mexican soldiers. Uris gives his readers an idealized portrait where old hatreds are easily discarded and where all Americans pull together for the greater good. And again, as was pointed out in 1953 by Merle Miller (author of *That Winter*), we find in Jake Levin the disturbing trope of the "self-sacrificing Jewish boy who has turned up in every war novel so far."[70]

When first encountering Jake Levin, Speedy calls him a "Jewboy" and tells the other men that "I don't like kikes." Immediately, a fellow soldier, Marion, who is a novelist, but in direct contrast with Wouk's Keefer, is kind and ethical, challenges Speedy by asking him "What has Levin ever done to you?" When Speedy continues to vent his antisemitic vitriol, Marion asserts "you don't like Levin because he's Jewish. You don't like Pedro because he's Mexican. You don't like New Zealanders because they talk funny. You don't like colored people — who do you like, Speedy?" Speedy's only response is to call the other men "nigger lovers" (451). In Uris's rendition of the military, the racist antisemite is quickly cut down by the other men. Speedy is from Texas, and only Texans are antisemites (all the racism as well is caused by them), while the majority of soldiers are fair minded and their main concern is to be good fighters and supportive of their fellow soldiers. Although most of the men do not at first like Levin because he lets them know that he was drafted (rather than volunteering like the rest of them), he soon gains their respect by doing all the worst jobs on the base in Wellington without any complaint. Levin's service changes him from a whiny draftee into a tough and uncomplaining marine. Even as he undergoes a constant tirade of antisemitic assaults from Speedy, he does not fight back, choosing to show his mettle by being an extremely hard worker. While all the other men learn to respect Levin, Speedy continues to abuse him until Mac, the Sergeant narrator, realizes that this is bad for platoon cohesion and finally decides to confront Speedy. He tells Speedy that the humble, quiet, hardworking Levin who has taken his abuse with barely any complaint was the "Golden Gloves welterweight champ of New York for two years" (453). This immediately shuts Speedy up.

Levin is thus the ideal Jew according to this construct of Jewish American masculinity. Where the Jewish people in Eastern Europe may have defined men positively for their levels of learning and intellectualism, here again the idealized postwar American Jewish man is extremely physical and tough: he is a boxer, brave, and hardworking. (This theme of tough, fighting Jews would continue in Uris's *Exodus*.)[71] Jake's Jewishness is entirely a form of ethnicity which faces discrimination (like Mexican Americans), rather than a form of religious identity.

And as with the novels of 1948, Levin's life is sacrificed in order to bring out the humanity of the other soldiers. In this case, in a terrifying surprise attack by the Japanese on Tarawa atoll, Levin runs away, seemingly proving that he is the cowardly Jew that Speedy has accused him of being. However, rather than fleeing, he is actually heading into the most dangerous point of battle to retrieve a radio so the men can call for help. By so doing, Levin sacrifices his life to save the platoon. Speedy of course realizes how wrong he has been to be antisemitic, and refuses to leave the bullet-riddled Levin. In a scene oozing with melodrama, Levin makes his dying request to Speedy that he be buried with a Star of David, rather than a cross, since his father would want that. Levin dies as a heroic Jew who has sacrificed himself for the men of the platoon and brought humanity to Speedy.

Levin also dies because as a Jewish soldier he has had to work harder than the others to prove himself. Mac realized this about Levin earlier, when he said to him, "Look, Levin. I know you've been busting your ass to prove yourself . . . Levin, why are you trying so hard? Is it because you are a Jew?" (432). In response to this correct assessment of his actions, Levin "turned pale." Levin then told Mac that Speedy had been saying that "we're fighting the war because of Jews. He says Jews are yellow" (434). Although this Jewish soldier feels that he must prove that he is not "yellow," even when it means risking his life, ultimately Levin's act is seen within the context of the book as being extraordinarily heroic. There is no hint in the text of the darker reason impelling his actions and that Speedy's tenderness toward Levin during his dying moments is hypocritical since he was the one who drove Levin to sacrifice himself. The novel steers clear of any such complex presentations, instead establishing a simplistic cause and effect where the Jewish soldier's bravery brings on his death and by so doing proves to others that Jews are worthy.

Levin was not the only victim of Speedy's hate. As in *The Naked and the Dead*, the Mexican soldier also faces racism, and there is a third ethnic character, a Native American called "Shining Lightower," whom Uris describes by using, seemingly without any awareness, a variety of caricatures about American Indians.[72] The Mexican soldier Pedro Rojas describes how incredibly happy he is to be in New Zealand since he is treated so much better than in the United States. As Pedro explains it, "even in San Diego they look at me like I was a leper. People here they smile and they say, 'Hello Yank'" (442). In other words, for some Americans Pedro is first and foremost a racial inferior, while the New Zealanders see him positively as an American. Even in New Zealand, however, American soldiers continue to be racist:

> You know what happen tonight? Pedro will tell you. I went to a
> dance at the Allied Service club and some colored sailors from

a ship come in and the girls, they just dance with them and treat them like anybody else. And then some goddam Texans they go to the hostess and demand the colored boys leave the club. Instead, all the girls refuse to dance with Marines at all and they walk out. (445)

In the final section of *Battle Cry*, Speedy will also amend his previous hatred for Mexicans by offering to visit Pedro's family to bring them their dead son's uniform. Uris is showing his readers that they must disavow racism and antisemitism in light of the multiple sacrifices made by a variety of ethnic Americans during World War II (and in the current conflict in Korea). He is suggesting that the military transforms men for the better by making them discard their hates and prejudices. Finally, Uris is demonstrating the common struggle of Jews in the 1950s who sought to balance their pro-American, anti-Communism stance with their desire to remain true to their egalitarian ideals.[73]

These are quite similar themes to those found in *The Naked and the Dead*, where Mailer as well depicts the abuse that ethnics face in the military, and suggests that Americans need to stop acting in such a manner. The difference is that in Mailer's work the military is rife with characters who dislike ethnics, while in Uris's take, there are merely a few bad apples (from Texas) and the majority culture is accepting of differences.

Jake Levin, who sacrifices himself for the sake of his fellow marines, is not the only Jewish soldier portrayed in the novel. Where Jake's transformation and eventual death mimic those of Jewish soldiers in the novels of 1948, Uris also introduces a new type of Jewish character: Captain Max Shapiro. Shapiro is a near mythical figure to the marines because of his brave, brilliant, yet often risky manner of leading his men to victory:

My squad gathered around the large shack which housed the Battalion office. There was rampant excitement. Captain Max Shapiro had been transferred into the Second Battalion to take over Fox Company. The notorious and glorious Two Gun Shapiro from Coleman's Raiders who had earned his first Navy Cross in the Makin raid — and a courts martial. He had more decorations and courts-martial than the next three officers in the Corps combined. He was a legend. (518)

When the officers first spot Shapiro, one comments that he "looks like a rabbi" since he "sure doesn't look tough" (519). Yet Shapiro's actions prove that he is the toughest man around, regardless of his "Jewish" physique. He may look weak, but he combines his great intellect with his fortitude to make himself into a tougher and braver leader than all the other officers.

Shapiro is Uris's means to revise "the stereotypes of Jews as weak and easy victims."[74] After having fearlessly led his men through a series of harrowing battles, Shapiro is finally killed in a scene reminiscent of a showdown in an American Western. Shapiro's death inspires his men, called "Huxley's Whores," to fight in their most ferocious manner, leading to their success over the Japanese and the end of the battle:

> Max Shapiro sank to his knees, his pistols empty. He threw them at the enemy. "Blood!" he screamed. "Blood!" The men of Huxley's Whores were petrified. A legend was broken! The invincible captain, the man bullets could not touch, the man they believed was almost divine, lay there writhing in agony the same as any human being. The blood gushed from his mouth and ears and nose and he rolled over defiantly, trying to crawl to his enemy to kill with bare hands, the same ghastly word on his lips . . . Huxley's Whores rose to the heights of their dead captain. They no longer resembled human beings. Savage beyond all savagery, murderous beyond murder, they shrieked, "Blood!" "BLOOD!" . . . "BLOOD!" The enemy, who were mere mortals, fell back. (681)

Here the Jewish soldier dies to bring out the latent warrior spirit of the non-Jewish men and to turn them into fighters out for blood vengeance. Max Shapiro is the Jewish warrior, a new type of tough Jew who will become the dominant figure in the rest of Uris's corpus. Uris has completely erased from his representation men facing fears in combat, instead evoking a version of war as an epic heroic battle that men gallantly undertake to prove how tough they really are. Where previous war novelists such as Mailer and Shaw delineated the terror men confront in combat and infused into their portraits of soldiers intellectualism and emotionalism, here Uris is returning to the type of masculine hero who suffers no fears. In this case, however, the ultimate hard guy is a Jew.

This is a remarkable remaking of the American Jewish male into a gun-slinging, fearless fighter. Here there is nothing overtly Jewish about him — the only time he is referenced as such is as looking like a rabbi. Uris has transformed the Jewish American into the Sabra fighter who can outfight and outwit the enemy. Where the other Jewish soldiers died to bring about the Jewish American liberal belief in a brotherhood of men, in Uris's 1951 reconfiguration, Shapiro's death is a new Zionist vision of the Jew as the ultimate fighting machine who inspires others to battle. While *Battle Cry* lacks the overt conservative agenda of *The Caine Mutiny*, it shares with that novel a clear desire to promote a patriotic vision of the American military, particularly at a time when a new generation of men were going off to the Korean War.

Uris's extremely idealistic portrait of the military was hugely popular with readers. Perhaps this was because the novel spoke to the postwar desire of Americans to feel good about the sacrifices of their young men, particularly at a time when the country was undertaking a new war in Korea. Also Uris's extremely charged, macho, tension-filled writing style made his book hard to put down, especially since it described a range of exciting things such as close fighting, sex, and scenes of violent death.

The Caine Mutiny and *Battle Cry* were published nearly a decade after the war and their aim was not to get the information of the Holocaust out to a broad readership as had been the case with the earlier novels. Rather, in these works the Holocaust is a symbol of how good America and the armed forces have been to the Jews, by beating the Nazis, treating Jews as equals, and enabling them to attain leadership positions. Because of this, these novels suggest, American Jews want the public to know that they are profoundly grateful for how much the country, and its military, has done for them.

Part and parcel with the aim to present a patriotic vision of military service is the reconstruction of masculinity in the novels in a very different way than it was written of in the novels of 1948. Where the earlier works drew Jewish soldiers as complex men who did their service bravely yet were also intellectual and emotional, in Wouk's and Uris's portraits the Jewish soldier's masculinity is less complex and textured. Captain Shapiro, in fact, is the paradigm of the tough, active, unemotional leader who loves fighting and does not suffer fear. He shows the American public that the Jew is just as much a tough guy as the ideal Hemingway soldier. These types of male icons, however, suggest that there were deep insecurities impelling Jews to prove to the world that the Jewish man was equal to the American Christian one. Where the men of the previous novels act tough even when they feel scared, in Wouk and Uris the men do not suffer any internal battles. They are strong through and through.

Like Mailer in *The Naked and the Dead,* Uris uses two Jewish characters to give to his readers a deeper understanding of the Jewish soldier: a city boy who through war service becomes a hero, and a captain who is tough and brave from the start. In both instances, the Jewish soldier dies, and by so doing, saves the other men and furthers the war effort, and in Jake Levin's case, also teaches an antisemite to respect Jews. Unlike Mailer, however, who gave one of his characters, Goldstein, Jewish cultural and religious aspects, Uris makes his soldiers Jewish in name only.

Wouk presents a more nuanced representation of Jewishness, where the novel itself evokes Jewish textual strategies, such as Talmudic discourse, that question the laws and codes in order to understand their deeper meaning and to extrapolate from them rules for conducting one's life. The meta-narrative critique of legalistic versus novelistic discourse that Wouk embeds in his novel makes *Caine* far less "closed" than critics claimed it to be, since it enables the text to be open to a potentially frustrating range of contradictory interpretations.

This is epitomized by Greenwald who is a very contradictory type of Jewish soldier, outwardly representing liberal tendencies such as fighting for Native American rights, yet whose ideological position is deeply conformist and conservative. Like Queeg, Greenwald is double-sided and his inconsistencies highlight the dual positioning of Jews at the time: in court, by brilliantly arguing that the men were right to do the mutiny, Greenwald evokes an America where all men are free to rebel against their oppressors. Later, when reprimanding those same men, Greenwald connotes the American ideal of protecting the weak. Greenwald depicts the tension felt by many Jews about how to understand what it means to be American when the Holocaust has called into question previous notions about rebellion and belonging. For their immigrant parents and grandparents, things were more clear-cut: the socialist impulses which many brought with them from Europe fit into the American tradition of rebellion as evident in the Revolutionary War against the British. Now with the Holocaust, and America's successful war effort against the Nazis, the idea of rebelling against any aspect of the United States caused some to feel like traitors. This was of course intensified by the Cold War climate where any type of dissent made one seem suspect. Wouk's novel therefore uses a mutiny as a trope with which to delve into American and Jewish concepts of belonging and breaking free.

In the years after the war, when the full weight of the Holocaust was being processed, Jewish responses were diverse and complicated. There were those Jews who said there was no longer a God, or that God was dead or utterly useless. There were others who held the Manichaean belief that the Holocaust was a struggle between good and evil, and evil had won. Some saw it as a historical calamity that could only be rectified through the creation of a Jewish state, while others responded by disavowing all forms of nationalism. But certainly one reaction Wouk and Uris encapsulated in their novels was the assertion that American Jews were safe because the U.S. Army had stopped Hitler's murder machines. So whether or not the Holocaust brought about a deep questioning of one's beliefs, this truth had been validated for the Jews of the world who owed a great debt to the U.S. servicemen who had defeated the Axis enemies.

Both Wouk and Uris were deeply patriotic, conservative-minded men who had an uncomplicated view of their own military service, seeing it as the best experience of their lives. In the conservative, anti-Communist climate of the 1950s, the time was ripe for these types of American Jewish portrayals of World War II to become dominant.

CHAPTER 5

1961 and the New Liberalism: *Catch-22*

Yes, Yossarian was very Jewish, but I didn't know that until years later. But I didn't plot that. That comes from the unconscious.

—1991 INTERVIEW WITH JOSEPH HELLER

Joseph Heller's *Catch-22*, published in 1961, is considered one of the most important American novels of the twentieth century. It was a massive best seller that sold more than ten million copies, went through multiple editions, and introduced a new phrase into the English language for an unsolvable conundrum or paradox.[1] The novel became hugely popular during the Vietnam War because it was embraced by many as an antiwar manifesto. *Catch-22* was groundbreaking because it was the first broadly successful American novel that offered a modernist, satirical take on World War II.

In *Catch-22*, two aspects that were prevalent in all of the other Jewish war novels that I have discussed — Jewish soldiers and the Holocaust — are missing and ostensibly the novel has nothing whatsoever Jewish about it beyond the ethnicity of its author. Instead it is about the Assyrian or Armenian protagonist, Yossarian, a U.S. Army Air Force (USAAF) bombardier in the European theater. The large corpus of scholarship on *Catch-22* generally sees the novel as a challenge to conformism, as an antiwar document, or as heralding an absurdist vision of war.[2] Why then include it in a study of Jewish war novels? As I will argue, while outwardly the novel aims to represent the war and the protagonist as "American" rather than "Jewish," the work is, in fact, packed with signs and signals that it is about a Jewish airman, Yossarian, confronting the Holocaust. Heller's attempt to hide this was part of a tradition that arose with Jewish authors in the postwar years who sought to distance themselves from their ethnicity in order to speak to "universal" themes of rebellion. However, to overlook the Jewish semiotics of *Catch-22* is to miss many of its major themes. I am thus offering a Jewish reading of the novel that will delineate what it tells us about postwar Jewish life in America.

Ten years before the publication of *Catch-22*, Herman Wouk had tapped into the conservative ethos of his time in *The Caine Mutiny*, voicing the outlook of Jews who wanted to conform and be accepted. In contrast, Heller's novel spoke for the rebellious urges of the late 1950s. Where Wouk's novel viewed the military as a positive organization and suggested that men must obey its rules and not rock the boat, Heller's book attempted to show that the armed services were in fact completely corrupt and moribund. Where Wouk's writing was highly patriotic and suggested that Americans in general and Jews in particular should be profoundly grateful to the military, Heller challenged the basic premise that American efforts during World War II were noble. Where Wouk's novel was rendered in "middlebrow," straightforward, unembellished prose, Heller's narrative voice was experimental, comic, and completely destabilizing to any idea of a rational, teleological world.

Catch-22 helped to initiate a trend of individualistic, countercultural, bohemian literature.[3] When Heller used his surreal literary style he was instituting a narrative rebellion against the "middlebrow" voice of best sellers such as Wouk's *The Caine Mutiny* and his follow-up *Marjorie Morningstar* that a range of American intellectuals were attacking as dumbing down American life and making it turn away from authentic art.[4] And in spite of employing a high literary narrative style the book was extremely popular. This shift in narrative voice can in part be explained by changes then under way in American cultural life. In the ten years between the publication of the two novels the United States had continued to experience an economic boom, but major cracks were showing in the idealization of suburban, middle-class life. Intellectuals were starting to wake up from their previous complacency toward and support of domestic and international Cold War politics. From 1957 onward, liberal ideologies began to overtake the conservative ethos of the previous decade and these included renewed calls for civil rights for African Americans and challenges to the nuclear proliferation of the Cold War.

As Kirsten Fermaglich has documented, when liberalism began to again dominate intellectual life, prominent Jewish thinkers started to espouse two central mandates as underpinning their liberal ethos: a call against the mass conformism of the type that was exemplified in William Whyte's *Organization Man*, and an embrace of a universal mandate over racial or ethnic specificity. This Jewish liberal take of the late 1950s was therefore rooted in seemingly contradictory ideologies — universalism and individualism. The call for universalism was part of the civil rights belief that all people shared traits that were more central than one's ethnic specificity, including one's Jewishness. The individualistic aspects were that intellectuals needed to fight against the bureaucracies that squashed personal freedoms.[5] Joseph Heller's *Catch-22* was thus rooted in this complicated push and pull between the desire for individual rebellion against the corporation, and the downplaying of Jewish aspects for a universal stance. By using a modernist narrative style Heller was reasserting the importance of an artistic, individualistic reading of the current political landscape while distancing himself from the "middle-brow" style of the populist writers Wouk and Uris.

The individualistic ethos of Heller's novel connected it to a rebellious trend in Jewish American writing that used young men to voice anger with the status quo, as evident in J. D. Salinger's *Catcher in the Rye*[6] and Norman Mailer's 1957 iconic essay "The White Negro." Mailer's piece was published by the journal *Dissent*, which had been founded in 1954 by a group of New York Jewish intellectuals including Mailer and Irving Howe, an outspoken critic of the type of complacency and Cold War consensus dominating Jewish intellectual life. The journal expressed a disillusionment with Stalinism and Communism, but also aimed to assert a "radical" perspective not tied to any single political persuasion. It was the place that intellectuals and artists could turn when they found the *Partisan Review* and *Commentary* too conventional, as was made evident in the editorial statement in the journal's first edition that began, "The purpose of this new magazine is suggested by its name: to dissent from the bleak atmosphere of conformism that pervades the political and intellectual life of the United States."[7] "The White Negro" was Mailer's radical rejection of white middle-class mainstream culture. However, by locating his "hipster" as being primarily the counter image of the middle-class suburban man, Mailer was propagating a form of rebellion that negated the prewar radical focus on helping those who are discriminated against by the mainstream society.

The rebellious hipster that Mailer described in his essay had arisen out of the shadows of nuclear war and concentration camps and was born "in such places as Greenwich Village" where "the bohemian and the juvenile delinquent came face-to-face with the Negro." The hipster's aim was to break free from the conformist pressures and to chart his own path, and the hipster's language did this by evoking jazz cadences that disrupted all the old rhythms.

The same year that Mailer's essay was published, the construct of the hipster was underlined when Jack Kerouac's alter ego Sal Paradise described the lure of African American life in the novel *On the Road* : "At lilac evening I walked with every muscle aching among the lights of 27th and Welton in the Denver colored section, wishing I were a Negro, feeling that the best the white world had offered was not enough ecstasy for me, not enough life, joy, kicks, darkness, music, not enough night."[8] Evidently a broad range of young men who viewed themselves as outsiders were seeking to use black culture to reinvigorate their own bland lives. Kerouac and Mailer were part of a tide of rebellious young male icons such as Elvis, James Dean, and Marlon Brando who were challenging the status quo. Yet in all these cases the rebels were essentially depoliticized, and rather than confronting real, devastating American problems such as racism or economic disparity or even McCarthyism, they were rebelling simply for its own sake. And the form that the rebellion took with its sexuality and youthful rage made critics such as Alfred Kazin very uncomfortable: he likened it to the perversity of figures like the Marquis de Sade.[9] Moreover, because America was still experiencing a major economic boom, the apolitical rebellions were primarily directed against middle-class suburban conformity rather than the American institutions that discriminated against African Americans or the poor. It would only be in the 1960s that the energy of rebellion would take on political aspects that broadened the focus from a challenge to bourgeois middle-class norms to fighting for civil rights or against the war in Vietnam.

Mailer's essay went beyond a simple longing for "darkness" to include an atavistic and troubling description of violence, including one notorious passage where he describes a murder:

> It can of course be suggested that it takes little courage for two strong eighteen-year-old hoodlums, let us say, to beat in the brains of a candy-store keeper, and indeed the act — even by the logic of the psychopath — is not likely to prove very therapeutic, for the victim is not an immediate equal. Still, courage of a sort is necessary, for one murders not only a weak fifty-year-old man but an institution as well, one violates private property, one enters into a new relation with police and introduces a dangerous element into one's life. The hoodlum is therefore daring the unknown, and so no matter how brutal the act, it is not altogether cowardly.[10]

Mailer's intention was obviously to show the courage and rebelliousness of such a violent act, but as Morris Dickstein noted, "he does not mention that the storekeeper, like the psychoanalyst, is likely to be Jewish, representing a rejected part of his own identity. (Mailer's maternal grandfather kept a grocery in Long Branch, New Jersey, besides being the town's unofficial rabbi.)"[11] Mailer's embrace of the rebellious spirit was therefore in part predicated on a denunciation of his Jewish heritage.

For Mailer, Jewishness was "too white" and other forms of identity, such as African American culture, were sought as a pathway toward revitalization. At the same time as Mailer and others were reaching out to alternative forms of selfhood, many young Americans saw Jewishness as the site for experiencing oppositional energy, since the Jew was a more acceptable type of rebel than an African American. It was at this time, then, that Jewish American literature became hugely popular.[12] The new central role of Jewish literature was evident when Jewish writers began winning major book awards in disproportion to their numbers. Even though Jews were just over 3.5 percent of the overall population, male Jewish writers won virtually every American literary prize of note during the 1950s: the most prestigious prize in American letters, the National Book Award, was given to Saul Bellow in 1954, to Bernard Malamud in 1958, and to Philip Roth in 1960. And the Pulitzer Prize went to Herman

Wouk in 1952, Arthur Miller in 1957, and to Stanley Kunitz in 1959. When conformity was the norm, ethnic writers could offer their readers an escape into more complicated portraits of self and otherness, and writers like Saul Bellow and Philip Roth used Jewish "outsider" protagonists, only marginally outside of the norm, to speak of difference and struggle and transformation.[13]

So where authors such as Bellow and Roth were putting the Jewish experience on center stage, others like Mailer and Heller were evoking a type of rebelliousness that sought to deny any Jewish aspects. This contradictory form of individualism which negated Jewishness was, as I have pointed out, a dominant aspect of late 1950s Jewish liberalism in America that stressed commonalities over differences. The disappearance of the Jew in the literature written by some Jews was also perhaps impelled by the rising dominance of television, a medium that in the 1950s erased from view Jews and other ethnics (except for the odd exception like Desi Arnaz of *The Lucy Show*).[14] Unlike *Point of No Return* and *That Winter*, where the Jewish character eventually "comes out" and proclaims his true identity, in Heller's novel, Yossarian remains outwardly "Armenian," although as I will show, the quest he undertakes during the novel converts him from an everyman ethnic into a Jew.

Like Mailer's hipster, *Catch-22*'s protagonist, Yossarian, destabilizes the larger system and has nothing overtly Jewish about him. He is a figure whose role is to undermine and break down the hierarchy, and he is almost entirely shorn of any biography or background, instead existing solely in the present moment as a destabilizing force. The system he challenges, reaching back to *The Naked and the Dead*, is the military, which in Heller's outlook becomes a stand-in for American corporate culture.

Catch-22 was published in 1961 when there was a renewed popular interest in World War II, with, for instance, the movie *The Bridge over the River Kwai* having won the 1958 Academy Award for best picture. Moreover, the year before the novel's publication, John F. Kennedy was voted into office as president, a veteran who seemed to effortlessly unite his war experience with his liberal ethos. With the rise of television as a major cultural force during the 1950s, *Catch-22* was also the first Jewish war novel to have precedents in televisions shows.

In this case, the comic take on military life was on display in programs such as the popular *The Phil Silvers Show* (commonly called *Sgt. Bilko*) which ran from 1955 to 1959 and focused on a fictional army base in Kentucky.[15] As Stephen Whitfield notes: "Joseph Heller's unique novel crossed the wires of zaniness and dread, as though the dialogue that Sgt. Bilko's motor pool crew delivered in the 1950s television series starring Phil Silvers had suddenly been altered by a new team of writers named Dostoevsky and Kafka."[16] Sgt. Bilko, played by Phil Silvers, who was the Jewish son of Russian immigrants, is a comic schemer who constantly tricks the officers in charge by running a series of scams to make money and avoid work. Typical of Yiddish comedy, the Jewish *macher*, Sgt. Bilko, is far smarter and more verbally adept than anyone else on the base and is the real power behind the scenes even though his rank is low.

In a typical episode, "Blue Bloods of the Bilkos," broadcast on January 8, 1957 (series 2, episode 16), Bilko wreaks havoc on a family of "blue bloods" that have refused to allow Bilko's friend to their big fancy wedding since he is "only a sergeant." To get even, Bilko turns everything upside down by showing that the "undesirables" are not the low-ranked army conscripts, but instead the "blue blood" family that may have Nazi and/or Communist sympathies. The episode is typically subversive, using the (Jewish) outsider, Bilko, to establish that the "undesirables" are in fact the better people, while the wealthy WASPs cannot be trusted. At the same time the show makes fun of the McCarthy witch hunts by showing the dangerous trend of labeling innocents as Communists as a means to destroy them. Sgt. Bilko (like the main protagonist in *Catch-22*, Yossarian) is a character who wreaks havoc on the established hierarchy and does so from a Jewish outsider's perspective, although he is never identified as such. (And Bilko's otherness is also amplified because he is only a lowly enlisted man.) It is from a position of perceived weakness that Bilko takes down the leaders and runs circles around them. We know Bilko, like Yossarian, is Jewish because he exhibits so many traits associated with Jewish Americans: his speech cadences, mannerisms, and sense of humor are straight out of the Borscht belt. Sgt. Bilko shows the foibles and stupidities of the WASP power structure but does so while avoiding mention that he is a Jew.

Although Heller is remembered as the first novelist to present a comedic take on World War II, in fact writing about the war in a humorous way was widespread from the 1940s onward. The trend initially began with the huge 1942 best seller, Marion Hargrove's nonfiction account of his basic training, *See Here, Private Hargrove*. This was followed by the massive best-selling comedic novel, Thomas Heggen's *Mr. Roberts*, which although it ends on a dark note, nevertheless presents the daily life of servicemen in a funny way.

In the 1950s there were a string of best-selling comic novels, beginning with Mac Hyman's *No Time for Sergeants* (1954), which landed on the best seller list and remained there for most of 1955 (the movie version would launch Andy Griffith's career). *No Time for Sergeants* is about a Georgia country bumpkin in boot camp and the humor is based on his simplistic redneck take on things. Hyman died young, and only had this one hit, so there is scant biographical information, but his novel is important, not because of any overt Jewish ties, but because it launched a mini-publishing trend of military comic novels in the mid-1950s.

During the 1950s and early 1960s, there followed a string of paperbacks that continued in the vein of *No Time for Sergeants*, turning boot camp and combat into the subject of comedy and presenting a "wacky" take on military service: William Brinkley's 1956 *Don't Go near the Water* (that was also made into a movie) about naval officers on a fictional Pacific island; Robert Fuller's 1959 *Danger! Marines at Work!* about a U.S. Marine parachute battalion in New Caledonia; Robert Duncan's 1959 *If It Moves, Salute It*, about the American military in Japan in 1945, and George Bluestone's 1960 *The Private World of Cully Powers*, about life in a Southern boot camp. The comic novels use the military setting to play up the cultural clash and fish-out-of-water themes of naive young men attempting to follow the complex and myriad laws of life in service. The comedic aspects also often revolve around attempts by recruits to subvert the rules and undermine the military.

There was also a popular, comedic late 1950s war novel about a Jewish conscript, Mark Harris's 1957 *Something about a Soldier*. Harris (born Mark Harris Finkelstein) was the well-known author of four popular baseball novels, including *Bang the Drum Slowly*. The autobiographical novel describes Jacob Epp undergoing basic training in the Deep South in 1943. Jacob is a wisecracking, intellectual, funny Jewish eighteen-year-old who is so stunned by the racism he encounters in the South that he organizes a petition against the Jim Crow laws. Like the author himself, Jacob ends up deserting because he cannot stand the racism and intolerance; he is first put in the stockades and then in a psychiatric hospital where he is diagnosed as a neurotic. Eventually he is discharged, and fifteen years later he learns that every member of the group that he trained with in the camp was killed during the war.

The tone from the outset is sarcastic, funny, and caustic as Jacob tries to get a handle on the antisemitism in the army and the racism of the locals. The absurdist aspects, which we will see in Heller's novel too, riddle the book, with Adolf Hitler showing up from time to time in and around the training camp. Moreover, in the tradition of Charlie Chaplin's *The Great Dictator* and later Mel Brooks's *The Producers*, Hitler is a figure of derision and comedy who has been deflated from his monstrous powers. *Something about a Soldier* evinces a comfort and ease with its Jewish outlook, with conversations littered with Yiddish phrases and jokes, and Jacob constantly making fun of his own Jewishness (at times using his full Jewish last name, Epstein, and at other times condensing it to Epp). Jacob confronts the paradox that he is derided as a Jew but is being asked to fight as an equal for the country: "It was really disheartening, no sooner swearing to uphold the Constitution than to hear those derogatory remarks."[17]

Living in the deep South and seeing firsthand the brutal treatment of African Americans cause Jacob to realize that while in the North he may be a Jewish ethnic, in the South he is a member of the white race that victimizes blacks:

> He now saw how parochial he once had been. Whereas he had once felt himself to be, because he was a Jew, oppressed, he now knew an opposite and more terrible emotion: he was no longer oppressed but oppressor, persecutor, no longer of the minority but of the majority, no longer weak but shamefully strong. (*Something about a Soldier*, 52–53)

With this knowledge comes an exploration of what makes blacks and Jews different, and his conclusion is that Jews can hide themselves by, for instance, changing their names, while African Americans have no means of escaping their despised status. His mission, then, is to try and help to put an end to the racism in the South, since he views himself as a fellow member of a victimized minority.

Rather than delivering his punches against American racism in a serious manner, the novel uses humor to expose the deep wells of hatred that blacks experience directly, and Jews undergo in a more peripheral way. Typical of the earlier war novels, Jacob is a wisecracking city Jew, but here, because of the novel's focus on the racial politics of the American South, he is unsure what his role really is and how he should understand his status. Jacob even learns that he has something to lose by no longer being the "Jewish victim" since it requires him to reevaluate the role of Jews in an American racial system where the African Americans are the real victims, segregated and suppressed in both their homes and in the military.

Miller's novel exemplifies a clearly articulated liberal perspective on the military. Making the mistreatment of African Americans the book's main focus, the novel conflates the military with Southern racism and challenges both to improve in their treatment of blacks. However Miller, unlike Heller, makes his attack from an overtly Jewish standpoint, never letting the reader forget that as a Jew he has a particular insight into inequity and why it must be overcome in America. Heller, by contrast, writing slightly later, ostensibly expunges the Jewish perspecrtive from his call for a subversion of the military.

Another type of comic Jewish take on war service was evident in Philip Roth's 1959 short story for the *New Yorker* entitled "Defender of the Faith," although the humor here is less "wacky" and more bathetic. The tale presents a cynical view of what it means to be a Jewish soldier: it is 1945 and the protagonist and narrator, Sergeant Nathan Marx, has just returned to the United States to work on a training base for new recruits, having served in many harrowing battles in the European theater during the previous three years. On base he is spotted as a Jew by a new recruit, Sheldon Grossbart, who seeks to manipulate Marx to give him and his two Jewish friends a series of special accommodations. Reluctant at first to admit he is a Jew and to use it to pass on any privileges, Marx discovers that reconnecting with his identity enables him to get back in touch with his own humanity which he has suppressed in service. At the end of the story, after discovering how much Sheldon has been lying and manipulating him, Marx gets even. Sheldon has pulled strings so that he will be the only recruit who will not be sent to the Pacific and Marx intervenes and has Sheldon's special privilege revoked so that he will be sent to battle.

The short story presents a stark contrast between the positive figure of the elder statesman, Marx, and the young upstart, Sheldon, who could not be further from the image of the heroic Jewish soldier that dominated the previous war novels. Sheldon is weak, fearful, cowardly, and has no desire to support the great American war effort. He is only concerned with himself, and he will manipulate anyone and do anything to have his way. By contrast, Marx is a good soldier and a good man who struggles to understand how to be both a Jew and an American. Published fourteen years after the end of the war, Roth's story draws Sheldon as the opposite of the Jewish American soldier who is intrinsically heroic or patriotic. Sheldon lives without adherence to any larger ideological, religious, or moral belief systems, and his aims are entirely selfish. While Marx holds onto his dignity at the end, and is Roth's representation of the older generation of Jewish soldiers, Sheldon suggests that the new Jewish soldier has nothing redeeming about him, except perhaps the ability to survive in any situation. As Sheldon says of the Jews in Europe who were killed in the Holocaust, "They let themselves get pushed around,"[18] and he has no intention of allowing this to happen to him.

In Roth's late 1950s take on a Jewish soldier, the Holocaust is the dominant trope and motif, overriding previous concepts such as American patriotism. The young Jew in America, like his counterpart in Israel, is a Jew first and foremost and his brothers are fellow Jews rather than fellow comrades in arms. Only ten years after the first wave of Jewish American war novels, with their serious and earnest attempts to portray the heroism of Jewish soldiers, Roth shows that this type of man, as represented by Marx, is in danger of being supplanted by the new generation of men like Sheldon. No longer concerned with showing Jewish patriotism to America, Roth's young soldier is only concerned with himself. His Jewishness is just as much a sham as his Americanism, and he has broken free of any ties to anything but his own concerns. The ultimate rebel against any code of behavior, larger system of loyalty, or religiosity, Sheldon is a young man adrift and dangerous because his selfish acts put others at risk. Jewishness for him is a costume that he wears but which is empty of meaning.

Joseph Heller's *Catch-22* follows in the tradition of comic World War II writing, evoking elements of the wacky style of Hyman, the absurdist vision of Harris, and the dark satire of Roth. Heller's approach, however, was more literary than populist, and its style would initiate the subversive trend in the heroic tradition of war writing later found in novels such as Kurt Vonnegut Jr.'s *Slaughterhouse-Five* (1969) and Thomas Pynchon's *Gravity's Rainbow* (1973).[19] This type of writing had an anarchic world-view that developed out of the massive forms of destruction wrought by the Second World War. As Alfred Kazin pointed out, for those who had experienced World War II, the unprecedented scale of the horrors, from extermination camps to nuclear bombs, were viewed in increasingly apocalyptic terms: "War as an actuality, bound by space and time, an event that literature could do justice to, soon yielded to an apocalyptic sense of the possible destruction of mankind, the boundlessness of its enmities."[20] James Dawes labels this manifestation of an apocalyptic reality in the arts as the "aesthetics of the grotesque."[21]

In *Catch-22*, Heller employs a groundbreaking narrative style that goes against the prevailing linear plot of American war novels while describing a series of farcical, perverse, and absurd occurrences.[22] Heller tells the story in a circular manner with time jumping forward and backward, and with the same event retold from numerous temporal perspectives. Time's arrow is subverted constantly throughout the text, undermining the notion of war as a grand, forward-moving event with clear winners and losers. Instead, it is a chaotic, jumbled, and random mess that the men must simply survive without necessarily understanding. Indeed, what Heller seems to be suggesting is that order was only imposed upon these events in retrospect, after the fact, when the great narratives about the war were being told by historians and journalists and novelists; none of these outsiders, however, was capable of telling the truth of what it was like to be in the USAAF during World War II, when there seemed to be no order or rationale for anything that was done.

Heller's approach received a mixture of adulatory and scathing reviews, as some critics loved the subversive stance while others hated its nonlinear, chaotic timeline.[23] Typical were the reviews in the *New York Times*. First, there was a negative write-up in the newspaper's *Book Review* (which Heller obsessed about for many years),[24] which called the novel an "emotional hodgepodge" whose author was "like a brilliant painter who decides to throw all the ideas in his sketchbooks onto one canvas, relying on their charm and shock to compensate for the lack of design."[25] The next day, the paper's daily edition contained an extremely positive review by the *Times* chief critic, Orville Prescott, who described *Catch-22* as "wildly original, brilliantly comic," and asserted that it "will not be forgotten by those who can take it."[26]

Joseph Heller (1923–1999) was born and raised in Coney Island, Brooklyn; his parents were poor Russian Jewish immigrants.[27] His father died when he was five, and his mother struggled to support her three children by working as a seamstress. When the Depression hit it made little impact upon the already impoverished family. In 1942, at the age of nineteen, Heller enlisted in the Army Air Force. He was instructed at bases around America for the next two years: basic training at the Lowry Field in Denver, aviation cadet training school in Santa Ana, California, and advanced flight training in Columbia, South Carolina. Heller received his first (and only) posting as a bombardier in May 1944 to the Alesan Air Field in Corsica from which he participated in bombing runs over occupied Europe. Once he completed his sixtieth mission in October 1944, he spent a few months hanging around the camp in Corsica until he got his ticket home.[28] Time on the island was broken up by leaves to Rome where Heller, who described himself as a "boyish and ravenous satyr," sought out sex with a variety of Italian women.[29] In January 1945 Heller was finally shipped back to America for an honorable discharge; he received a Presidential Unit Citation and an Air Medal.

Once back in the United States, Heller married Shirley Held with whom he had a daughter, Erica, and a son, Ted. Under the GI Bill, Heller studied literature, receiving an M.A. from Columbia University (where he took a course with Lionel Trilling) and was awarded a Fulbright to attend Oxford. He taught university English courses at Penn State University while writing short stories that were published in *Esquire* and the *Atlantic Monthly*. In the early 1950s Heller left academia to work as an advertising publicist for a range of magazines.

The idea for *Catch-22* came to Heller one night in 1953 "as a seizure, a single inspiration," and for the following eight years he worked on it while employed at a small ad agency.[30] In 1957 he received a contract and advance from Simon and Schuster's young editor Robert Gottlieb (who would eventually become the editor of the *New Yorker*). The novel was finally published in 1961, and the Mike Nichols film version came out in 1970.

Catch-22 was Heller's sole major critical and popular success, although during his life he wrote six additional novels, two plays, and several credited and unaccredited screenplays such as *Sex and the Single Girl*. Heller supported himself from his royalties and by teaching creative writing courses. His gregarious and ebullient personality made him deeply loved by his children, and throughout his life he had a group of loyal friends, including Mel Brooks and Mario Puzo.

During 1981 and 1982, Heller was hospitalized with the rare and debilitating Guillain-Barré syndrome, a nervous system disease, which left him paralyzed for a time. While sick, he narrated a book about his experiences, entitled *No Laughing Matter*. By 1984 Heller had recovered, whereupon he divorced his wife of thirty-nine years to marry the nurse who had taken care of him while he was sick, Valerie Humphries. In 1994, thirty-three years after *Catch-22*, Heller published a follow-up entitled *Closing Time*. *Closing Time* describes the life of the protagonist of *Catch-22*, Yossarian, and a few other main characters of the first novel, who are now elderly veterans. The book was neither a critical nor a popular success.[31] In 1999 Heller died of a heart attack in his Long Island home, having just completed his final novel, the autobiographical *Portrait of an Artist, as an Old Man*.

The plot of *Catch-22* is actually quite simple, although the events are complicated by being dictated out of sequence. The story covers the period from July through December 1944, opening in the hospital on the island of Pianosa where the main character, Yossarian, is trying to stay as long as possible in order to avoid having to fly more combat missions. Yossarian is an Armenian American with an Assyrian name and is a lead bombardier on B-25 runs over targets in northern Italy and France.

The bombing runs rarely bring the men into direct combat with German aircraft; instead they have to weave through terrifying fields of surface-to-air fire, known as flak: "flights of planes were making the same hazardous journey over the target, threading their swift way through the swollen masses of new and old bursts of flak like rats racing in a pack through their own droppings"[32] (*Catch-22*, 150). The airmen are led by the evil and inept Colonel Cathcart who is "in the service of himself" (188) and rather than being concerned with winning the war, is waging a campaign "to become a general" (215). The colonel's rank means he can wield his power and use it abusively whenever and wherever he chooses to. The intellectual Yossarian is Cathcart's complete opposite, and he has become "his nemesis" (210) because Yossarian is constantly undermining Cathcart's self-serving attempts to make a name for himself.

In fact, Colonel Cathcart's sole aim is to stand out from the other commanders in order to be noticed for advancement. He cares so little about the men serving him, that at a whim he will increase the number of bombing runs that the men are required to complete in order to be sent home. Every time Yossarian is near to finishing his required number of missions, the colonel raises the number, from fifty to sixty to seventy. To Yossarian it seems that it is only a matter of time until he will be killed on a bombing run. Cathcart is not alone in his selfish pursuit of glory — in fact none of the senior officers are doing their duty to try and protect the men, and all are motivated by their own agendas. Yossarian becomes increasingly aware that his "only mission each time he went up was to come down alive" (29). His survival instinct has even made him consider options such as killing Cathcart, hiding out in the hospital to have a break from the bombing runs, or deserting.

In the recent past Yossarian, however, had bravely undertaken his role as lead bombardier, but he had finally "lost his nerve on the mission to Avignon" (225). This event is revisited repeatedly throughout the novel from a variety of angles, until the final pages of the book when Yossarian graphically describes each moment of the tragedy. The trauma occurred when a fellow member of Yossarian's flight, Snowden, was hit by flak and subsequently died in Yossarian's arms after his intestines poured out of him. After this, Yossarian refused to wear his uniform, which had been covered with Snowden's blood, and went around naked for a time, including when he received his Distinguished Flying Cross. Yossarian's refusal to wear clothes marks an important symbolic shift for him, for when he stopped wearing the army uniform he rejected his membership in an organization that decided every aspect of his life, including the clothes that he wore. He broke free, releasing himself from the shackles of the corporation, destroying the link between his corporality and their ownership of him.

Scenes of terrifying bombing runs are interspersed with life on the island base and furloughs to Rome. In Rome men are constantly having sex with prostitutes and partaking in orgies. These scenes read like the last days of the Roman Empire when everything is breaking down into a hedonistic, primal state of sex and debauchery. The novel moves between starkly contrasting landscapes: Pianosa, which is male-dominated and where the men wait around for their potentially deadly missions; the terrifying bombing runs; and Rome, which is a world of women, sex, and fun. As Heller noted about these alternating scenes, "Yossarian's sex urge is strongest right after he has been close to death."[33] Heller is giving his readers an exciting, titillating romp through war as a site of extremes of psychological and physical drama, with a lot of sex thrown in. These scenes would have spoken to readers bored with late 1950s American life. Here young men get to fulfill all their sexual desires, play with guns, and deride the elders who are in charge. It is a young, male fantasy of rebellion against stability and quiet conformism. Catch-22 therefore offers an accentuated world of gender divisions, where the men are the fighters and the warriors, and the women are their hyper-sexual, earthy, fecund playthings.

Yossarian's only moment of truly unethical behavior is when he gropes a nurse (293), yet within the system of Catch-22, where women exist solely for the pleasure of the men, his act does not seem abusive but rather comic. All women are whores for the men and they readily strip off their clothes. Only the chaplain has a completely positive relationship with his beloved wife, yet he is drawn as effeminate and weak in comparison with the macho Colonel Cathcart, and his love of a woman is a comic example of this. For the men, and for the women, this primal landscape has brought them to extremes — warrior-like, muscular men and sexual women — with both sides having sublimated intellects.

In the last section of Catch-22 the tone changes markedly, becoming much darker as Yossarian undertakes a frightening journey through an apocalyptic Rome that culminates with his comrade, Aarfy, raping and killing a maid who worked at the brothel. The nightmarish mood remains as Yossarian then tries to avoid being killed by a knife-wielding prostitute who can magically appear everywhere and anywhere. She wants to kill Yossarian because she blames him for the death of her boyfriend (and Yossarian's friend), Nately.[34]

At the end of Catch-22 Yossarian is offered a deal by Colonel Korn and Colonel Cathcart whereby they will promote him and send him home and in return he will "be one of the boys" and will talk about the great heroism and leadership skills of the senior officers (428). If he refuses their offer he will be court-martialed. Yossarian accepts, and leaves the meeting with an "exhilarated air" but is stabbed by "Nately's whore"; an act subsequently seen as rough justice, since by joining the evil empire of Korn and Cathcart, rather than continuing to rebel against it, he became the fair recipient of her vengeance. Recovering from the nearly critical stab wound in the hospital, Yossarian tells the doctors his name is Yo-Yo (symbolic of course of his flipping to the side of the evil senior officers), and while talking with the chaplain about the deal he had accepted, like a Yo-Yo he flips again and decides he will refuse their offer. After vividly recalling the full horror of Snowden's death, Yossarian tells Major Danby that he is going to go AWOL. As Nately's whore tries to take one final stab at him, Yossarian flees, aiming to get to neutral Sweden as his friend Orr had done.

The novel's focus on USAAF airmen, who had very high mortality rates, means *Catch-22* has a far greater number of deaths of main characters than the other war novels I have been discussing, although following the absurdist tenor of the book, the men frequently die in ridiculous ways or outside the field of battle: Hungry Joe is smothered by a cat while he sleeps; McWatt flies into a mountain; Clevinger's B-25 permanently disappears in a cloud; Kid Sampson is cut in half when a plane flown by his showboating friend accidently clips him.

The cumulative experience of having multiple friends die, being at the whim of corrupt senior officers, and regularly facing his own mortality in terrifying bombing runs has transformed Yossarian into an angry, hardened man with a cynical take on the world. He is the polar opposite of Leon Uris's and Herman Wouk's protagonists, who come out of the war feeling a deep appreciation for and attachment to their military comrades. Instead, Yossarian, like Sheldon in Roth's "Defender of the Faith," is not tied to anyone and only desires to save himself. Where Sheldon, however, has a cynical attitude going into the military, Yossarian learns it from his experiences at war as he discovers the central role of selfish desires in motivating people's actions, especially those in leadership positions. He sees that patriotism and heroism are empty words, and he develops an even greater dislike for religiosity. In the end he only wishes to meet God in order to punch him in the face for all the evil that he has spawned.

Finally, in the heartbreaking reiterated scene where Snowden dies in his arms, Yossarian has his deepest revelation, that, paraphrasing Shylock's speech in *The Merchant of Venice*: "Man was matter, that was Snowden's secret. Drop him out a window and he'll fall. Set fire to him and he'll burn. Bury him and he'll rot, like other kinds of garbage. The spirit gone, man is garbage" (440). War has shown Yossarian that humans are nothing but sacks of bones, disposable matter, trash. In this nihilistic landscape, devoid of God, all one can do is try to outrun the weapons aimed at one's body. For readers seeking to break free of the shackles of late 1950s nine-to-five life, *Catch-22* offers no obvious solution or hope. Instead it asserts a clear-sighted acknowledgment of how doomed we all are. In this worldview, all larger systems, be they corporations, political, or religious, are seemingly false and misleading. Each man is his own little island, a physical site in constant danger of destruction. Like Holden Caulfield in *The Catcher in the Rye*, all the young men can do is challenge the phoniness of the system, without offering an alternative. In Holden's case, his complete loss of faith leads him to an insane asylum, while for Yossarian, to the decision to desert. Both are running away but there is nothing that they are running toward.

The year before the publication of *Catch-22*, John Updike's *Rabbit, Run* came out, with a similar challenge to life in the corrupt corporation. The story focuses on a young man fed up with the constraints of nine-to-five life in the conformist suburb who decides to flee from it in order to experience a richer life. After a series of mishaps and tragedies, he returns to his wife, rather than continuing to search for meaning in a stream of empty experiences. While the plea of the ultimate WASP writer, John Updike, was to remain in the established system although it is intolerable, outsider authors such as Jack Kerouac (a working-class French Canadian), Norman Mailer, and Joseph Heller were showing that even if there is nowhere to run it is better to move than to stay still, conform, and die. Rather than knuckling under and conceding to the system, these writers were asserting that, even if it leads to nothing, it is still better to rebel against the power structure than to accept it.

Catch-22 not only challenges life in the bureaucracy, but subverts many aspects of the war novel genre. Heller both undermines the conformist systems lauded in Uris and Wouk and satirizes the range of characters that typically make up platoon novels. For instance, in *The Naked and the Dead* and *Battle Cry* the Texas characters are tough rednecks, while in *Catch-22* the Texan is a friendly goofball whom the other characters dislike because he is so chatty and nice. And the intellectual, ethnic Yossarian, rather than being bullied by the Texan, joins with the others to torment him (11). Or there is the Native American character who, instead of being a fierce warrior facing others' discrimination, is a murderous intimidator who likes to scare fellow soldiers and uses racial slurs himself (43–44). Heller also satirizes the Hemingway tradition of using war as a backdrop for love stories between American GIs and Italians by making Yossarian's lover not an earthy and heroic Italian country girl, but an angry Roman prostitute.[35] Yossarian also subverts the standard trajectory of war novels where the protagonist evolves from a fearful soldier to a courageous one. Here the opposite is the case.

Throughout the novel Heller uses language as a weapon to destabilize coherent forms of meaning: "Words, Heller reminds the reader, do not necessarily capture reality. Language is artificial and gratuitous, and on occasion it misleads."[36] Judith Ruderman labels this "the language of deficiency" wherein the reader cannot trust the words being used to describe the actions. This makes the novel "a farce — as well as a tragedy — of miscommunication" particularly because in the military the misuse of language can lead to the death of soldiers.[37] The only buffer against the organization's misuse of discourse is the individual, Yossarian, struggling to formulate his own vocabulary and seeking to authentically speak about his reality.

Although *Catch-22* seems to attack all forms of stable discourse, it is nevertheless driven by the ideological imperative of using military culture as an allegory for corporate life, and Heller attempts to show both as oppressive systems. Its aim therefore is to subvert aspects of both the past and the present: the military officers who oversaw World War II and abused their power, and the current corrupt corporate world. Heller claimed he evoked this double position of past and present when he "deliberately seeded the book with anachronisms like loyalty oaths, helicopters, IBM machines and agricultural subsidies to create the feeling of American society from the McCarthy period on."[38] Yossarian, in fact, straddles both decades. He is a 1950s man, bored in a corporation whose rules he must follow, and seeking a way to have an exciting and fulfilling life. But in the moments of intense combat he reverts to the 1940s soldier man who lives most fully when in the most extreme danger, and who has no reason to undergo an existential search for the meaning of life, since he knows that the meaning is simply to live and survive.

The title of the novel suggests another set of tensions that permeates the work: is it a true account of the war, or is the war being used to signify other things? The book was originally titled *Catch-18* but Heller's publishers made him modify it since the best-selling writer Leon Uris was about to release his novel *Mila 18*. Heller changed the number to twenty-two after his editor, Robert Gottlieb, told him "I've got the perfect number. Twenty-two, it's funnier than eighteen."[39] In Uris's case, *Mila 18* was a historical novel that focused on the Jewish experience in the Warsaw ghetto with "Mila 18" the name of the real street address where Jewish resistance fighters were housed. Uris's novel, then, described the war from the perspective of Jews, and offered a historically based, realistic account. This is emblematic of the radically different takes on the war of these two major Jewish novelists: Heller is interested in using his work as a site on which to explore meaning, language, and culture in general, while Uris aims to describe the real historical war against the Jews. Nevertheless, while Uris created the illusion that it was a historically accurate novel, his book presented the Jews of Europe in an idealized manner as bold warriors rather than victims.

In Heller's case, *Catch-22* is a young man's attack on the generation that had brought on the war and was now creating an equally repressive postwar society.[40] The book displays the evils of hierarchies and how powerless those on the lower echelons feel when they are pawns to the bosses' needs. The novel attacks as absurd and pointless the rituals that are used by those who are in charge. For instance, where marching in line would ideally serve to create a united platoon, Lieutenant Scheisskopf (meaning "shithead") is so obsessed by his men winning the weekly parade contests that he has seriously considered "nailing the twelve men in each rank to a long two-by-four beam of seasoned oak to keep them in line" (73). Or there is Captain Black, who has started a "Glorious Loyalty Oath Crusade" (113) as a McCarthyistic means to discern how patriotic the men are. This, of course, like every other aspect of military ritual in the novel, evolves into an absurd fight between the men to prove their loyalty: "The more loyalty oaths a person signed, the more loyal he was; to Captain Black it was as simple as that, and he had Corporal Kolodny sign hundreds with his name each day so that he could always prove he was more loyal than anyone else" (113). The combatants are so busy doing these ridiculous militaristic rituals that it impacts upon their time spent fighting the war. The multiple, pointless decrees are also reminders to readers of the ludicrous edicts of the McCarthy witch hunts, which were also a tremendous waste of time and served no real purpose except to intimidate those who were under scrutiny.

Where the other Jewish war novels I have discussed went to lengths to show the virtue of battling an enemy who was trying to kill Americans generally, and Jews specifically, in this case there is no real external adversary, and Germans are mentioned as just another group, some of whom are even trade partners with the senior officers and in the black market of the camp cook, Milo. Rather than creating a binary universe where the positive figures are the Americans and the negative ones are the Germans or Japanese, in *Catch-22* the positive ones are the enlisted men and the junior officers, and their enemies are the senior officers who are raising the required number of bombing missions without concern for their men. And even though Yossarian is an officer, he has gained his advancement arbitrarily, and he has no real power. "The enemy," as Yossarian says, "is anybody who's going to get you killed, no matter *which* side he's on, and that includes Colonel Cathcart" (124). This is quite a stunning challenge to the entire concept of the noble war and the soldier's mission: here the combatant is no longer a member of a group that is heroically serving their country, but is an island unto himself whose only concern is for his own life.[41]

As I will discuss in more detail, *Catch-22* goes out of its way to avoid mentioning the Holocaust and that the Nazis are killing Jews. This, instead, is a generic battle where neither side is better or worse, and because it is situated in a strange, ahistorical void, this war lends itself to symbolic readings. Further adding to the generic quality of the war that is being described is the fact that that bombing runs dehumanize the enemy into distant targets seen from far above. In the novel there is, in fact, only one time that the target becomes specified as human. In this case, it is the bombing of an Italian hilltop town in order to make it fall over the cliff and create a barrier on the road. Peckem is not ordering this attack on civilians because of any larger war aim, but merely in order to create a good photo opportunity for himself (328). In this one instance in which real human targets are specified, the men are horrified and some respond by dropping their bombs away from the village.

This war has been expunged of a larger meaning, and its title, "Catch-22," points to this in its range of definitions. Foremost the term attacks the heroism of combat by asserting that "anyone who wants to get out of combat duty isn't really crazy" (46). To further quote from the novel on the implications of catch-22, "Orr was crazy and could be grounded. All he had to do was ask; and as soon as he did, he would no longer be crazy and would have to fly more missions. Orr would be crazy to fly more missions and sane if he didn't, but if he was sane he had to fly them. If he flew them he was crazy and didn't have to; but if he didn't want to he was sane and had to" (46). In other words, the illogical system of warfare means that crazy people who seek out missions are deemed sane, and sane people who want to avoid service because it entails risking their lives, are deemed to be crazy.

Throughout the course of *Catch-22* it becomes evident that there is a profound tension between a representation of combatants as anarchic actors without cause or purpose, and a deeper system of good versus evil that provokes the narrative. This tension plays out in Yossarian's own reading of the term "catch-22" as evoking the moral issues related to flying missions: "To die or not to die, that was the question" (68). If Yossarian ditches his bombing runs by playing sick in the hospital, running away, or simply refusing to go out on them anymore, then someone else, likely a friend, will be sent in his place and may end up being killed. So either he offers up his life, or he saves himself and sends someone else to his death (407).

While Yossarian is viewed as insane and rebellious and nearly anarchic in his worldview, he is in fact guided by a strict moral compass and he acts ethically on numerous occasions, including when he chooses to continue to fly his missions so that someone else will not have to go in his place. Yossarian's final decision to desert is largely motivated by his desire to try and rescue the missing twelve-year-old sister of Nately's prostitute lover. Almost in spite of himself, Yossarian is a good man and a good soldier. Moreover, Yossarian is a character who mourns the loss of his friends and enables the reader to feel the personal tragedy of each individual death.

Catch-22 was based directly on Heller's own war experiences, although for a time he denied it,[42] but when he wrote his autobiography *Now and Then* in 1998, he was comfortable making explicit ties between his past and the novel.[43] Heller, however, always vacillated between admitting and denying that Yossarian was a stand-in for himself.[44] There are, nevertheless, myriad similarities between Heller's and Yossarian's lives in the USAAF. For instance: Heller was also an Army Air Force bombardier based on an island from which he undertook missions in B-25s to sites in northern Italy and southern France; the number of runs he was required to do kept increasing (although, unlike with Yossarian, once Heller completed his sixtieth run, he was rotated back to the United States);[45] he shared a tent with a "dead man" — a soldier who had been killed but whose things were still there; and Heller also lost his nerve after a run over Avignon when his copilot went crazy and dove the plane into a flak field. At that moment, Heller, like Yossarian, feared his life was over, and he realized that "they were trying to kill me, and I wanted to go home. That they were trying to kill all of us each time we went up was no consolation. They were trying to kill *me*."[46] (Unlike Snowden, Heller's gunner survived his hit by flak.)

While Heller's experiences were clearly the basis for many of the events in the novel, there is no indication that Heller experienced the USAAF as being run in a poor, corrupt, or evil manner as it is portrayed in the novel. Moreover, even though *Catch-22* was embraced by antiwar activists during the Vietnam War, Heller claimed throughout his life that he was not a pacifist and that he had supported World War II:

> I still feel it was a necessary war. *Catch-22* was criticized because Yossarian justifies his participation in World War Two until the outcome is no longer in doubt. It offended some people, during the Vietnam War, that I had not written a truly pacifist book. But I am not a true pacifist. World War Two was necessary at least to the extent that we were fighting for the survival of millions of people.[47]

For Heller, "the antiwar and antigovernment feelings in the book belong to the period following World War II."[48] If Heller saw World War II as a just war, and in his autobiographical writings did not describe bad senior officers, where did his extraordinarily dark portrait of the American military come from? One answer may be the possibility that Heller used the setting of war merely as a canvas on which to paint an ugly portrait of the corporate hierarchies of the 1950s. His attack, then, is not against the armed services, but against American business culture.

Also, writing the novel may have enabled Heller to work through many of his own experiences as a naive and idealistic young man who thought that the war would be a big fun adventure, and discovered that although this was true it was also bloody, terrifying, and tragic.[49] For instance, Heller admitted in a 1998 interview that one of the most horrific scenes in the book had indeed happened: bombing the Italian village to make it fall off the cliff and become a roadblock and in the act killing countless innocent civilians. Heller asserted:

> I was aware we were bombing civilians, but I can't say it had much of an effect on me. Even when I got to that part of Catch-22 — it was almost ten years to the day — the writing didn't affect me. But thinking about it did. Thinking about it certainly affects me now.[50]

Within the context of the novel Heller's alter ego Yossarian finds the action deeply troubling, but unlike Heller makes sure his bombs miss the village. The novel was perhaps the place where Heller could write out all the emotions that, as he said, "didn't affect me," at least consciously, and have Yossarian experience them in his place.

If Yossarian is Heller's alter ego, why is he an Assyrian with an Armenian name? Or does the text suggest that he is, in fact, really Jewish?[51] Alternatively, perhaps we should read the novel as "a Jewish book because its sensibility and humor are Jewish"?[52] Over the years, Heller offered contradictory statements about Yossarian's ethnicity, while acknowledging that "the sensibility of Yossarian and the chaplain and the sympathetic characters in Catch-22 was mainly an urban Jewish sensibility."[53]

In an interview from 1962 Heller claimed that the reason that he made Yossarian Armenian or Assyrian, rather than Jewish like himself, even though Yossarian's experiences are largely autobiographical, was that he wanted to stress the "otherness" of Yossarian and make him into a real and authentic outsider:

I wanted somebody who would seem to be outside the culture in every way — ethnically as well as others. Now, because America is a melting pot, there are huge concentrations of just about every other kind of nationality. I didn't want to give him a Jewish name, I didn't want to give him an Irish name, I didn't want to symbolize the white Protestant — but somebody who was almost a new man, and I made him Assyrian (but what I was ignorant of, for one thing, his name is not Assyrian; I've since been told it's Armenian). But I wanted to get an extinct culture, somebody who could not be identified either geographically, or culturally, or sociologically — somebody as a person who has a capability of ultimately divorcing himself completely from all emotional and psychological ties.[54]

Yossarian, then, would be the ultimate outsider, the "new man" untied to anyone or anything and therefore able to operate as a force breaking down the established cultural patterns.

Right before stating this in the interview, Heller noted that the idea for making Yossarian Armenian or Assyrian came "frankly, from James Joyce's placing Bloom in Dublin."[55] So Heller's original model was Leopold Bloom, the Jewish inhabitant of the predominantly Irish Catholic city of Dublin. By the late 1950s, when Heller wrote his book, Jewish characters had, however, become so mainstream in American literature that they no longer connoted the exotic outsider status of previous generations, as had Bloom in Joyce's *Ulysses*. To make Yossarian an ethnic outsider Heller needed to reach much further afield than an American Jew. *Catch-22* showcases a moment in American cultural life when some Jews were shifting from being exotic to mainstream, and when a Jewish writer had to create a non-Jewish character to make him have aspects of Jewish "otherness." This mirrors Norman Mailer's desire in "The White Negro" to reinfuse ethnicity into his bland life by embracing African American culture.

In 1974 James Nagel discovered two manuscript sketches that Heller had written in preparation for *Catch-22* that help to illuminate some of these issues. In the first sketch, labeled "A Perfect Plot," and with the word "Hemingway" scrawled above the text, Heller wrote: "Now that they had just about everything to make a perfect plot for a best-selling war novel." Heller further notes the stereotypes that were common in war novels (such as "a clean-cut young lad who was doomed to die") and how a Jewish character would fit into the picture:

> They had everything there but the sensitive Jew, and that was enough to turn them against the whole race. They had a Jew but there was just nothing they could do with him. He was healthy, handsome, rugged, and strong, and if anybody else in the ward wanted to make something out of anything he could have broken them in time, anybody but Yossarian, who didn't want to make anything out of anything. All he cared about was woman [sic] and there was just nothing in the world you could do with a Jew like that.[56]

As Nagel points out, the "healthy, handsome, rugged, and strong" Jew is likely a wink to Hemingway's Robert Cohn from *The Sun Also Rises*. It is unclear from the sketch, however, if the "Jew like that" refers to Yossarian, and Heller had at one point intended to make Yossarian overtly Jewish, or instead if it points to the Robert Cohn–type Jew the passage opens with.[57]

Whether or not Heller originally considered Yossarian Jewish, this sketch suggests that Heller had a negative view of the ethnic stereotyping typical of World War II novels, and in particular the genre's inability to present a Jewish character that was not simply a "sensitive Jew."[58] Heller's rejection of all stereotypes is further delineated in his manuscript notes when he describes how the Texan, quite against typecasting, will be one who asserts "I don't have any best friends . . . because I love everybody equally, but if I did have any best friends some of those best friends would be Jews."[59] As Nagel observes, the "limitation of the characters to ethnic dimensions certainly would have restricted the universal thematic dimensions of the novel," which makes it "understandable then that in nearly a decade of revision and expansion Heller was ultimately to portray his characters in other than ethnic terms."[60]

In the second manuscript sketch discovered by Nagel, Heller continues to challenge the standard portrayal of Jewish characters in war novels:

This time they had close to a perfect unit. Even the Jew was almost exceptable [*sic*]. His one weakness was that he was stronger than the antisemite, who was afraid to pick on him, which left the Jew a static character. As if that weren't bad enough, he didn't wear glasses. Furthermore, he had never been to City College and had never been interested in socialism.[61]

By overtly distancing Yossarian and other characters from these types of ethnic stereotypes, Heller undermines the war novel tradition of the platoon as a mixing pot where a group of different types came together for the common cause of fighting the Good War. And by making Yossarian into an Armenian or Assyrian, Heller has him become a member of groups that have not been stereotyped in war novels, where the ethnic types are generally Jews, Italians, Texans, Mexicans, Native Americans, and Irish.

This aim to distance his protagonist from overt ethnic stereotypes is also part and parcel of the liberal mandate dominant in Jewish America in the late 1950s, as I mentioned earlier.[62] The call for equality for all meant a universal vision that aimed to suppress ethnic difference and unite all men. By making Yossarian an "other" but not a Jew, Heller could have it all. He could use him to be a rebel against the system, which was a standard liberal call of the era. At the same time, by not specifying him as Jewish, his otherness could take on more universal aspects than the inherent "typecasting" of platoon novels. In other words, Yossarian could be a stand-in for *all* liberal-minded rebels who aim to challenge and subvert the conservative hierarchy.

Instead of making Yossarian overtly Jewish, Heller hides him in plain sight. Or as Sanford Pinsker puts it, "Yossarian is a Jew under his comically 'Assyrian' skin."[63] He has an Armenian name: a population that, like the Jews, underwent a genocide in the previous war. He is Assyrian who, like the Jews, were largely wiped out in World War II. Moreover, in perhaps a subconscious twist, he gives Yossarian the ethnicity of the group that overran the Israelite kingdom and deported many Israelites (and which was immortalized in Lord Byron's famous poem "The Destruction of Sennacherib" with which Heller, a literature major, would have been familiar). Symbolically, like the Assyrians who dispersed the Hebrews, the Assyrian Yossarian displaces the Jew.[64]

Yossarian's Armenian and Assyrian characteristics are solely in his name rather than any explicit cultural heritage, family background, or personal history; he is given no biography, comes from nowhere, and exists solely in the context of war. This makes it much easier to read him as Jewish since the reader knows him only by how he functions in the novel, and his actions have numerous qualities that are often ascribed to Jews. As Josh Greenfeld wrote in 1968, Yossarian has "a Jewish Talmudic mind."[65] He is an intellectual, master wordsmith, a person fully of the book and texts, who amuses himself by playing around with the letters he is asked to censor. And his references frequently have Jewish cultural resonances. For instance, Yossarian's description of America is New York Jewish in tone: "The hot dog, the Brooklyn Dodgers. Mom's apple pie. That's what everyone's fighting for" (9).

Yossarian's sense of humor and his use of it also came straight out of the "traditional Jewish humor" found in Yiddish literature[66] and the Marx Brothers, which according to Judith Ruderman, "stamp this novel [as] indelibly kosher."[67] Moreover, Heller's use of constant repetitions was likened by Sanford Pinsker to the "rapid-fire shpritz" of comedian Lenny Bruce.[68] Additionally, Yossarian's highly tuned ethical stance is a common marker of Jewish soldiers in all the novels that I have discussed. The Jewishness is also manifested during the scene of Snowden's death when "impelled perhaps by the unconscious Jewish identification, Heller paraphrases the famous 'humanizing' speech of Shylock" ("If you prick us, do we not bleed? if you tickle us, do we not laugh? if you poison us, do we not die?").[69]

The reader, having picked up on many signs of Yossarian's underground ethnicity, understands that when the novel asserts that "they hated him because he was Assyrian" (18) this meant that they hated him because he was a Jew. This is made evident in Cathcart's tirade against Yossarian's name, in which he uses terms such as "suspicious" and "socialist" that are typical slurs against Jewish Americans:

> It was like *seditious* and *insidious* too, and like *socialist*, *suspicious*, *fascist* and *Communist*. It was an odious, alien, distasteful name, a name that just did not inspire confidence. It was not at all like such clean, crisp, honest American names as Cathcart, Peckem and Dreedle. (Italicization done by Heller, 210)

However, since Heller has not specified Yossarian as a Jew, he becomes a stand-in for all those who have been victimized by McCarthyism.

Furthermore, even though Jews were becoming accepted members of the middle class, and most of the barriers were down, for Heller nevertheless it may have been still problematic to create a Jewish soldier who was overtly critical of the military, the war, and American patriotism in general. This novel was written during the McCarthy hearings, and Heller also may have been worried about putting his criticisms against the United States in the mouth of a Jew.

Moreover, specifying Yossarian as a Jew would have transformed the critique from a general challenge to "the organization" to the specific wrath of a disaffected Jew. So by making Yossarian Armenian or Assyrian, Heller could have it all: Yossarian is both an ethnic outsider and a universal everyman. His full name, John Yossarian, connotes this since it is "a rather unseemly combination; an almost extraordinarily ordinary first name coupled with a 'foreign-sounding' surname."[70] It is a name that locates the protagonist as both the everyman American, John, and the specific ethnic.

On the one hand, Yossarian's outsider status enables him to stand on the sidelines and have a critical stance toward what he sees, while on the other hand, because he is a member of an ethnic group, the Assyrians, that no longer exists, he cannot be pinned down by general American readers as having petty ethnic gripes. It also allows Heller to establish that there are two sides to American culture: the insiders, like Colonel Cathcart, who hold the power and are part of the boys' club that is corrupt; and the outsiders, like Yossarian, who challenge them. This is part of the broader portrait of evil hierarchies, ruled by insider WASP types, and the rebels who are trying to bring them down.

Heller, who did not want his novel read as autobiographical, also likely chose to make Yossarian Assyrian because it would make it harder for readers to see Yossarian as a stand-in for himself. By distancing himself from the Jewish aspects of the text Heller could take on the stance of being an "American" or "universal" writer, rather than a Jewish one focused only on Jewish concerns. In the 1950s, to be labeled a "Jewish" (or female or black) author still could carry the stain of parochialism, as was evident as I discussed earlier when John Aldridge attacked Jewish, African American, and homosexual writing as not being "universal." While many white youth saw these discourses of "otherness" as sites of authenticity and rebellion, for the writers themselves, many sought to be embraced not as an "other" but as an unhyphenated "American." For Jewish writers, this meant linking one's literature to the tradition of Fitzgerald or Hemingway, rather than the "minor" one of "immigrant" authors such as Abraham Cahan, Chaim Grade, or Sholem Aleichem. And it was only in 1991 that Heller mentioned that Yossarian was "very Jewish."[71]

Although Yossarian is a Jew in all but name, he seemingly has no connection to the Holocaust, since Heller goes out of his way to avoid mention of it. For instance, when Yossarian gives a litany of how people are currently dying, from "being shot to death in hold-ups" to "plummeting like dead weights out of hotel windows," there are no allusions to the Holocaust (166).[72] In spite of this, the novel nevertheless presents a post-Holocaust "Jewish expression of the imagination of disaster, which means paranoia confirmed by history."[73] As Alfred Kazin noted, this feeling of death looming everywhere and "this sense of oneself not as a soldier in a large protective group but as an isolated wretch doomed to die unaccountably is more and more a feature of literature about World War II. It haunts all fiction by Jews since the war, even novels which do not deal with the war."[74] We see the shadow of the Holocaust when Yossarian repeatedly asserts that everyone is trying to kill him, which of course has a resonance with any Jew located in Europe during this period of time. Yossarian's journey, then, is also a Jewish one through a world which has been blighted by mass death.

All of this plays out, I believe, in one of the final chapters in *Catch-22*, "The Eternal City," about Yossarian's nightmarish wanderings through Rome. Heller originally called the chapter "Night of Horrors" but changed it to "The Eternal City," a term used for Rome that reminds the reader that this is taking place in the heart of Roman Catholicism. This strange chapter, which seems very out of character with the tone of the rest of the novel, transmutes Rome, which had been the place where the men went for sex and fun, into a dark, violent, and terrifying place.[75] It is almost as if Heller could no longer repress the shadow of the Holocaust, and as Yossarian walks through the city, he traverses a place that *resonates* as a Jewish ghetto. While the novel makes no direct mention of the Holocaust, the journey through Rome signifies and suggests that it can be read as a ghetto. Yossarian's walk through Rome is thus an *allegory* for an American coming face to face with the Holocaust. Rome was in fact home to the longest-lasting Jewish ghetto, and was directly affected by the Holocaust when nearly two thousand Jews were rounded up in late 1943 and deported to Auschwitz.[76] I am using a long quote here to convey this transformation of Rome into a location that suggests that it has been touched by the Holocaust. Here the innocent are brutalized while the majority, including Yossarian, are bystanders who watch and do not intervene:

> At the next corner a man was beating a small boy brutally in the midst of an immobile crowd of adult spectators who made no effort to intervene. Yossarian recoiled with sickening recognition . . . Nobody moved. The child cried steadily as though in drugged misery. The man kept knocking him down with hard, resounding open-palm blows to the head, then jerking him up to his feet in order to knock him down again. No one in the sullen, cowering crowd seemed to care enough about the stunned and beaten boy to interfere . . . Yossarian crossed quickly to the other side of the immense avenue to escape the nauseating sight and found himself walking on human teeth lying on the drenched, glistening pavement near splotches of blood kept sticky by the pelting raindrops poking each one like sharp fingernails. (415)

The city has become claustrophobic and horror-filled, and Yossarian can find no escape. Everywhere he encounters death and mobs chasing and beating innocent victims. Heller makes the transformation into a Jewish ghetto glaringly clear when Yossarian brushes by a man who evokes a Jewish victim of the Nazis: "a gaunt, cadaverous, tristful man in a black raincoat with a star-shaped scar in his cheek" (417).

In the early 1960s, Richard Brooks requested that in preparation for directing *Catch-22*, Heller give him detailed information about the novel.[77] (Mike Nichols would eventually take over as director when Brooks pulled out.) Heller provided Brooks with a paperback version of the novel on which he wrote up a series of explanatory comments on the page margins.[78] Heller's notes to "The Eternal City" chapter give useful insights into his aims. What stands out most is that during the night covered in the chapter, Yossarian plays the role of a guilty spectator, a bystander, who does not intervene to stop the horrors that he is witnessing. As Heller scrawled along the margin of page 403 (which is page 411 in the modern 2004 edition):

> Yossarian's sadness and feelings of guilt will grow as he walks back to the apartment. He will pass incident after incident that will shock and sicken him, but he will do nothing to intervene and his guilt will be increased by each failure to act.

In Heller's annotations for Richard Brooks there are in fact three times that he mentions Yossarian's guilt, including his note to the scene on page 407 (page 416 in the 2004 edition) when Yossarian watches an old woman fail in her chase of a young woman:

> Here all his feelings of guilt are crystalized for a moment in the poor old woman, whom he could have helped easily had he chosen to become involved in an injustice that was not directly his own.[79]

Yossarian in "The Eternal City" is a guilty and passive witness of the horrors. It is my belief that in this part of the book, Heller suggests, perhaps unintentionally, the profound guilt felt by those who were unwilling or unable to intervene in the destruction of the Jews.[80] Walking through a ghetto, with skinny, pale individuals with "star-shaped" scars on them, and with grotesque and terrible violence being enacted against the weak, children, and women, Yossarian watches the events without attempting to stop them. In this way, Heller actualized the (unfair) sense of guilt felt by many American Jews who were unable to intervene in the destruction of Jewish life in Europe, while also indicting those who were actual bystanders during the Holocaust and did nothing to help the Jews. The chapter indicts not only the bystanders to violence, but also those who perpetuate it, particularly the police, who should be figures of law and order, but like the SS, hurt the weak.

After fleeing from the horrors, Yossarian discovers Michaela, the maid at the whorehouse, lying dead on the street. Her name resonates with St. Michael, who was the patron saint of soldiers. With Michaela lying dead in the street, there is no more order, evil seems to have won, and evil's adversaries, the American soldiers, have joined the cult of death.[81] Yossarian's fellow airman, Aarfy, readily acknowledges that he raped, brutalized, and killed Michaela and then threw her corpse out the window. Aarfy is the most WASP of the junior officers in the novel: he attended prep schools and his main desire after the war is to seek social status and wealth. Yossarian tries to explain the evil of what Aarfy has just done, but the nonchalant young man is certain that he will not be in any trouble since the maid was merely a lowly servant. They hear sirens and two policemen arrive, but rather than arresting Aarfy for having raped and murdered an innocent young girl, the police arrest Yossarian for not having a pass, and take him away.

This is one of the most unexpected and shocking moments in the book and the reader does not see it coming, since they expect that Aarfy, the brutal rapist and murderer, rather than Yossarian, the innocent man, will be arrested. With Yossarian's arrest, the absurdist aspects of the novel suddenly twist from discursive sites of destabilization to connoting a real world that has transformed into one of utter insanity. The ultimate cause is the Nazi regime which has brought on an upside down and evil world where the innocent "Jew" is carted off while the brutal "Aryan" Aarfy remains free. At this moment, Heller's generic, anarchic, and pointless war becomes specified as real, horrific, and brutal. The war is part of a clearly defined system of good and evil, where the Nazis are evil, and those who oppose them are good.

This also could be an example of the novel having mid-1950s notions embedded within it, particularly the fear of Stalinist totalitarianism and a police state.[82] At the same time, the arrest reiterates Heller's condemnation of corporate culture. In this case, Yossarian the rebel is arrested while Aarfy the ultimate company man is left free because the conservative institution of the military has of course sided with its loyal member. Heller is showing here the inherent corruption of the conservative elite, who side with their own. This returns us to Yossarian's earlier description of America: "The hot dog, the Brooklyn Dodgers. Mom's apple pie. That's what everyone's fighting for" (9). The Brooklyn Dodgers symbolized the best aspects of the liberal perspective since they were the team that broke the color barrier in 1947 when they allowed Jackie Robinson to play for them. This was a major moment in civil rights history, and Heller would have been absolutely aware that by putting "Brooklyn Dodgers" with "Mom's apple pie" his readers would know that the America he has been fighting for is New York liberal in tone. Yossarian is arrested because the conservative hierarchy of the (military) American organization can no longer tolerate his rebellious actions.

These events help lead to Yossarian's transformation from a figure who has seemingly not cared about beating the enemy, to one who can avow that all along he had been fighting not to save himself, but to save his country: "Don't talk to me about fighting to save my country. I've been fighting all along to save my country" (446). Critics have challenged this statement as false and out of place with the rest of the novel because of its investment of Yossarian with "a totally unexpected idealism."[83] However, I think that Yossarian's assertion of patriotism makes absolute sense when considered as a reaction to his journey through a Rome that is being destroyed by the Holocaust. He has come out of that horrific experience transformed from a bystander to a participant who will now assert his role in fighting evil. He is ready to admit that this is not a generic war of a corporation versus an individual, but a specific war of an American (Jew) fighting against the Nazi enemy. Yossarian has grown through his rite of passage, turning from the anonymous ethnic everyman to a symbolic Jewish soldier who must fight evil. In Heller's handwritten notes to the final chapter of the book (page 432; 442 in the 2004 version), he wrote that "Yossarian now knows that he does have a responsibility to all the other men, even though they take no action to save themselves." And a few pages later (page 437; 447 in the 2004 version), Heller wrote that "Yossarian has learned by now that it is not life alone that is important, but life of a certain moral quality." Yossarian has become a fully ethical being, rather than merely being an oppositional force of rebellion to the status quo. Yossarian will still choose to desert but, as the novel makes clear, he only does so once the Germans are in retreat and the war in Europe is nearly over (446).

Heller has used a liberal perspective to subvert the conservative mandate of "the organization" by using the extreme image of a rape to showcase the corruption of those who are in charge. With the power elite now undermined, Yossarian can move forward and act ethically because the corrupt system has been disassembled and reconstituted according to his liberal perspective.

Catch-22 resonates with some aspects of Franz Kafka's *The Trial*: in both works the main characters are deemed guilty and are put into absurd worlds where the administrators make arbitrary decisions that curtail their lives and choices. Heller's "Eternal City" chapter, however, shifts the work from the Kafkaesque realm of allegory to a world where the Nazis are exterminating Jews: here everyone is trying to kill Yossarian since all Jews are deemed to be guilty. As I said, although the journey through Rome does not explicitly show the Holocaust, it is suggestive of the events and becomes a location that is infused with its evils. While initially *Catch-22* seems to point out the complete lunacy of war, the selfish impulses that drive the leaders, and the Kafkaesque absurdities and craziness of military life, the Roman ghetto scene challenges this by showing real evil and suffering straight out of the events of the Holocaust: a child whipped brutally in front of a large crowd of bystanders, a girl raped and thrown out a window, streets running with blood and body parts. If Yossarian had been overtly Jewish then the connection to the Holocaust would have been obvious; it instead becomes an experience undergone by the not Jew who is really a Jew, who feels the horror of it, and responds to it as the everyman facing total evil. Heller employs a rhetorical strategy in *Catch-22* that at one and the same time enables the text to be a commentary on war and evil corporations in general, and in the person of Yossarian, an account of the Jew during the Holocaust who hides in the everyman but who cannot truly escape his particular and despised status.

Kirsten Fermaglich has demonstrated that in the late 1950s prominent Jewish American intellectuals began to use the imagery of the Holocaust to denote liberal concepts, such as the need to end the mistreatment of blacks, but did so in a way that erased completely mention of Jewish victims.[84] *Catch-22* is part of this trend of presenting the imagery of the Holocaust while seeming to erase from it any Jewish specificity which would deflect from using it to showcase liberal notions. Yet at the same time, the act of obfuscation fails because so much of the novel generally, and the Rome section particularly, has signposts that mark its Jewishness.

As demonstrated, this novel which is not about a Jewish soldier or the Holocaust is about both. As much as Heller sought to distance *Catch-22* from its Jewishness, the specificity of the experience of the Jewish soldier overlays the book. By including a novel such as *Catch-22* in the framework of Jewish American literature, we can read it as expressing a common conflict between an author's aim to distance his writing from a

Jewish position and the text's semiotics, which have an intensely Jewish flavor. To read this text as Jewish requires using a broad range of textual strategies to ascertain when Jewish perspectives are cloaked in costumes of universalism. By so doing, we see that some Jewish American writing in the postwar era was just as much about hiding as it was about self-exposure.

Catch-22 demarcates the desire of Joseph Heller to have an assimilated "everyman's" take on the war, and to create the great American war novel, when in fact, the Holocaust "haunts the text," to again quote from Kazin. Unpacking the Jewishness of the novel gives us a new range of insights into one of the most important novels of the twentieth century, as well as the unique stresses undergone by a postwar Jew seeking to rewrite his army service into a universal yet individual narrative of a liberal's rebellion.[85]

Conclusion

> Now that fifty years have gone by since *The Naked and
> the Dead* was published in May 1948, I think it might be
> interesting to talk about it as a best-seller that was the work of
> an amateur . . . it thrived on its scenes of combat — and it had
> a best-seller style. The book was sloppily written in many parts
> (the words came too quickly and too easily) and there was
> hardly a noun in any sentence that was not holding hands with
> the nearest and most commonly available adjective . . .
>
> — NORMAN MAILER

Norman Mailer, whose story is woven throughout *The Young Lions*,
wrote in the introduction to the fiftieth-anniversary edition of *The Naked
and the Dead* that his novel's success was due in part to the scenes of
combat. Mailer, who had chosen to be an enlisted man rather than an officer because he thought it would enable him to experience combat and
then write his great war novel, backed down when given the possibility of
serving on the front line. He wrote home to his wife Bea that he chose office work because he thought to himself "You ass, you're playing around
with your life." It was an extremely hard decision for him:

> In a way, Bea, I'm an utterly incurable adolescent. For although
> I was glad and relieved when I heard of the headquarters' assign-

ment, for it did assuage the pain every time I thought of you and wondered if I should never return, as I realized was so possible for the few days I thought I was an infantryman — still I felt a little heartsick, for in back of the fear there had been an anticipation of combat too. In some respects, darling, it was the toughest quick decision I ever had to make.[1]

By not seeing fighting, Mailer was like the majority of men and women who served in World War II, the clerks, dentists, base cooks, logistics officers, and members of support staff, and so on. In order to overcome a lack of experience on which to draw from for his novel, Mailer created his landscapes of war based on the information he gathered from the men with whom he served, by watching how they spoke about battle, by hearing from a distance the sounds of artillery, by interviewing the men about their private lives. Mailer then used his imagination to create his version of the war, giving himself and his readers (many of whom had also not been there) a chance to enter the heroic, intense world where men tested themselves and overcame their darkest fears.

What if Mailer had, instead, written an honest account of what he had actually gone through? A narrative about being on the periphery of battle, since this was, in fact, much closer to the real experience of most American servicemen? A novel about choosing to do office work during some of the most deadly campaigns in the Pacific; of wanting desperately to be on the front line or on combat patrols but being too scared of death to volunteer himself, while others, such as his friend Martinez, offered themselves up for the most dangerous duty? What if Mailer had written a brutally frank account of the terrors men feel about warfare, and how the desire for and fear of battle forced them to confront their manhood? What if he had described the anguish of intellectual men determined to prove that they were tough guys in an era that required combat as their rite of passage? Perhaps this would have been a more authentic novel than the one Mailer looked back upon late in life and faulted for its naive, overwrought style; a book that Mailer could have written if he had not been so desirous of creating a popular story about soldiers on the front lines where he himself could not find the courage to go.

In 1944 elements of a novel like this had in fact been published as the first major work of a giant of postwar American fiction, Saul Bellow's

Dangling Man. As an erudite, multilingual street kid, it was intelligence rather than toughness that Bellow valued most. *Dangling Man* delineates the existential dilemma of the intellectual in wartime, showing the deep self-loathing felt by a Jewish thinker who, like Mailer, is too scared to offer himself up for combat. In Bellow's novella, Joseph embodies the story of men like Mailer who are on the sidelines of the war and can only be "real men" by playing at it rather than offering themselves up for front-line combat. Since Bellow's novella was written when the war and the Holocaust were still under way, the distress he feels about not enlisting is twofold, because there is still the possibility that by joining the military he can help stop the destruction of his people.

Bellow began work on "Notes of a Dangling Man" when he was jobless, writing all the time, and awaiting conscription after having been deferred twice. "Notes" was first published as a story in the *Partisan Review* in 1943 and then extended into a novella, his first major work, retitled *Dangling Man* and published in 1944.[2] The novella is structured as a diary written by Joseph (who, like Joseph K. in *The Trial*, has his last name hidden) about his day-to-day life from December 15, 1942, seven months after his draft deferment order, until April 9, 1943, his final day as a civilian. Reviewed at the time as "an uncannily accurate delineation"[3] of American men waiting to serve, Joseph spends his days obsessing over small things, fighting with his wife, friends, and neighbors, visiting coffee houses, smoking, having an affair, going to parties, and overall being desperately lost, lonely, and unhappy. Joseph ends up volunteering because after nearly a year of waiting to be called up he decides he would rather face death in combat than life as a "dangling man." The novella offers an insightful and dark account of a Jewish American intellectual who is desperate to become a soldier but who holds himself back from enlistment.

The opening paragraph of *Dangling Man* establishes the type of masculinity that men in this era feel they must have in order to enlist:

> For this is an era of hard-boiled-dom. Today [it's] the code of the athlete, of the tough boy . . . If you have difficulties, grapple with them silently, goes one of their commandments. To hell with that! I intend to talk about mine . . . The hard-boiled are compensated for their silence: they fly planes or fight bulls or catch tarpon, whereas I rarely leave my room.[4]

The dichotomy of men who overcome their fears and go to war, and those who wait it out, is actualized in the discourse itself, with "hard-boiled" referring to the terse third-person prose style of tough, cool, independent, and hyper-masculine protagonists who are driven by action and untroubled by violence. (This style of writing reached its pinnacle in the popular pulp detective and film noir works of the 1920s and 1930s from authors such as Dashiell Hammett, James Cain, and Raymond Chandler.) By remaining on the sidelines, Joseph's discourse is instead aligned with Dostoevskian self-exposure, and he composes his diary in the first person, recounting endless days where little to nothing happens.[5]

In his diary, verbosity reigns, in contrast to the taciturn tough guys of whom Joseph asks:

> Do you have an inner life? It is nobody's business but your own.
> Do you have emotions? Strangle them . . . They are unpracticed
> in introspection, and therefore badly equipped to deal with op-
> ponents whom they cannot shoot like big game or outdo in dar-
> ing. (*Dangling Man*, 3)

In other words, as an intellectual Joseph is unable to quell his thoughts and jump into the requirement of the day that only by fighting can he become a real Hemingwayesque man. And the longer that Joseph waits to serve, the more "feminine" he becomes. In *Dangling Man*, where the hard-boiled man is a protean version of a soldier, the Jew Joseph, by contrast, is emotional, chatty, and introspective and has all the aspects of a stereotypical woman, even writing a "female" form of literature, the journal, rather than the "male" novel. By not enlisting, and remaining away from the center of where real men are made, he is transforming into a "housewife" who conducts his affairs in the private realm of the home.[6] This is the opposite of the hard-boiled man who lives in the public sphere and dominates his environment, be it the battlefield or the mean city street. Eventually Joseph figures out ways to become more "masculine" and "hard-boiled" and, when he does so, he begins to describe his exploits in the third-person form of the "male" novel.

Joseph's play-acting at masculinity begins with his first diary entry: whereas in the "old days" he "read constantly" now he has stopped since "books do not hold me. After two or three pages or, as it sometimes happens, paragraphs, I simply cannot go on" (4). In this era of war there is no room for the indoor man who pursues scholarly endeavors. Joseph, therefore, embodies the culture clash between American masculinity, which privileges toughness over smarts, and Eastern European Jewish culture, which instead idealizes intellect over physicality. In order to distance himself from his femaleness and Jewishness, to transform into a real American man, he will need to assert his masculinity in a stereotypical hard-boiled way, based on the values of the soldier. As he understands it, being a soldier makes him embody a type of hyper-masculinity that causes him to treat women poorly. Joseph's transformation into a tough guy/soldier will, however, be so clumsy, unnatural, and inept that, in the end, rather than becoming a heroic man of action he will become a pathetic bully.

Like Mailer, Joseph's sexuality also takes on an element of play-acting, although in his case he loses control, as is evident in a troubling scene in which he picks a fight with his wealthy teenage niece after she needles him about being poor. First Joseph verbally abuses her, then he pulls her over his knee and spanks her:

> I did not release her at once. She no longer fought against me but, with her long hair reaching nearly to the floor and her round, nubile thighs bare, lay in my lap. Whether this was meant to be an admission of complicity and an attempt to lighten my guilt, or whether she wished them to see and savor it fully, I did not know at first. (50)

Rather than coming off as a tough macho man, able to seduce women, the scene shows Joseph to be an unsympathetic bully.

Joseph's torment over wanting to have the will to enlist and thereby potentially die in battle, or stay on the sidelines where he is safe, even infiltrates his nights, when he has terrible dreams about massacres. Joseph's nightmares about the war bring him, like his biblical namesake, to interpret his dreams. Joseph finally realizes that it is better to kill or be killed in battle than to remain dangling in America while others are slaughtered:

But it is even more important to know whether I can claim the right to preserve myself in the flood of death that has carried off so many like me, muffling them and bearing them down and down, minds untried and sinews useless — so much debris. It is appropriate to ask whether I have any business withholding myself from the same fate. (122)

Joseph decides that he can no longer withhold himself from the same fate as myriad young American men, and he volunteers. Although mimicking the existential angst of Russian novels such as Fyodor Dostoevsky's *Notes from the Underground* (after which Bellow gave the original title of the novella: *Notes of a Dangling Man*) or Nikolai Gogol's *Diary of a Madman*, Bellow's version is rooted in American Jewish life during the war years.[7] *Dangling Man* is a portrait of an American Jewish intellectual on the edge of the war and unable to act, but becoming increasingly convinced that he needs to do so. By enlisting, he will do battle for the Jews of Europe, while also fully immersing himself in the war (137). His diary entry concludes with:

I am no longer to be accountable for myself; I am grateful for that. I am in other hands, relieved of self-determination, freedom cancelled. Hurray for regular hours! And for the supervision of the spirit! Long live regimentation!

Joseph's long days of freedom from work, rules, and bosses have brought him to a crisis of selfhood that the army will resolve by immersing him in a structured environment.[8] While some critics have viewed Joseph's decision to enlist as "ironic,"[9] Morris Dickstein rightly sees it as a serious reflection of Bellow's "fundamental conservatism" that was wary of individualism and bohemianism.[10] In the end, the only way to turn from the thinker into the actor, to transform into the ideal of masculinity, is to jump in and let the army teach him how to do this, since his own attempts have failed. His anguished journey has led him to evolve from a feminized Jew on the sidelines of battle to an American man who offers himself up. Joseph's transformation suggests the extraordinary torment that many, including Mailer, must have felt between wanting to be in the middle of things, but also being so self-introspective that they could not simply turn into the hard-boiled men that they, and the era, needed and desired.

In an era when Hemingway still dominated American letters, it must have been a breath of fresh air for a generation of readers, Jewish and non-Jewish alike, to come across Bellow's "dangling man," whose verbose self-examinations and attempts to become more manly spoke to the myriad fears of young men trying to prepare themselves for the inconceivable possibility that by becoming soldiers they could be killed. It makes sense that a Jewish writer, standing on the cusp between a Jewish European vision of intellectualized masculinity and an Anglo one of action, could use his writing to unpack the fears and promises of the American ideal of masculinity. As Bellow renders it, when the Jewish intellectual tries to wear the costume of the soldier he becomes unbalanced and unable to maintain relationships with women, culture, and the public world. In the process of embracing American masculinity, he loses as much as he gains. Bellow's Jewish protagonist heads off to enlist but we do not see what happens once he becomes a soldier — whether he continues to stay on the sidelines, as Mailer did, or instead puts himself forth for dangerous, direct combat missions.

The Jewish war novelists that I have discussed take the next step and bring the Jewish intellectual into the setting of war where he is reconstructed as a man of action, capable of slaying an enemy who wants to destroy his entire people. In most of the cases, the transition of the Jew into the soldier has many positive elements, since it allows him to become a true American hero, and in some instances even marry a Christian wife, while also allowing him to shed the negative weak aspects of his immigrant parents. This positive reconstruction of the Jew's masculinity into one based on physicality and toughness rather than intellectualism was evident in *The Young Lions*, *An Act of Love*, *Point of No Return*, *The Crusaders*, and *Battle Cry*.

For writers such as Bellow, Mailer, Wouk, and Heller, the depictions of how Jews transform into soldiers were more complicated and less clearcut. As Bellow, Mailer, and Heller showed with their characters Joseph, Roth, and Yossarian, becoming a soldier could mean the obliteration of their true selves, either symbolically or literally. Mailer's protagonist Roth is the most extreme example: he shows the attempt to be respected as a brave soldier is so self-destructive that it can lead to death. In the case of

Yossarian, he represents the impossible paradox, or "catch-22," which says that in order to be heroic in war he must sublimate his intellect and blindly follow corrupt leaders, even at the risk of his life. Wouk's *The Caine Mutiny* further delves into the dissonant and uncomfortable duality of the Jew at war in an organization that requires blind obedience, while Jewish culture encourages Talmudic questioning. Wouk solves this dilemma by seeking to allow his Jewish soldier to have it both ways: as a lawyer he uses his intellect to question and then rationalize the laws of war.

In fact there seems to be no effective resolution of this binary universe, and perhaps this is why in so many instances in Jewish American war novels the Jewish soldier dies outside the realm of combat, since he cannot successfully live as a soldier man-of-action and as a Jewish intellectual. This splitting of Jewish masculinity into incompatible extremes of physicality and intellectualism did not just take place in Jewish American war novels, but was so widespread in twentieth-century Jewish writing that Hebrew scholars came up with terms to describe it: the *talush* is the overthinking inactive intellectual (whom Joseph begins as in *Dangling Man*), and the *bal-guf* is the man of the body (whom Joseph becomes in preparation for going to war).[11] In Jewish American war writing, the tensions between these two extreme visions of masculinity are accentuated since the Jewish intellectual must become a *bal-guf* in order to survive, but as Heller shows in *Catch-22*, to survive he must outwit his commanders by using his intellectual *talush* characteristics.

The tension between seeking to reinvent Jews as men of action, and a culture that is sexually conservative, also plays out in Jewish American war novels. On the one hand, we see writers like Bellow, Mailer, and Heller creating characters with extremely strong sexual impulses who treat women as playthings, and who attenuate their own masculinity (and the women's femininity) in ways that contrast with the conservative ethos of Jewish immigrants. (Mailer, in fact, evinced his true naiveté when interviewing his fellow soldiers to gain access to lives he assumed were promiscuous.) Nevertheless, the positive aspects of a heightened sexuality are complicated by the texts themselves. Examples include *Dangling Man* when Joseph's sexuality takes on troubling aspects as it plays out in his inappropriate actions with a teenager, or in *The Naked and the Dead* when Goldstein and Martinez, who have the most finely tuned ethical compasses, are also the characters who are not sexually promiscuous and remain true to their wives and girlfriends. We also see this in *Catch-22* when Yossarian is deeply anguished when the twelve-year-old sister of Nately's girlfriend begins to take on aspects of a prostitute. It is as if these characters reveal the stresses their authors felt about wanting to prove that they were sexual macho men in an era when the soldier was the ideal figure of maleness, rather than being seen as effeminate Jewish asexual weaklings.

Young Lions joins the trend of challenging the assumption that the trope of the strong Jew was invented in Israel with the rise of the Sabra hero, by reiterating that in America as well Jews were reconfiguring the idea of masculinity to mimic the soldier: strong, tough, physically adept.[12] The "Jew as a Soldier" *Collier's* essay from April 1944 discussed earlier, where Jewish American soldiers, Jews in Palestine, and Warsaw partisans were all conflated, exemplifies this widespread trope of the Jewish soldier who effortlessly combines brains and brawn to outwit his enemy, be he Arab or otherwise.[13] Yet by 1961 in Jewish American literature we have Heller rejecting the icon of the tough Jewish soldier, instead presenting him as a complex character who is almost paralyzed by his existential doubt.

The literary trajectory of the greatest non-Jewish war novelist, James Jones, author of *From Here to Eternity* (1951) and *The Thin Red Line* (1962), parallels the literary transformation of the Jewish soldier as I have documented it. Jones's novels therefore serve as examples of the widespread infiltration of the trope of the Jewish soldier into American literature, where Jones would recycle the character type in his own novels.

As Mailer labeled him, James Jones was "a real article in terms of the Army,"[14] who fought in some of the worst campaigns in the Pacific, including Guadalcanal, where he suffered a serious head wound. Jones's novels offer a good counterpoint to the ones I have discussed, not only because they were the most important war novels by a non-Jew during the period this book considers, but also because Jones was a friend of and influenced (and was influenced by) writers such as Irwin Shaw, Norman Mailer, and Joseph Heller. For instance, Irwin Shaw and Jones were extremely close friends throughout their lives, and Shaw mentored the much younger Jones.[15] Norman Mailer asserted that "the only one of my contemporaries who I felt had more talent than myself was James

Jones . . . [and] *From Here to Eternity* has been the best American novel since the war."[16] Moreover, according to Morris Dickstein, in *The Naked and the Dead* and *From Here to Eternity*, Mailer and Jones "wrote the same novel from opposite points of view,"[17] with Jones in fact writing as the "thirties anarchist" and Mailer as the "postwar Freudian and existentialist." Dickstein further notes that Jones's *The Thin Red Line*, also about a patrol on a mission on a Pacific island, was "essentially a tighter, more disciplined rejoinder to *The Naked and The Dead*."[18] Joseph Heller as well measured his abilities against Jones's, and like Mailer, believed they paled in comparison: "So I had written thirty, forty, fifty pages of [a] novel, and then I read *From Here to Eternity* . . . I said, 'No chance of that.' . . . I did not have the vocabulary. I didn't have the patience. I didn't have the knowledge. I didn't have the talent."[19] Reciprocally, Jones was one of the readers of the manuscript version of *Catch-22* who told Art Buchwald that he thought it "one of the greatest war books."[20]

From Here to Eternity takes place at the Schofield Barracks of the U.S. Army near Honolulu in the months before the attack on Pearl Harbor, and describes the daily life and intrigues of the men housed there. Jones's novel was published three years after Mailer's, and like him he offers two very different types of Jews: the central character Isaac Nathan Bloom, who mimics Mailer's Roth and who does all that he can to prove he is as tough as the others, and the more minor character Sussman, like Mailer's Goldstein, who seeks out friendships with non-Jews and tries to make everyone like him. Isaac is a boxer and he has enlisted in the army in the hope that it will transform him into the all-American heroic leading man:

> When he joined the Army he had visions of coming home bronzed by southern seas like Errol Flynn, a world traveler like Ronald Colman, an adventurer like Douglas Fairbanks Jr, a man to be reckoned with like Gary Cooper, a man of the world like Warner Baxter, a man people would listen to respectfully like President Roosevelt.[21]

In G-company where boxing is a major focus, Bloom becomes the regimental middleweight champion. Matching the way Jewish soldiers were drawn in all the novels of 1948 I have discussed, Bloom's Jewishness is defined by his being the victim of antisemitism, rather than by him having any cultural or religious ties to Jewish life. And matching as well the typical fate of Jewish soldiers in the other novels, Corporal Bloom dies prematurely and outside the theater of war, and by so doing, awakens the other soldiers to a higher moral stance.

In the scene where Bloom ruminates on his life and then decides to end it, he first bitterly recalls the humiliation he felt when the brothel madam Sue "had called him Jewboy to his face in front of all her girls" (558). This leads Bloom to consider, similarly to the other Jewish soldier characters, that no matter what he has accomplished and no matter how much of a tough guy he has proved himself to be, in the eyes of Christians he is always first and foremost a Jew:

> He was Isaac Nathan Bloom. And Isaac Nathan Bloom was a Jew. It did not make any difference that he had made corporal and become a noncom. It did not make any difference that he had won the Regimental middleweight division and become a Schofield Class 1 fighter. He was still Isaac Nathan Bloom. And Isaac Nathan Bloom was still a Jew . . . But in the end it hadnt [*sic*] any of it made any difference. And he knew it never would make any difference. Instead of liking him, the more honors he gained the more they hated him . . . He had thought it was going to be different, for once, when he enlisted in the Army. But it wasn't ever going to be any different, any place. (563)

Acknowledging the terrible and inescapable burden he carries as a Jew leads Bloom to consider the other "dark" truth he is facing: that he may in fact be homosexual. Bloom, who has sex with both women and men, but nevertheless considers himself to be heterosexual, has been the subject of a search to root out homosexual activity. This tarring of him as a "queer" has been doubly painful because it has made him realize that his Jewishness is now fodder for the others' hatred of him for being "queer."

As with the 1947 Academy Award-nominated film *Crossfire*, Jones's novel comingles Jewishness and homosexuality. *Crossfire* was based on Richard Brooks's novel *The Brick Foxhole* (1945), in which a soldier is murdered because he is a homosexual. When the novel was turned into a movie he becomes a Jew who is murdered by an antisemite, although there are hints in the film that he had brought on his killer's wrath by flirting with him. In both the film and in Jones's rendition, the broader culture is critiqued for viewing Jewishness and homosexuality as making men effeminate. In other words both homosexuality and Jewishness are feminizing traits that contrast with the masculinity of straight, non-Jewish men. As I mentioned earlier, Merle Miller unpacked this assumption in his groundbreaking 1971 essay "What It Means to Be a Homosexual."[22]

Bloom feels utterly torn, believing that for those like him, there are only two choices: to be the types of Jews like Sussman "who would rather be Gentiles and therefore smiled queasily and sucked the ass of every Gentile who would drop his pants" or those of his parents' generation "who would never let anybody forget they would rather be Jews than anything else in the world." What Bloom really longs for, and has been unable to achieve, is to be "accepted as a man, according to his individual virtues and vices." This can never happen, however, "as long as this open advertisement of a nose hung dangling out from his face" (566).

Bloom's long, emotional, pained speech ends with his decision to do the ultimate act of toughness, blow his own head off, since this will make them finally "be sorry for the Jewboy" and will prove that he was not "yellow then. Or a queer" (567). Yet at the moment in which he is dying, Bloom regrets the act, not only because he realizes how much life is left to be lived, but also because he should have pulled the trigger in front of the others so he could have seen their reactions to his death.

Jones is reiterating the struggles of Jewish soldiers as described throughout the novels of 1948, and in particular that of his friend and literary competitor, Norman Mailer, while also offering a version of Robert Cohn from Hemingway's *The Sun Also Rises* — although in Jones's case there is nothing but empathy for his Jewish character. Like those of the other Jewish soldiers of the novels of 1948, Bloom's death is the ultimate sacrificial act that proves himself to the other soldiers. Yet in this case, in contrast with the death of Roth in *The Naked and the Dead* who hides the act in a heroic gesture, the suicide is overt and cannot be construed as anything else. Jones's Jewish soldier reiterates all the themes of the Jewish war novels, and offers another impassioned expression of how hard Jewish servicemen find it to fit in. Moreover by making Isaac Nathan a boxer, a tough guy, who also has homosexual tendencies, Jones is blurring gender lines of what constitutes masculine and feminine. Jones, like Mailer, is showing that the idealized "brotherhood in arms" is in fact filled with hatred, and that many young men respond to it with deep confusion and fear. Bloom had thought that in the army he could reinvent himself as a New American male, but instead as Jones showed, he found himself far from home in a hate-filled world where he was seen as a Jew first and foremost. Jones's novel revisits the Jewish soldier stereotype of the other books, with one major change, the blurring of his ethnicity with his sexuality, both of which he feels himself unable to escape and is utterly despised for.

More than a decade after the publication of *From Here to Eternity*, in 1962, Jones published his masterpiece, *The Thin Red Line*, based on his own experiences on Guadalcanal. Here the Jewish soldier is so transformed that he is barely recognizable from his previous incarnation. *The Thin Red Line* describes C-for-Charlie Company on Guadalcanal in the final weeks of that horrific, game-changing battle against the Japanese. Focusing on a broad range of characters, with no clear protagonist, the novel outlines in graphic detail the close combat against the Japanese, highlighting the range of ways that soldiers attempt to overcome their own fears in battle. The novel does not shy away from, nor judge, the many atrocities that soldiers on both sides commit in the name of war, from beheading captives to dismembering corpses for fun. And as with *From Here to Eternity*, Jones also describes the prevalence of homosexuality in the platoons. Where the novels of the previous generation showed the company as a community where divided men had to find a way to come together, in *The Thin Red Line*, we find men so enmeshed in their own inner battles and fears that they rarely connect with one another.

The Jewish soldier in this novel is the much loved leader of the company, Captain Stein, who is an intellectually minded, ethical man, and the character who shows the most positive traits overall in the book. The emotional and metaphysical turning point of *The Thin Red Line* is when Stein refuses to follow the orders of his commanding officer, Colonel Tall, a WASP West Point graduate, who wants his men to advance across a hilly terrain filled with Japanese machine gun nests. All the scouts that Stein had sent across the area had been killed, so he requests that his men take the hill by using a flanking maneuver. Colonel Tall, a classic old man in a hurry, refuses Stein's suggestion and insists on a frontal assault, even though Stein explains that if he sends his company over the hill they will be slaughtered. Tall responds by stating that it is a direct order that Stein must obey.

Realizing that to refuse a direct order will mean a court martial, Stein asks for witnesses, and understanding the seriousness of Stein's intentions, Tall responds that he will come to the front lines to see things for himself. As Stein awaits Tall's arrival, he ruminates on whether he is making the correct decision, knowing that his father, who served as a Jewish officer in World War I, would have obeyed. Worried that he is a man who thinks too much and is therefore a lesser soldier and man than those like Tall and his father who require in themselves and others blind obedience, Stein finds himself humiliated since by the time Tall arrives things on the line have changed and become less dangerous. Stein's actions now look like cowardice rather than a tactical strategy.

Where to Tall it seems that Stein has made the wrong decision, and Stein in fact questions himself as well, the reader knows that he was correct about requesting the flanking maneuver, and that in his actions he aimed to do the right thing. By rejecting what the army leadership wanted him to do because it would have led to the slaughter of the men he cared deeply about, Stein became the moral locus of the book. As with Willie Keith in *The Caine Mutiny*, Stein was torn between following the orders of his senior officer, and the reality on the ground which required a different response. Unstated is that as a Jew he may have felt a unique pressure to prove that he was acting for a moral reason, rather than out of cowardice, especially since his father was the type of Jewish soldier who obeyed unquestioningly. In the end, Stein is rotated from active duty since he is deemed not tough enough to make the necessary decisions required by a combat leader. Against the protests of his soldiers who want to fight his discharge, Stein accepts the order to be sent back to Washington to take a noncom desk job.

Captain Stein is miles away from Captain Max Shapiro in *Battle Cry* who has no qualms about any of his leadership choices, since in Uris's literary world commanders only make correct decisions and they never suffer self-doubt or fears of death. In *The Thin Red Line*, the Jewish soldier has done a complete turnaround, reflecting the changing times: he is no longer the exotic ethnic, defined solely as a victim of hatred, but is a well-fleshed character driven by a range of impulses. Where in *From Here to Eternity*, Bloom is the paradigmatic young man desperate to prove his bravery and unable to do so (because of his Jewishness), in *The Thin Red Line*, Stein is even willing to act in a "cowardly" way by having his men (and therefore himself) avoid a battle that will become a bloodbath. No longer desperate to prove his toughness, his "Jewishness" is found in his being an ethical thinker whose main aim is to make the right decisions to protect his men. In this way he shares many aspects with Joseph Heller's Yossarian. In a marked change as well, none of the men even consider the fact that he is a Jew, and they judge him entirely on his leadership, although it is an unstated fact that his Jewishness likely motivates his actions.

The manner in which Jones's portraits of Jewish soldiers mimicked so directly those in the Jewish-authored novels suggests that there were clear formulae about the trope of the "Jewish American soldier" that Jones could readily tap into. As Jones's works make clear, in order to write a novelistic account of the war, the Jewish soldier had to play a central role as a foil illuminating the misguided notions of other GIs. Mailer and the other Jewish war novelists had therefore successfully taught postwar writers that the genre of the World War II novel required that the Jewish soldier be a central character.

Moreover, while Jones's shifting representation of the Jewish soldier may have come about as a response to the changing manner in which Jewish soldiers were drawn in other novels, it also may have reflected Jones's own evolution as a man and as a writer, since Jones wrote that he aimed in *The Thin Red Line* to reorient how people understood the whole concept of "bravery" because

> there're so many young guys, you know — young Americans and, yes, young men everywhere — a whole generation of people younger than me who have grown up feeling inadequate as men because they haven't been able to fight in a war and find out whether they are brave or not. Because it is in an effort to prove this bravery that we fight — in wars or in bars — whereas if a man were truly brave he wouldn't have to be always proving it to himself.[23]

Jones further noted of *The Thin Red Line*: "I think that in my life I'm less afraid of being thought a coward than I used to be."[24] Interestingly, when Terrence Malick made his movie version of the novel in 1998, he changed Captain Stein from a Jew into another dark-skinned ethnic, a

Greek: Captain James "Bugger" Staros. By deracinating him of his stereotypically Jewish aspects, the Talmudic questioning and compassionate action, Malick robbed the movie of the moral locus found in the book. In fact, this is typical of what occurred when Jewish soldiers were turned into movie characters, illustrated by four of the Jewish novels discussed in this book that ended up being made into films: *The Caine Mutiny*, 1954; *Battle Cry*, 1955; *The Naked and the Dead*, 1958; *The Young Lions*, 1958.

In all the films made of the war novels, the Jewish characters and what they represent are altered. While a detailed analysis of the shifts in representation is beyond the purview of this study, overall the topic of Jewishness is downplayed. For instance, in the 1954 film version of *The Caine Mutiny*, Barney Greenwald's court address deletes the mention that men like Queeg saved his Jewish grandmother from being turned into soap, and therein makes his speech no longer about a specifically Jewish form of gratitude to the military, but a general one. Moreover, in the 1958 movie of *The Young Lions*, the Jewish intellectual protagonist Noah Ackerman is played by Montgomery Clift, an actor as far from ethnically Jewish as one could conceive of, but who had played the lead in the 1953 Academy Award–winning war film *From Here to Eternity*. Moreover, the sadistic, completely evil Nazi Christian Deisl is portrayed in the movie by Marlon Brando, who depicts him as a lost soul whose evil is not the natural state of Germans, but something he has learned under National Socialism. The film even has a happy ending, in which Noah returns to America to marry his Christian girlfriend, Hope. Mike Nichols's 1970 film version of *Catch-22* reversed the trend of negating Jewish aspects by reinfusing the Jewishness that Heller had cloaked: when it came time to cast the lead, he chose the Brooklyn-born Jewish actor Alan Arkin as the essential Yossarian, then went on to cast Art Garfunkel as Captain Nately, Buck Henry (Henry Zuckerman) as Colonel Korn, and Richard Benjamin as Major Danby.

With the exception of *Catch-22*, the general retreat from Jewish aspects in the film versions perhaps came about because war movies were made along a set of distinct guidelines with the aim to appeal to popular audiences.[25] As a topic, war was ideally suited to the genre since it was an extremely visual event that filmmakers could use to portray moments of spectacular intensity as well as issues about how individuals cope with their inner fears. It also readily engaged larger questions about how individual soldiers and groups in platoons were representative of America. As with the novels, in war movies the platoon became a sort of mini-American "melting pot,"[26] although here it was idealized as a place resonating with a range of positive American values related to individuals working and living together in a multiethnic society. Since war films were also a form of propaganda to incite patriotism at home, they idealized military service, focusing on American heroism and victory.[27]

Generally in American World War II films, the Jewish character in platoon films is one ethnic stereotype among many, and usually a funny street kid from New York. Most important, as it relates to this study, as Patricia Erens notes, "he is generally well-liked by his comrades. In no film is antisemitism an issue among the men in the combat unit or even a subject for conversation. Similarly, the old myth of the Jew as Coward does not appear in a single work."[28] Even though many studio heads were Jewish, they were understandably reluctant to document antisemitism in the American military, instead using the genre as a form of entertaining propaganda that incited the public to root for American soldiers.[29]

By the early 1950s, the portrayal of Jews in film changed as Hollywood became the target of the House Un-American Activities Committee, and studios were fearful of addressing any topic that could be construed as "radical" such as antisemitism, instead choosing to have their films focus only on "light drama."[30] This shift toward depicting the country as unified, patriotic, and without problems is reflected in the Jewish war novels of that period by Herman Wouk and Leon Uris, which describe Americans in highly idealistic and patriotic tones, and negate the theme of antisemitism.

In Hollywood movies, the portrayal of the Jewish soldier comes full circle. First the early films depict the platoon as a positive community where Jews face no discrimination. In part as a reaction, Jewish novelists show the platoons as negative communities where Jews are treated poorly. Finally, when the novels by Jewish authors are turned into films, their powerful messages are muted, the sting taken out of them, and the Jewish aspects generally erased.

Throughout this book I have labeled the novels as "Jewish American." But what does this really mean? What is the rubric for including a work under this label? Is it "Jewish" if the author is? A series of critics and scholars have tried to tackle this issue from a range of angles. Twenty years ago, Hana Wirth-Nesher challenged the idea that Jewish literature was simply "literature written by Jews" because "such a reductive approach, by its indiscriminate inclusiveness and its biological determinism, begs the question of what constitutes Jewish culture as a matrix for Jewish literary texts."[31] In other words, to decide that a work is "Jewish" if its author is reduces Jewish literature to the locale of individual identity rather than the much richer, broader matrix of culture. A more limited definition is offered by Ruth Wisse in *The Modern Jewish Canon*: "I mean simply that in Jewish literature the authors or characters know and let the reader know that they are Jews."[32] By contrast, Ben Schreier argues for more awareness of the political motivations involved in labeling texts as Jewish (or not).[33] The editors of the three most recent major surveys of Jewish American literature also struggled with the term, and their nuanced considerations suggest that their aim was for more inclusive definitions that moved beyond labeling a text as Jewish if the author or content was overtly so.[34]

My own theoretical belief is that the label "Jewish American" should be broadly inclusive, allowing for works without overt Jewish content, such as *Catch-22*, or even perhaps those by writers who are not Jewish, but who use Jewish characters such as the war novels of James Jones. I believe that by opening the theoretical doors it enables us to reorient the field from one based on a minefield of identity to a theory of "family resemblances," in which works that fall under the rubric of "Jewish American" share certain traits, including in many instances the aim to hide the Jewish aspects in the clothing of universalism.[35] The trend of cloaking is emblematically Jewish American and is typical of a range of postwar writers who felt an intense pressure to distance their work from the previous generation, and by so doing, give their literature an intense Jewish feel without any overt Jewish content (much as was the case in Europe as well with the work of Franz Kafka).[36]

To exclude works such as *Catch-22* from Jewish American literature because there is nothing overtly Jewish about it turns a blind eye to an extraordinary moment when a Jewish outsider was rewritten as an Assyrian or Armenian because his Jewishness no longer connoted an exotic otherness. It also means overlooking how the Holocaust cast a huge shadow over even this most "American" of novels. An inclusive policy as well rebuts the idea of a pure Jewish text, since Jewishness can be something beyond simply overt signposts to strategies of meaning. In my mind, there is nothing more typical of "Jewish literature" than the multilayered, circular, and often polyphonic discourse that challenges a clear, univocal reading, and in order to understand Jewish American writing specifically, we need to accept that many authors evinced their Jewishness in insecurities, cloaking, hiding. To require that they be explicit in their Jewishness is to read the American experience in a way that ignores the profound insecurities that many felt, even in a postwar "golden era," to publicly claim oneself as a Jew. In fact, the question of whether to claim or negate the Jewish story, to embrace it as exotic and rebellious or to deny it and assert a universalism, to struggle with whether it is cultural or religious or ethnic, is the essence of what it means to be a Jew in the postwar era, and to fully reckon with this requires that we expand upon how we understand and read the literature that was produced in response to these myriad competing pulls.

Conversely, American studies also needs to broaden its scope to recognize the central role of Jewish writers. Although American literary studies has acknowledged the Jewish origins of many writers, with the exception of some theorists such as Morris Dickstein, Leslie Fiedler, Werner Sollors, and others, it has not fully reckoned with the enormous impact of Jews in shaping American writing.[37] Jewish American war novels blur the border between the Anglo and Jewish traditions, and in fact make the stance of the outsider Jewish soldier the dominant one, as is evident when the sole major non-Jewish American war novelist, James Jones, mimics these representations. To submerge Jewish American literature into the broader genre of American war writing, without considering how insistently and forcefully the works speak about the unique status of the Jewish soldier, is to miss whole layers of meaning in these novels. However, there is a drawback to using soldier novels to consider the transitions in Jewish life after the war, since military service generally excludes women and with it the possibility of female writers to undergo experiences about which to write popular war stories. This is why there is only one female author of the genre, Martha Gellhorn, whom I chose to include in my 1948 chapter even though her novel was not a best seller like the others (it did sell extremely well though). The unfortunate outcome of the dominance of war novels on best sellers lists is that it relegates female authors to an auxiliary status, in contrast to immigrant writing where they were more central.

World War II was both a disaster and an opportunity for American Jews. The disaster was the destruction of European Jewry. The opportunity was the chance to integrate fully into the American military and thereby have easier access to all facets of American life after the war ended. Out of these dual trends — disaster and opportunity — the Jewish American war novels were born. To return to the question of what makes these books "Jewish," the answer lies less in the personal identity of the authors or of the characters they created, and more in the very specific context of a war that forced Jewish men and women to grapple with a unique set of issues. These novels were "Jewish" because they were created in response to the specific experiences of Jewish soldiers and journalists during the war. They became "American" as those experiences were translated for larger, mainstream audiences and affected how the war was understood.

Jewish American war novels of World War II show that the late 1940s and 1950s were precarious times for young Jews seeking to understand their role in a country undergoing rapid economic, social, and political changes. As Jewish life in America entered a "golden age," soldier protagonists explored the geography of insecurity — the tensions that young men felt about becoming adults in a culture that rewarded conformity and physicality. These novels underline again the central fact that the Holocaust was a shadow over everything, and that war service taught Jewish soldiers and authors that this event needed to be reckoned with by all Americans, indeed all citizens of the world. Yet, as I have discussed, the intense focus in the novels on the Jewish victim was perhaps also a means to convince postwar readers to overcome all forms of hatred and embrace liberal notions of equality and pluralism. During an era when there was a shift to the right, many American readers must have found deep solace in the war novels for presenting a faith in the country's democratic institutions.

These war novels were also part of the American Jewish tradition of using Jewish military participation to transmit two concepts: Jews were active participants in the country's battles and were therefore fully assimilated members of the United States, and, in the military Jewish men were able to "reinvigorate" their masculinity along an American model.[38]

Yet as I have shown, the form the masculinity took evolved to match changing ideas about gender in the postwar era. In the novels of 1948, the Jewish soldier stood in opposition to the other members of his platoon because he had a complex range of emotions: weak yet strong, cowardly but often brave, impulsive and highly strung but deeply thoughtful. The Jewish soldier mines new ideas of heroism by using both his brains and his brawn to succeed in battle.[39] He thus becomes a positive symbol of a complex masculinity that subverts standard notions about ideal manhood. In the novels of the mid-1950s, the Jewish soldier loses much of his emotionalism and intellectualism, becoming a tough warrior and re-establishing Jewish men as icons of Hemingwayesque manhood. Yet by the late 1950s, the trope again changes radically with Heller's Yossarian who is an intellectual, constantly challenging and subverting the ideals of blind, heroic, masculinity by showing that the bureaucracy is using these concepts to manipulate soldiers to risk their lives for an "absurd" war. Where masculinity evolves in the novels, with the exception of *The Caine Mutiny*, femininity remains limited with women generally cast in traditional roles as men's playthings while having little or no agency of their own.

Both World War I and World War II were fought overseas and the literature that was written in response aimed to bring elements of the war home to readers safely ensconced in a country outside the zone of battle. As John T. Matthews wrote: "In important respects, American writing of the war *was* the war."[40] Because of its distance from the events it described, American war writing was therefore deeply allegorical and could serve to put forth a series of moralistic and political concepts since readers had to rely on the literature as their source of direct insight into events that Europeans experienced firsthand.

World War II literature, then, became a medium for imparting two important lessons that contrasted sharply with the individualistic nihilism of the earlier war writing: World War II had served the good of humanity, and the positive effects of the war must continue into the future in the form of pluralism. By so doing, World War II literature juggled two seemingly opposing viewpoints. On the one side it espoused liberal tendencies in its rhetoric of pluralism and equality, while, on the other side, the conservative aspects were manifested in its desire to present a positive image of war service as a force for good. Readers of the novels therefore were offered a complex duality that spoke directly to the double tendencies of liberalism and conservatism struggling to dominate in the postwar era. By the time we get to the final novel considered here — Joseph Heller's *Catch-22* — liberal impulses have won out.

Yet by making two themes central to their novels: the war as a battle against totalitarianism, and the platoon as a symbol for the ideal pluralist, liberal society, the war novels of the postwar years were documenting two of the central trends of Jewish life during the Cold War era. On one side was the battle against totalitarianism, which in the postwar years shifted from the fight against Nazism to the war against Communism. On the other side was the assertion of liberal values and the fight for social democracy. In the World War II novels these two trends are elided into a broad platform that calls for defeating totalitarianism *and* fighting to improve life at home in America. As the authors shifted in their relationships with postwar liberalism, the manner in which they wrote about the war and the military changed to match their ideological and moral agendas.

The authors of the war novels used a remarkable array of inventive narrative forms to get their messages across and by so doing challenged the idea that the genre of the popular novel was unworthy of critical attention. With the novels of 1948, the literary forms range from the terse, hard-boiled prose of Merle Miller to the elegant and compelling portraits of war found in Martha Gellhorn. For Mailer, in order to get his political messages across, he returns to the polyphonic text, ideally suited to embodying a range of American voices. In the mid-1950s, during the heyday of the Cold War and McCarthyism, we have Uris and Wouk seemingly mastering the "middlebrow" form to such an extent that their next two novels, *Exodus* and *Marjorie Morningstar*, would become two of the biggest American best sellers and models of the genre — high emotion, heavy action, deep sentimentality, straightforward prose. Yet *The Caine Mutiny* also has a complex layering of voices, based on Talmudic discourse, that creates a meta-commentary on the relationship between legalistic and novelistic forms of narrative. With Joseph Heller, we get a narrative that reflects the typical late 1950s Jewish liberal backlash against the mass, populist voice, preferring the individualistic, modernist one and by so doing heralding in a new trend in American writing of the absurdist text.

Because all the novels were written after the war they were employing their varied narrative styles to work on two fronts: teaching Americans how to look back and understand the war effort, and also showing them how to understand the current times. The lessons of these novels changed in step with the trends that had an impact on Jewish American life. In the late 1940s, during the first wave of war novels, a major effort was to get the news of the Holocaust out to Americans. In addition, the works make it clear that Jews had been mistreated in the military, and that hatred was an ugly scourge that hampered the war effort. Finally, the novels taught that as Americans moved forward, they needed to embrace pluralism and see the model of the ideal platoon, where diverse men learned to live together, as a basic American premise.

In the 1950s, with a new war under way in Korea, Jewish war novels presented military service as a largely positive means of turning boys into heroic men. In addition, with McCarthyism on the rise, Jewish war novels insisted that Jews were the most patriotic Americans, and that the Holocaust was an incentive for Jews to profess their gratitude toward the country that had saved them. But by the early 1960s, *Catch-22* reflected a new trend, a liberal call for rebellion that put Jews into the untenable position of both signifying acceptable forms of exotic otherness and at the same time being too mainstream to stand in as sites of rebellion. In this case, as Jewish aspects went underground the Holocaust overshadowed attempts to show the war as an ahistorical symbol of postwar bureaucratic life. As the Jewish soldier changed in these novels from a victim of hatred who tries (and often fails) to overcome it, to a patriotic hero, to a symbol for rebellion, he shows the struggles of second-generation Jews to understand their place in the world.

In non-Jewish-authored literature, Jewish soldiers played a central role and were similarly used to challenge the prevalent, macho ethos of the military. Moe, in John Horne Burns's *The Gallery*, contests the exploitative culture of GIs in Italy, and Captain Stein in James Jones's *The Thin Red Line* espouses intellectualism and ethics when confronted with the rash actions of senior officers who unthinkingly put their men in danger. The Jewish soldier therefore becomes a central trope generally for exploring, challenging, and imparting to readers the complexity of military service where calls for blind obedience and heroic action caused many men to reevaluate how they understood themselves. Best-selling Jewish-authored war novels taught Americans generally, and writers specifically, that the "outsider" Jew was the prototype of the individual who stands separate from the group, looks in, and then defies its basic premises.

One of the most remarkable things about the Jewish American war novels of the 1940s through the 1960s is the largely unspoken fact that although Jews were only 3.5 percent of the population, they created the template through which Americans saw World War II. Even though there were many different forms of media — films, television shows, radio, plays — the dominant genre for a serious discussion of the war was still the novel. The GI Bill and basic training in the military had enfranchised millions of men and women and sparked an interest in college education and reading like no other generation in U.S. history. In Jewish-authored works, members of this statistically marginal population therefore became the central figures through which the story of World War II was told. And mainstream Americans, hungry for an explanation of all they had gone through in the war years, got those experiences first through the best-selling war novels discussed here.

NOTES

Introduction

The epigraph is as found in *Jewish Youth at War: Letters from American Soldiers*, ed. Isaac Rontch (New York: Marstin, 1945), 141.

1. Charles Poore, "For the Reader's Christmas List: A Retrospective Look at the Results of a Prolific Year along Publishers' Row," *New York Times*, December 5, 1948.

2. The dominance of these five books about Jewish soldiers is even more surprising when one considers that none of them were chosen as Book of the Month Club selections, which often had an impact on the best seller list (in fact, no books by Jewish writers were chosen that year). For the list of the 1948 selections, see Charles Lee's *The Hidden Public: The Story of the Book-of-the-Month Club* (New York: Doubleday, 1958), 181–82.

3. By the following year the book was in its second printing.

4. The most famous example is that *White Christmas*, starring Bing Crosby, was an Irving Berlin creation and was directed and written by a group of Jews. For analysis of the roles of Jews in Hollywood, see *Entertaining America: Jews, Movies and Broadcasting*, ed. J. Hoberman and Jeffrey Shandler (Princeton, N.J.: Princeton University Press, 2003); and Neal Gabler's *An Empire of Their Own: How the Jews Invented Hollywood* (New York: Anchor Books, 1989). Murray Friedman discusses the extraordinary impact of Jews in a range of areas during the postwar era in *The Neoconservative Revolution: Jewish Intellectuals and the Shaping of Public Policy* (Cambridge: Cambridge University Press, 2005), 12–27.

5. See Deborah Dash Moore's *GI Jews: How World War II Changed a Generation* (Cambridge, Mass.: Harvard University Press, 2004), 9.

6. Beth S. Wenger's chapter "War Stories: Jewish Patriotism on Parade" in her book *History Lessons: The Creation of American Jewish Heritage* (Princeton, N.J.: Princeton University Press, 2011) shows the varied ways that American Jews from the Revolutionary War forward "crafted a public image" to counteract this idea about Jewish soldiers.

7. There are numerous critical studies of American war literature, including *The Language of War: Literature and Culture in the U.S. from the Civil War through World War II* by James Dawes (Cambridge, Mass.: Harvard University Press, 2002); *Writing War in the Twentieth Century* by Margot Norris (Charlottesville: University Press of Virginia, 2000); *Writing after War: American War Fiction from Realism to Postmodernism* by John Limon (New York: Oxford University Press, 1994); *American War Literature: 1914 to Vietnam* by Jeffrey Walsh (New York: St. Martin's, 1982); *War and the Novelist: Appraising the American War Novel* by Peter G. Jones (Columbia: University of Missouri Press, 1976); *The American Soldier in Fiction, 1880–1963: A History of Attitudes toward Warfare and the Military Establishment* (Ames: Iowa State University Press,

1975); *An Armed America: Its Face in Fiction: A History of the American Military Novel* by Wayne Charles Miller (New York: New York University Press, 1970); and *American Novels of the Second World War* by Joseph Waldmeir (Paris: Mouton, 1969).

8. Derek J. Penslar's *Jews and the Military: A History* (Princeton, N.J.: Princeton University Press, 2013) aims as well to extend our understanding of the long tradition of Jewish soldiers and by so doing to challenge the dominant notion that the "Jewish soldier" is a new model born in Palestine and matured in the State of Israel. Moreover, Wenger traces the numerous ways that Jewish Americans chronicled their "participation in the military . . . as one of the building blocks of Jewish heritage in the United States" (97). See the chapter "War Stories: Jewish Patriotism on Parade" in her book *History Lessons*, 96–134.

9. For good overviews of postwar Jewish life in America, see Wenger, *History Lessons*; Hasia R. Diner, *The Jews of the United States 1654–2000* (Berkeley: University of California Press, 2004), 259–358; Arthur A. Goren, "A 'Golden Decade' for American Jews: 1945–1955," in *The American Jewish Experience*, ed. Jonathan D. Sarna (New York: Holmes and Meier, 1997), 294–311; and Edward S. Shapiro, *A Time for Healing: American Jewry since World War II* (Baltimore: Johns Hopkins University Press, 1992).

10. Edward S. Shapiro notes that "the census of 1940 was the first to note that a majority of American Jews were native-born." In *A Time for Healing*, 125.

11. See Marc Dollinger's *Quest for Inclusion: Jews and Liberalism in the Modern Era* (Princeton, N.J.: Princeton University Press, 2000). Michael E. Staub discusses the shifts in ideas about the form liberal action should take in the postwar era in his book *Torn at the Roots: The Crisis of Jewish Liberalism in Postwar America* (New York: Columbia University Press, 2002).

12. Richard H. Pells's *The Liberal Mind in a Conservative Age: American Intellectuals in the 1940s and 1950s* focuses on the "retreat from radicalism" in intellectual circles (New York: Harper and Row, 1985), 119. Alan M. Wald examines the evolution of the postwar anti-Stalinist left in his book *The New York Intellectuals: The Rise and Decline of the Anti-Stalinist Left from the 1930s to the 1980s* (Chapel Hill: University of North Carolina Press, 1987), which "documents the process by which the views of former revolutionaries came into harmony with the dominant ideology of the liberal intelligentsia during the Cold War" (8). While Wald's "political sympathies are with Marxist commitment" (22), his book compellingly argues for a greater focus on the cultural events that lay at the heart of the postwar political transformations of the New York intellectuals. Marc Dollinger's *Quest for Inclusion* focuses instead on Jewish organizations and presents a strong case for the centrality of liberalism in Jewish life in the postwar era, while detailing how it transformed in reaction to the anti-Communist efforts that dominated American life. See in particular his chapter "The Struggle for Civil Liberties," 129–63. Hasia Diner's *We Remember with Reverence and Love: American Jews and the Myth of Silence after the Holocaust, 1945–1962* (New York: New York University Press, 2009), which focuses more broadly on Jewish communal organizations and popular discourse, argues that "despite the new opportunities that opened up and their high levels of suburbanization, they remained stalwarts of American liberalism, ardent supporters of liberal causes" (267).

13. Michael Kimmage discusses the rightward movement of the time in *The Conservative Turn: Lionel Trilling, Whittaker Chambers, and the Lessons of Anti-Communism* (Cambridge, Mass.: Harvard University Press, 2009).

14. Dollinger discusses this in *Quest for Inclusion*, 129–63. He labels this trend "lib-

eral anti-Communism"; see p. 162. Friedman also discusses this in *The Neoconservative Revolution*, 26–27.

15. See Caroline Moorehead's *Martha Gellhorn* (London: Chatto and Windus, 2003), 309.

16. See Ruth Prigozy's "The Liberal Novelist in the McCarthy Era," in *Twentieth Century Literature* 21, no. 3 (October 1975): 253–64.

17. Friedman discusses the tie between pluralism and liberalism in *The Neoconservative Revolution*, 18–19.

18. Jean Baumgarten's chapter "Books of Morality and Conduct" in his *Introduction to Old Yiddish Literature*, ed. and trans. Jerold C. Frakes, discusses the range of old Yiddish literature that had moralistic intentions (Oxford: Oxford University Press, 2005).

19. Dollinger discusses the manner in which a liberal ethos served American Jews in their aim to transform America into a country fully accepting of them in *Quest for Inclusion*, 3–10.

20. Capitalization in the original. Norman Mailer, *The Naked and the Dead* (New York: Picador, 1998), 277.

21. Morris Dickstein, *Leopards in the Temple: The Transformation of American Fiction, 1945–1970* (Cambridge, Mass.: Harvard University Press, 2002), 17.

22. See James T. Patterson's *Grand Expectations: The United States, 1945–1974* (New York: Oxford University Press, 1996), 328.

23. See Diner's *The Jews of the United States*, 283–304.

24. For a good overview of the positives and negatives of suburbanization during the 1950s, see Patterson's *Grand Expectations*, 333–42.

25. For an excellent overview of postwar suburban American notions of masculinity, see the chapter "'Temporary about Myself': White-Collar Conformists and Suburban Playboys, 1945–1960," in Michael S. Kimmel's *Manhood in America: A Cultural History* (New York: Oxford University Press, 2009), 147–69. James Gilbert gives a nuanced and convincing account of the complexities of postwar masculinity in American suburbia in his book *Men in the Middle: Searching for Masculinity in the 1950s* (Chicago: University of Chicago Press, 2005).

26. I am consciously simplifying the tropes of the suburban man versus the soldier to establish the binary that existed, although the two icons are obviously much more complicated. For an account of the complexities of postwar masculinity in America, see Gilbert's *Men in the Middle*.

27. The Jewish soldier with his complex evocation of masculinity would fit in with James Gilbert's premise that rather than masculinity becoming a simplified category during the postwar era, in fact middle-class men "had a rich and often contradictory range of images and personality aspirations available to them in public culture." See *Men in the Middle*, 33. Michael Davidson also asserts the variety of notions about masculinity in *Guys like Us: Citing Masculinity in Cold War Poetics* (Chicago: University of Chicago Press, 2004).

28. Elaine Tyler May's *Homeward Bound: American Families in the Cold War Era* (New York: Basic Books, 1988) documents the full scope of the manner in which women were pushed into these new, and often difficult, gender roles in the postwar years.

29. For a discussion of the huge success of the Kinsey Report, see Kenneth C. Davis's *Two-Bit Culture: The Paperbacking of America* (Boston: Houghton Mifflin, 1984), 130–32.

30. Gilbert asserts that "the 1950s were unusual (although not unique) for their relentless and self-conscious preoccupation with masculinity, in part because the period followed wartime self-confidence based upon the sacrifice and heroism of ordinary men." See *Men in the Middle*, 2.

31. For a history of the liberation of Dachau, see Robert H. Abzug's *Inside the Vicious Heart: Americans and the Liberation of Nazi Concentration Camps* (Oxford: Oxford University Press, 1987), 87–104. Deborah Dash Moore gives an account of the liberations from the perspective of Jewish soldiers in *GI Jews*, 200–247.

32. See for instance Tony Kushner, *The Holocaust and the Liberal Imagination: A Social and Cultural History* (Oxford: Blackwell, 1994), 245; and Alan Mintz's *Popular Culture and the Shaping of Holocaust Memory in America* (Seattle: University of Washington Press, 2001), 9–11; and S. Lillian Kremer, *Witness through the Imagination: Jewish American Holocaust Literature* (Detroit: Wayne State University Press, 1989), 15.

33. See, for instance, the edited volume *Jewish American and Holocaust Literature*, ed. Alan L. Berger and Gloria L. Cronin (Albany, N.Y.: SUNY Press, 2004); and Emily Miller Budick's essay "The Holocaust in the Jewish American Literary Imagination," in *The Cambridge Companion to Jewish American Literature*, ed. Hana Wirth-Nesher and Michael Kramer (Cambridge: Cambridge University Press, 2003), 212–30.

34. Saul Bellow's July 19, 1987, letter to Cynthia Ozick is found in *Saul Bellow: Letters*, ed. Benjamin Taylor (New York: Viking, 2010), 437–40.

35. See, for instance, Mintz, *Popular Culture*, 12.

36. Hasia Diner gives an extensive list of textual responses, including in the mode of popular culture, that made the Holocaust central and which started coming out right after the war. By so doing she counteracts the idea of a tiny literary response in her chapter "Telling the World" in *We Remember with Reverence and Love*, 86–149. In this chapter, she also points out that "mainstream publishing houses issued many of these books, which got marketed no differently than books on less-painful and less-Jewish topics" (97).

37. Kremer, *Witness through the Imagination*, 20–23.

38. For a discussion of the standard "typecasting" see Paul Fussell's chapter "Typecasting" in *Wartime: Understanding and Behavior in the Second World War* (Oxford: Oxford University Press, 1990), 115–29.

39. By journalistic style I mean a straightforward account without embellishment or commentary. For instance, from Gellhorn's *Point of No Return*: "On the right was the pile of prisoners, naked, putrefying, yellow skeletons. There was just enough flesh to melt and make this smell, in the sun" (215). Pagination is from the 1948 edition of *The Wine of Astonishment*.

40. See Diner, *We Remember with Reverence and Love*, 89.

41. Novels that were not best sellers but that focused on the experiences of Jewish American soldiers include Gilbert Wolf Gabriel's *Love from London* (New York: Macmillan, 1946), Martin Dibner's *The Bachelor Seals* (New York: Doubleday, 1948), Morris N. Kertzer's *With an H on My Dog Tag* (New York: Behrman, 1947), Alan Marcus's *Straw to Make Brick* (New York: Atlantic Monthly, 1948), Murray Gitlin's *The Embarkation* (New York: Crown, 1950), Louis Falstein's *Face of a Hero* (New York: Harcourt, Brace, 1950), Mortimer Kadish's *Point of Honor* (New York: Random House, 1951), Joseph Landon's *Angle of Attack* (New York: Doubleday, 1952), Saul Levitt's *The Sun Is Silent* (New York: Harpers, 1951), Sam Ross's *Port Unknown* (New York: World, 1951), and Irving Schwart's *Every Man His Sword* (New York: Doubleday, 1951).

42. For a discussion of the change in sales once Mailer's and Heller's novels went into paperback editions, see Davis's *Two-Bit Culture*, 151 and 300.

43. See Trysh Travis, "Print and the Creation of Middlebrow Culture," in *Perspectives on American Book History: Artifacts and Commentary*, ed. Scott Evan Casper, Joanne D. Chaison, and Jeffrey David Groves (Amherst: University of Massachusetts Press, 2002), 357.

44. The main study of the growth of the paperback industry in America is Davis's *Two-Bit Culture*. See also Paula Rabinowitz's *American Pulp: How Paperbacks Brought Modernism to Main Street* (Princeton, N.J.: Princeton University Press, 2014). Rabinowitz shows how paperbacks contributed to progressive ideas about race, class, and sexuality in the postwar era.

45. See Travis, "Print and the Creation of Middlebrow Culture," 339–40; and Joan Shelley Rubin's *The Making of Middlebrow Culture* (Chapel Hill: University of North Carolina Press, 1992).

46. Jonathan Freedman, *The Temple of Culture: Assimilation and Anti-Semitism in Literary Anglo-America* (New York: Oxford University Press, 2000), 97.

47. See Pells's *The Liberal Mind in a Conservative Age*, 199.

48. Not only were many Jewish thinkers such as the New York intellectuals influenced by Marxist approaches that read literature as bound up with social issues, but for critics such as Leslie Fiedler there were also formal reasons for looking at art in context. For instance, as Fiedler argued in his groundbreaking 1952 essay for *The Sewanee Review* 60, no. 2 (April–June) entitled "Archetype and Signature: A Study of the Relationship between Biography and Poetry," a biographical approach to the study of poetry enables a more complex and fuller understanding of the deeper layers of the work.

49. Jean Baumgarten's chapter "Printing, Distribution, and Audience of Yiddish Books" in his *Introduction to Old Yiddish Literature*, ed. and trans. Jerold C. Frakes (Oxford: Oxford University Press, 2005), 38–71, discusses the broad publication and dissemination of Yiddish and Hebrew texts to Jewish readers in the early modern era.

50. Dan Miron's *A Traveler Disguised: The Rise of Modern Yiddish Fiction in the Nineteenth Century* (Syracuse, N.Y.: Syracuse University Press, 1996) is the classic work on the issue of how Yiddish fiction functioned and was received. Jeremy Dauber has a chapter on the history of the Haskalah and its relationship to fiction in *Antonio's Devils: Writers of the Jewish Enlightenment and the Birth of Modern Hebrew and Yiddish Literature* (Stanford, Calif.: Stanford University Press, 2004), 67–100.

51. Clement Greenberg, "The State of American Writing, 1948: Seven Questions," *Partisan Review* 15 (1948): 879. Five years later, Greenberg would reconsider his total disregard for the "middlebrow," asserting that although the "middlebrow" was still something he disliked, it had nevertheless been a barrier against the complete overthrow of culture by other forms such as film and television. See "The Plight of Culture," *Commentary* (June–July 1951): 28–30.

52. John Berryman, "The State of American Writing, 1948: Seven Questions," *Partisan Review* 15 (1948): 857.

53. Leslie Fiedler, "The State of American Writing, 1948: Seven Questions," *Partisan Review* 15 (1948): 872–73.

54. Walter Hölbling claims that there were between 1,500 and 2,500 American World War II novels published, although he gives no citation for this number. See his essay "The World War: American Writing," in *The Cambridge Companion to War*

Writing, ed. Kate McLoughlin (Cambridge: Cambridge University Press, 2009), 213. The most comprehensive bibliography that I could find of American World War II novels is found in Waldmeir's *American Novels*, 168–77. Waldmeir's bibliography has just over 300 entries.

55. Malcolm Cowley, *The Literary Situation* (New York: Viking, 1955), 23.

56. The term "middlebrow" reaches back to the nineteenth century in the United States, as Lawrence W. Levine documents in his book *Highbrow/Lowbrow: The Emergence of Cultural Hierarchy in America* (Cambridge, Mass.: Harvard University Press, 1988).

57. Rubin, *The Making of Middlebrow Culture*, xix.

58. Ibid., xiii–xv.

59. Much of the reconsideration of the "middlebrow" has come out of Britain. See for instance Nicola Humble's *The Feminine Middlebrow Novel, 1920s to 1950s: Class, Domesticity, and Bohemianism* (New York: Oxford University Press, 2004), which seeks to "rehabilitate" the British middlebrow novel because in her view these works were disdained by critics in large measure because they were written by women. See as well the edited collection *Intermodernism: Literary Culture in Mid-Twentieth Century Britain*, ed. Kristin Bluemel (Edinburgh: Edinburgh University Press, 2009) that focuses on a full range of "middlebrow," popular, noncanonical works. Sheffield Hallam University in Britain even runs an online scholarly "Middlebrow Network": http://www.middlebrow-network.com/. There was also a special issue of *Modernist Cultures* 6, no. 1 (2011) devoted to the topic, with a range of important essays discussing the devaluation of the "middlebrow" and its need for rehabilitation. The American journal *The Space Between: Literature and Culture, 1914–1945* is devoted as well to focusing on noncanonical works during the first, second, and interwar periods.

60. Arnold Band, "Popular Fiction and the Shaping of Jewish Identity," in his *Studies in Modern Jewish Literature: JPS Scholar of Distinction Series* (New York: JPS, 2003), 409–10. As Gordon Hutner points out, there is not a "critical conspiracy to keep these books from being read," but rather many books simply "slip through the cracks." See Gordon Hutner, *What America Read: Taste, Class, and the Novel, 1920–1960* (Chapel Hill: University of North Carolina Press, 2009), 32. See also the introduction to Laurence Roth's *Inspecting Jews: American Jewish Detective Stories* (New Brunswick, N.J.: Rutgers University Press, 2004); and Band's "Popular Fiction," 409–19.

61. Roth, *Inspecting Jews*. Paul Buhle also has done some work on popular literature such as the chapter "The Printed Word and the Playful Imagination," in his book *From the Lower East Side to Hollywood: Jews in American Popular Culture* (New York: Verso, 2004), 89–122. There are also a handful of interesting essays on the topic in Buhle's edited volume *Jews and American Popular Culture*, vol. 2 (Westport, Conn.: Praeger, 2007).

Chapter 1

The chapter epigraph appears as quoted in "The Naked Are Fanatics and the Dead Don't Care" by Louise Levitas in the *New York Star*, August 22, 1948, M5.

1. Ibid., M4.

2. Biographical information on Mailer can be found in *The Lives of Norman Mailer: A Biography* by Carl Rollyson (New York: Paragon House, 1991); *Mailer: A Biography* by Hilary Mills (New York: Empire Books, 1982); and Peter Manso's *Mailer: His Life and Times* (New York: Simon and Schuster, 1985). Mailer did well at Harvard,

although he was put on probation for a month for skipping his physical education classes. See the November 27, 1942, letter from the assistant dean of Harvard, R. W. Paul, as found in the Norman Mailer Archive, Container 511.5, Harry Ransom Center, University of Texas at Austin.

3. May 3, 1945, letter from Luzon to Mailer's wife Bea Silverman Mailer, Container 517.6, Norman Mailer Archive, Harry Ransom Center, University of Texas at Austin.

4. While Mailer found the military to be a great adventure, he grew tired of it over time, and even wrote to his parents asking them to write a letter falsely claiming that Mailer was losing his business as a means to get the army to release him before his term ended. Nothing came of this plan, and Mailer quickly accepted that he had to serve out his term. See his January 20, 1945, letter, Container 518.6, Norman Mailer Archive, Harry Ransom Center, University of Texas at Austin.

5. Norman Mailer, interview by Glenn T. Johnston, August 25, 2004, interview #OH 1560, transcribed, University of North Texas Oral History Program, University of North Texas, Denton, Tex., 43–44.

6. See Norman Mailer, *Advertisements for Myself* (New York: Putnam, 1959), 24.

7. As found in Mills's *Mailer: A Biography*, 75–76.

8. See Michael C. C. Adam's *The Best War Ever: America and World War II* (Baltimore: Johns Hopkins University Press, 1994), 70; and Michael S. Kimmel's *Manhood in America: A Cultural History* (New York: Oxford University Press, 2009), 148.

9. A good account of Mailer's war service is a little known interview that he gave in 2004 for an oral history archive on the 112th Cavalry of Texas. See Norman Mailer, interview by Glenn T. Johnston, August 25, 2004, interview #OH 1560, transcribed, University of North Texas Oral History Program, University of North Texas, Denton, Tex., 1–47. Manso's book *Mailer: His Life and Times* also provides an overview of his service. See also *The Lives of Norman Mailer* by Rollyson; and Mills, *Mailer: A Biography*.

10. As found in Manso's *Mailer: His Life and Times*, 74.

11. Container 518.5 at the Norman Mailer Archive, Harry Ransom Center, University of Texas at Austin, contains a group of letters that Mailer wrote to Bea that he wanted her to save for use by him later when writing *The Naked and the Dead*. In many of the letters he describes aspects of military life in short, cogent descriptions, with the note "save for use in novel."

12. Jay M. Eidelman, "Jewish GIs and the War against the Nazis," in *Ours to Fight For: American Jewish Voices from the Second World War*, ed. Jay M. Eidelman (New York: Museum of Jewish Heritage–A Living Memorial to the Holocaust, 2003), 14. Morris Dickstein discusses the profound impact of the Second World War on American literature in *Leopards in the Temple: The Transformation of American Fiction, 1945–1970* (Cambridge: Cambridge University Press, 2002).

13. *American Jews in World War II: The Story of 550,000 Fighters for Freedom*, under the directions of Louis I. Dublin and Dr. Samuel C. Kohs, vol. 2 (New York: Dial, 1947), 25–26.

14. *American Jews in World War II*, 26. Part of the reason that Jewish agencies went to such lengths to gather statistics on Jews in the military was in order to counteract "antisemitic propaganda" that downplayed how many and how well Jews served. See "Jewish War Records of World War II" by S. C. Kohs in the *American Jewish Yearbook* 47 (1946), 153.

15. See *American Jews in World War II*, vol. 2, 21.

16. Statistics quoted in "Jewish War Records of World War II" by S. C. Kohs in the *American Jewish Yearbook* 47, 1946, 153–72. The best overview of Jewish American World War II service is Deborah Dash Moore's superlative *GI Jews: How World War II Changed a Generation*. The statistics on Jewish war service were compiled by the Bureau of War Records of the National Jewish Welfare Board and are published in *American Jews in World War II*. There is also a good account of Jewish war service that was put out as a book in conjunction with an exhibition on the topic at the Museum of Jewish Heritage and which includes extensive photo documentation: *Ours to Fight For: American Jewish Voices from the Second World War*. On discrimination, as Edward S. Shapiro notes, "approximately 30% of the employment advertisements in 1942 in the *New York Times* and *New York Herald Tribune* expressed a preference for Christians." See *Modern Judaism* 10, no. 1 (1990): 69. On antisemitism in America during the 1940s, see Leonard Dinnerstein's superlative *Anti-Semitism in America* (New York: Oxford University Press, 1994), 128–49.

17. Moore, *GI Jews*, 260.

18. Beth Wenger discusses American Jews' ideas about service during World War I in *History Lessons*, 105–14.

19. The most extensive consideration of Jewish service in World War I is found in Nancy Gentile Ford's *Americans All! Foreign-Born Soldiers in World War I* (Houston: Texas A & M University Press, 2001).

20. For a discussion of the Jewish experience of basic training camp, see Moore's *GI Jews*, 49–85.

21. Ibid., 67.

22. March/April 1944 letter to Bea Silverman Mailer from Fort Bragg, Container 512.2, Norman Mailer Archive, Harry Ransom Center, University of Texas at Austin.

23. Norman Mailer, interview by Glenn T. Johnston, August 25, 2004, interview #OH 1560, transcribed, University of North Texas Oral History Program, University of North Texas, Denton, Tex., 11.

24. Mailer discusses how enamored he was of tough guy protagonists in the years leading up to his war service in *Advertisements for Myself*, 23.

25. See Glenn T. Johnston's opening comments in his interview of Norman Mailer, 2. In the 112th, Mailer also served under two exceptionally fair-minded and intelligent officers, one of whom was named "Lieutenant Horton" and was probably the inspiration for the protagonist Lieutenant Hearn in *The Naked and the Dead*, 19.

26. Undated letter, part of 1945 series of letters from Mailer in the Pacific theater to Bea, Container 518.5, Harry Ransom Center, University of Texas at Austin. And Leon Uris wrote of a similar transformation in a February 15, 1942, letter to his sister Essie from training camp, "So far I've gained about ten pounds, and it is solid rock, believe me. I'm as strong as a bull." Located in the Leon Uris Archive, Container 138.8, Harry Ransom Center, University of Texas at Austin.

27. Mills documents the full range of ways that Mailer tried to transform himself into a tough guy at Harvard in *Mailer*, 39–55. See also Manso, *Mailer: His Life and Times*, 60–61.

28. October 21, 1945, letter to Bea Silverman Mailer, Container 518.2, Norman Mailer Archive, Harry Ransom Center, University of Texas at Austin.

29. See Moore's *GI Jews*, xi.

30. Eidelman, "Jewish GIs and the War against the Nazis," 15.

31. A March 17, 1944, essay in *The Reconstructionist* by Edward T. Sandrow entitled "Jews in the Army: A Short Study" goes to lengths to show that "Jewish service men differ in no way, physically or mentally, from their fellow Americans of any other creed or national background" (16).

32. Dec. 2, 1945, letter from Tokyo to Bea Silverman Mailer, Container 518.3, Norman Mailer Archive, Harry Ransom Center, University of Texas at Austin.

33. For Mailer's denial, see his interview by Glenn T. Johnston, 76–84.

34. April 13, 1944, letter to Bea Silverman Mailer, Container 512.2, Norman Mailer Archive, Harry Ransom Center, University of Texas at Austin.

35. Undated letter from Fort Bragg, Container 513.12, Norman Mailer Archive, Harry Ransom Center, University of Texas at Austin.

36. To fully experience the vast difference in tone and feeling about war service between Jews and African Americans, compare the oral history accounts in Moore's *GI Jews* with those compiled in *The Invisible Soldier: The Experience of the Black Soldier, World War II*, ed. Mary Penick Motley (Detroit: Wayne State University Press, 1987).

37. March 29, 1945, letter to Bea Silverman Mailer, Container 517.5, Norman Mailer Archive, Harry Ransom Center, University of Texas at Austin. The major novel by an African American writer about the war, William Gardner Smith's 1948 *Last of the Conquerors*, describes the United States' occupation of Germany and depicts the Germans as better in their treatment of blacks than Americans (while at the same time being cognizant of the antisemitism of the Nazis).

38. John W. Aldridge, *After the Lost Generation: A Critical Study of the Writers of Two Wars* (New York: McGraw-Hill, 1951), 133.

39. Ibid., 134.

40. See Walter Höbling's "The World War: American Writing," in *The Cambridge Companion to War Writing*, ed. Kate McLoughlin (Cambridge: Cambridge University Press, 2009), 212.

41. Dickstein, *Leopards in the Temple*, 30.

42. See Adam's *The Best War Ever*, 70; and Michael S. Kimmel's *Manhood in America: A Cultural History* (New York: Oxford University Press, 2009), 148.

43. See Malcolm Cowley, *The Literary Situation* (New York: Viking, 1955), 26.

44. Hemingway described it as "one of the finest books of our literature" in his introduction to his edited volume *Men at War: An Anthology*. Originally published in 1942 (London: Fontanta Books, 1966), 11. Hemingway's introduction is on pages 7–19.

45. See Walsh, *American War Literature 1914 to Vietnam*, 77.

46. Mailer and Shaw both admired Hemingway deeply, while Gellhorn was married to him. As Werner Sollors pointed out to me, there is a difference between the mythic, uber-masculine Hemingwayesque hero, and some of Hemingway's characters, such as Jake Barnes, who could evince depth and anxiety.

47. Hemingway, introduction to *Men at War*, 16.

48. For a discussion of this broadly, see Vincent Sherry's introduction to *The Cambridge Companion to the Literature of the First World War*, ed. Vincent Sherry (Cambridge: Cambridge University Press, 2005), 1–11. Also John T. Matthews has an excellent discussion of the liberal trends that the war were seen to sublimate in his essay, "American Writing of the Great War," in *The Cambridge Companion to the Literature of the First World War*, ed. Vincent Sherry (Cambridge: Cambridge University Press, 2005), 217–20.

49. Matthews, "American Writing of the Great War," 220.

50. Hemingway, introduction to *Men at War*, 8.

51. Matthews, "American Writing of the Great War," 220–29. While Matthews demonstrates that most of these novels intended to teach their readers that the war would have a positive outcome on America, the novels don't describe the war as a good event for its own sake, as would the novelists of World War II.

52. John Dos Passos's *Three Soldiers* (New York: Modern Library, 1949), 8.

53. Hemingway's 1926 novel about a group of expatriate ex-soldiers in Europe, *The Sun Also Rises*, is also informed by a casual antisemitism in its treatment of the Jewish character Robert Cohn. The Jewish boxer/soldier would be revisited in James Jones's 1951 *From Here to Eternity* with Corporal Bloom. For a comparison of Robert Cohn and Corporal Bloom, see John Limon's *Writing after War: American War Fiction from Realism to Postmodernism* (Oxford: Oxford University Press, 1994), 129–33.

54. Erich Maria Remarque, *All Quiet on the Western Front* (no translator listed) (London: Triad/Grenada, 1982), 191–92.

55. For instance, even Norman Mailer, the author most reluctant of the five to claim his Jewishness, claimed to have enlisted as a means to oppose Hitler. See Rollyson, *The Lives of Norman Mailer*, 28.

56. Matthews reviews the populist novels in "American Writing of the Great War," 232.

57. Mailer was aware that his own novel would be read as part of the tradition of the platoon novel as established by Brown. He wrote about this in a letter to Bea: "And on artistry, I'm worried about the novel. I read where *A Walk in the Sun* is being cinemized. Damn bad, for too many people will be familiar with it now — and the surface resemblances — a patrol — will cause me grief perhaps in getting it published. I'm not really worried for mine will be so different, but publishers are queer people." Container 518.5, Norman Mailer Archive, Harry Ransom Center, University of Texas at Austin.

58. See David Margolick's "The Great (Gay) Novelist You've Never Heard Of," *New York Times Magazine*, June 11, 2013.

59. John Horne Burns's *The Gallery* (New York: Harper and Brothers, 1947), 323.

60. J. D. Salinger's story "For Esmé — With Love and Squalor," published in the *New Yorker* on April 8, 1950, has a similar soldier protagonist who is married to a shallow, materialistic New York wife he cannot relate to.

61. Leon Uris was a fan of the book while a soldier. See Ira B. Nadel's *Leon Uris: Life of a Best Seller* (Austin: University of Texas Press, 2010), 35.

62. Marion Hargrove's son, Stephen Hargrove, wrote to me that his father probably picked up the Yiddish words from fellow soldiers at Fort Bragg, and that part of Marion's extreme comfort with, and support of, Jewish culture likely had to do with his sense that Jewish humor was similar to his own self-deprecating and ironic way of looking at the world. From an e-mail to me from Stephen Hargrove dated July 20, 2011.

63. The major account of Pyle's life and work is James Tobin's *Ernie Pyle's War: America's Eyewitness to World War II* (New York: Free, 1999).

64. See Ernie Pyle's *Brave Men* (New York: Henry Holt, 1944).

65. Ibid., 40.

66. Overwhelmingly, Americans and their leaders backed the establishment of Israel: 1947 polls showed more than 80 percent of Americans supported the struggles of Zionists to create a state for the Jews. See Patterson's *Grand Expectations*, 152–53.

67. See Leonard Dinnerstein, *Anti-Semitism in America* (New York: Oxford University Press, 1994), 150–74.

68. Part of the decrease in antisemitism came about because major Jewish organizations such as the American Jewish Committee and the Anti-Defamation League mounted successful public campaigns against antisemitism. For a full discussion of this topic, see Stuart Svonkin's *Jews against Prejudice: American Jews and the Fight for Civil Liberties* (New York: Columbia University Press, 1997).

69. For a discussion of the Displaced Persons Act, see Dinnerstein's *Anti-Semitism in America*, 160–61. Tony Kushner compares the attempts in the United States and the United Kingdom to let in more survivors and views the DP act in a more positive light when contrasted with the negative British handling of the refugee crisis. See his *The Holocaust and the Liberal Imagination: A Social and Cultural History* (Oxford: Blackwell, 1994), 231–32. The manner in which the American Jewish community saw survivors through the lens of the fight over the DP act is evident when the *Jewish Book Annual* labeled literature about the Holocaust "Accounts of Displaced Persons." See Joshua Bloch "A Survey of American Jewish Books in English for 1948–1950," *Jewish Book Annual*, vol. 8 (1949/1950): 4.

70. See Nathan Reich's "The Year in Retrospect," in *American Jewish Yearbook*, vol. 50 (1948–1949): 115.

71. Joshua Bloch, "A Survey of American Jewish Books in English for 1947–1948," *Jewish Book Annual*, vol. 6 (1947/1948): 4.

72. For analysis of *Focus* and its relationship to postwar Jewish writing on antisemitism, see Donald Weber's *Haunted in the New World: Jewish American Culture from Cahan to the Goldbergs* (Bloomington: Indiana University Press, 2005), 98–125.

73. Arthur Miller, "Concerning Jews Who Write," in *Jewish Life* 2, no. 5 (1948): 7–8.

74. For a full discussion of this, see my essay "Just One of the Goys," *AJS Review* 34, no. 2 (2010): 180–83. For a discussion of the name change, see Christopher Bigsby's *Arthur Miller: 1945–1962* (Cambridge, Mass.: Harvard University Press, 2009), 325–26.

75. Pells includes Miller in a very short list of those intellectuals who actively opposed McCarthyism in *The Liberal Mind*, 265. Although Miller was blacklisted in Hollywood, he managed to produce his 1953 play, *The Crucible*, which was an allegory for the 1947 HUAC hearings when leading Hollywood players such as his previous friend Elia Kazan named names to the committee trying to root out Hollywood Communists. Because of Miller's anti-McCarthy work he came under the radar of the witch hunts, and was asked to testify in 1956 at the HUAC hearings in Washington D.C., during which time he was held in contempt for refusing to name names himself.

76. For a good examination of the complexities of this time period, see Edward S. Shapiro, *A Time for Healing: American Jewry since World War II* (Baltimore: Johns Hopkins University Press, 1992).

Chapter 2
The chapter epigraph appears in Norman Mailer's letter of November 10, 1948, Container B.67, Norman Mailer Archive, Harry Ransom Center, University of Texas at Austin.

1. This is made most evident in the personal letters of Norman Mailer composed in the months leading up to and during his war service, when he does not mention the war against the Jews of Europe, instead focusing his attention only on whether the

war in general was worthwhile. See for instance his December 8, 1945, letter to Bea Silverman Mailer from Tokyo, Container 518.3, Harry Ransom Center, University of Texas at Austin. In the letter Mailer discusses how the war was necessary in order to fight fascism, but avoids any mention of the Jews.

2. See "The Naked Are Fanatics and the Dead Don't Care" by Louise Levitas, 3. David Dempsey's review in the *New York Times* labeled it "the most ambitious novel to be written about the recent conflict, it is also the most ruthlessly honest" (May 9, 1948) while Orville Prescott described it as "the most impressive novel about the second World War that I have ever read." In *Books of the Times*, May 7, 1948. For a rebuttal to claims the book is pure "filth" with no artistic merits, see Orville Prescott's "Books of the Times," *New York Times*, December 20, 1948, p. 23.

3. See Paul Fussell, *Wartime: Understanding and Behavior in the Second World War* (Oxford: Oxford University Press, 1989), 251–67.

4. For a discussion of the decision to use "fug" see Peter Manso's *Mailer: His Life and Times*, 104–6. Interestingly, Mailer used the term "fug" when describing a scene from his novel in an undated letter to Bea: "Fug the Army anyhow, fug the goddamn mother-fuggin Army anyway." As found in the Norman Mailer Archives, Container 518.5, Harry Ransom Center, University of Texas at Austin.

5. See Raymond Rosenthal's book review "Underside of War" in *Commentary* 6 (1948): 91–92.

6. See Walsh, *American War Literature: 1914 to Vietnam*, 114–15.

7. Fussell, *Wartime*, 81.

8. For a compelling discussion of the manner in which Mailer recycled literary styles of the previous generation and a consideration of how his book compares and contrasts with James Jones's *The Thin Red Line*, see Dickstein, *Leopards in the Temple*, 28–39. For a consideration of how *The Naked and the Dead* fits into the genre of American naturalism, see Donald Pizer's *Twentieth-Century American Literary Naturalism: An Interpretation* (Carbondale: Southern Illinois University Press, 1982), 90–114. For an analysis of the impact of Dos Passos and Hemingway on Mailer, see John M. Muste's "Norman Mailer and John Dos Passos: The Question of Influence," *Modern Fiction Studies* 17, no. 3 (Autumn 1971): 361–74.

9. See Dickstein, *Leopards in the Temple*, 36.

10. For views about the impact of the Depression on the soldiers, see Alfred Kazin's *Bright Book of Life: American Novelists and Storytellers from Hemingway to Mailer* (Boston: Little Brown, 1973), 76–77; and Josephine Hendin's *Vulnerable People: A View of American Fiction since 1945* (New York: Oxford University Press, 1978), 120.

11. Norman Mailer, interview by Glenn T. Johnston, August 25, 2004, interview #OH 1560, transcribed, University of North Texas Oral History Program, University of North Texas, Denton, Tex., 21.

12. Ibid., 32–33. Mailer also discusses the "fake" patrols in an undated letter to Bea Silverman Mailer in the Norman Mailer Archives, Container 518.5, Harry Ransom Center, University of Texas at Austin.

13. See Nigel Leigh's *Radical Fictions and the Novels of Norman Mailer* (New York: Macmillan, 1990), 13–15. Not only did Hearn, like Mailer, attend Harvard but both refused to bow to authority. Thus Mailer describes how he refused to apologize to a captain and he "crawfished the way Hearn did." See Levitas, "The Naked Are Fanatics," 4. Although the similarities between Mailer and Hearn are many, Mailer denied the

connection. He wrote in an October 15, 1948, letter to a fan who asked about Hearn's death, "I'm getting a little weary of telling people that Norman Mailer does not commit suicide on page 602. Hearn is supposed to represent me I imagine, no more than Croft or Valsen or Cummings." As found in the Norman Mailer Archive, Container 519.13, Harry Ranson Center, University of Texas at Austin. Nigel Leigh is correct that Hearn is a hidden Jew, but I disagree with him that "Jewishness is by no means integral to the themes of *The Naked and the Dead* and has no force in the novel's relationships" (14). The Jewishness of Roth and Goldstein is absolutely crucial to the "novel's relationships" and leads to Roth's death, one of the central moments of the plot, while the constant chorus throughout the book of antisemitic statements leaves no doubt that Mailer is making the theme of Jewishness one of the most central concerns of his novel.

14. There is some excellent, albeit brief, discussion of the Jewish aspects of the novel in Pizer's *Twentieth-Century American Literary Naturalism*, 1982, 107–14.

15. See Hendin, *Vulnerable People*, 123–24.

16. See *The Lives of Norman Mailer* by Rollyson, 42.

17. Thank you to Deborah Dash Moore for suggesting to me the religious aspects of their quest.

18. Container 518.5, Norman Mailer Archive, Harry Ransom Center, University of Texas at Austin.

19. Rollyson, *The Lives of Norman Mailer*, 36.

20. While a student at Harvard, Mailer wrote an unpublished novel about a middle-class Jewish family, *No Percentage*, and a novella about the war with a Jewish protagonist, "A Calculus at Heaven." Mailer's first two works were thus about Jewish American characters. "A Calculus at Heaven" is reprinted in his collection *Advertisements for Myself*, 25–65.

21. Letter to Mailer's mother, May 21, 1944, Container 512.2, Norman Mailer Archive, Harry Ransom Center, University of Texas at Austin.

22. April 1944 letter, Container 512.2, Norman Mailer Archive, Harry Ransom Center, University of Texas at Austin.

23. Ibid.

24. April 13, 1944, letter to Bea, Container 512.2, Norman Mailer Archive, Harry Ransom Center, University of Texas at Austin.

25. May 8, 1944, letter to Bea, Container 512.2, Norman Mailer Archive, Harry Ransom Center, University of Texas at Austin.

26. April 26, 1944, letter to Bea, Container 513.12, Norman Mailer Archive, Harry Ransom Center, University of Texas at Austin.

27. Undated letter from Luzon to Bea, Container 518.5, Norman Mailer Archive, Harry Ransom Center, University of Texas at Austin. The letters on Martinez were part of a group that Mailer himself had sorted as ones he would use parts of for writing *The Naked and the Dead*, and in an undated letter from the group in Container 518.5, Mailer writes of Martinez "I think I could do him darling."

28. Undated letter to Bea from the Philippines, Container 518.5, Norman Mailer Archive, Harry Ransom Center, University of Texas at Austin.

29. He discusses this belief in a letter to Bea about some racist soldiers who come to respect blacks after working closely with them. See his July 5, 1945, letter from Luzon to Bea, Container 518.4, Norman Mailer Archive, Harry Ransom Center, University of Texas at Austin.

30. The real Martinez that the character was based on was less perfect than how he is portrayed in the novel. For instance, Mailer describes him as a "womanizer." See undated letter to Bea from the Philippines, container 518.5, Norman Mailer Archive, Harry Ransom Center, University of Texas at Austin.

31. For an overview of the critical reaction, see Robert Merrill's *Norman Mailer Revisited* (New York: Twayne, 1992), 11–29.

32. Mailer was sent a copy of the novel by Simon and Schuster to comment on, but he wrote back to them on November 18, 1948, that he wouldn't have a chance to read it since he was busy working on a new novel. Container 521.2, Norman Mailer Archive, Harry Ransom Center, University of Texas at Austin.

33. AP News dispatch, broadly disseminated in papers around the world, November 7, 1942.

34. The most extensive biographical and bibliographical information on Wolfert is found in Alan Filreis's introduction to *Tucker's People* (Urbana: University of Illinois Press, 1997), xv–xliv. There is also a 1997 obituary in the *New York Times* by Eric Pace.

35. For instance, Marc Brandel wrote that the novel is "so grossly out of proportion, so intolerably repetitious, that again and again through its length one cannot help wondering as Harry himself does at one point: 'Will there never be an end to the incoherence in him?'" See his review "Catharsis of Fear," in the *New York Times* (January 9, 1949), Book Review Section, 10.

36. The critic Granville Hicks made a list of the minor changes between the novels. These can be found in "The Granville Hicks Papers," Box 69, Folder Heading "Ira Wolfert" in the Syracuse University Library.

37. See "Letters from Readers" in *Commentary* 3 (1947): 589–90.

38. See "An Interview with Ira Wolfert" by Harvey Breit in the *New York Times* (February 6, 1949), Book Review Section, 16.

39. For a discussion of the standard "typecasting," see Paul Fussell's chapter "Typecasting" in *Wartime*, 115–29.

Chapter 3

The chapter epigraph appears as quoted in Stephen E. Ambrose's *The Victors: Eisenhower and His Boys: The Men of World War II* (New York: Simon and Schuster, 1998), 342.

1. Isaac E. Rontch, ed., *Jewish Youth at War: Letters from American Soldiers* (New York: Martin, 1945), 1.

2. Edward S. Shapiro, *A Time for Healing: American Jewry since World War II* (Baltimore: Johns Hopkins University Press, 1992), 1.

3. See Diner, *We Remember with Reverence and Love*. A recent collection of essays extends on Diner's project by challenging "the myth of silence" in a range of countries; see David Cesarani and Eric J. Sundquist, eds., *After the Holocaust: Challenging the Myth of Silence* (New York: Routledge, 2012). Jeffrey Sandler's *While America Watches: Televising the Holocaust* (New York: Oxford University Press, 1999) documents how the Holocaust was presented in television from the war onward. Michael E. Staub discusses how postwar liberals used the Holocaust to put forth certain ideas in *Torn at the Roots: The Crisis of Jewish Liberalism in Postwar America* (New York: Columbia University Press, 2002).

4. Diner, *We Remember with Reverence and Love*, 376.

5. See Phyllis Lassner's "'Camp Follower of Catastrophe': Martha Gellhorn's

World War II Challenge to the Modernist War," in *Modern Fiction Studies* 44, no. 3 (1998): 798.

6. This may have been based on a real incident in which the Hollywood director and U.S. Army Lieutenant Colonel, George Stevens, forced the non-Jewish inmates of Dachau to allow a Jewish service to be held there (which he filmed). See Moore's *GI Jews*, 237–39.

7. For a history of the liberation of Dachau, see Abzug's *Inside the Vicious Heart: Americans and the Liberation of Nazi Concentration Camps*, 87–104. Moore gives an account of the liberations from the perspective of Jewish soldiers in *GI Jews*, 200–247.

8. See Diner, *We Remember with Reverence and Love*, 277–78.

9. Mailer's discussion of his jealousy toward Shaw is found in Michael Shnayerson's *Irwin Shaw: A Biography* (New York: Putnam's Sons, 1989), 171.

10. See the interview conducted by John Phillips and George Plimpton with Irwin Shaw as recounted in "The Art of Fiction: Irwin Shaw," *Paris Review* 4 (Winter, 1953): 2.

11. For details of his service, see James R. Giles's "Interviews with Irwin Shaw: Summer 1980," in *Resources for American Literary Study* 18, no. 1 (1992): 10–11.

12. John Phillips and George Plimpton interview with Irwin Shaw as recounted in "The Art of Fiction: Irwin Shaw," *Paris Review* 4 (Winter, 1953): 8.

13. I am using pagination from the 2000 University of Chicago Press edition of *The Young Lions*.

14. See Giles, "Interviews with Irwin Shaw," 13.

15. See Marc Brandel's review "Three Men in the War," in the *New York Times* (October 3, 1948), while in contrast in 1961, William Startt asserted in his essay "Irwin Shaw: An Extended Talent," that Shaw had "over-stressed the theme of antisemitism." Moore's *GI Jew*, which documents the antisemitism in the armed forces, and the unrelenting way that antisemitism is portrayed in the armed services in Jewish war novels, suggests that this is not the case. Startt's essay can be found in the *Midwest Quarterly* 2 (1961): 325–37.

16. See Peter G. Jones, *War and the Novelist: Appraising the American War Novel* (Columbia: University of Missouri Press, 1976), 143.

17. Giles, *Irwin Shaw*, 103.

18. The 1958 movie version of *The Young Lions* chose to completely sublimate Shaw's portrayal of the horror of the Holocaust, with Marlon Brando making Christian into a sympathetic figure, and having Noah survive at the end.

19. A few years later Shaw would go to Israel to record a photo-documentary book with Robert Capa, as would Martha Gellhorn. See Caroline Moorehead's *Martha Gellhorn* (London: Chatto and Windus, 2003), 328–29. Moorehead takes quite a negative view of Gellhorn's Zionism; see for instance pp. 423–29.

20. Deborah Dash Moore pointed out to me that in many Hollywood movies of the time, the Jewish member of the platoon is killed off and the white Protestant hero remains alive, and perhaps Shaw's years in Hollywood suggested this to him.

21. See Orville Prescott in "Books of the Times," *New York Times* (October 1, 1948): 23.

22. See Brandel's "Three Men in the War," 5.

23. Alfred Kazin, "The Mindless Young Militants: The Hero-Victims of the American War Novels," in *Commentary* 6 (1948): 501.

24. Leslie A. Fiedler, "Irwin Shaw: Adultery, the Last Politics," in *Commentary* 22, no. 1 (July 1956): 71–74. This quote is from page 72.

25. For a harrowing account of an American attack in the Pacific where one of his friends died right next to him, see Miller's *Yank* essay "Mission's End in the Marshalls," collected in *Yank: The Story of World War II as Written by Soldiers*, by the Staff of *Yank* (New York: Brassey's US, 1984), 26–28.

26. Research data on the best sellers list compiled by Arlene Hawes Petersen, Hawes Publications, Brookfield, Wis., www.hawes.com.

27. Merle Miller, "What It Means to Be a Homosexual," *Sunday New York Times Magazine*, January 17, 1971, p. 49.

28. Merle Miller, *That Winter* (New York: William Sloane, 1948).

29. See James MacBride's book review "Reconversion Blues," *New York Times*, January 25, 1948.

30. See Miller, "What It Means to Be a Homosexual."

31. Werner Sollors kindly pointed out to me that Jake Barnes from *The Sun Also Rises* suffers the same types of soul anguish at night.

32. For biographical information on Heym, see Peter Hutchinson's book *Stefan Heym: The Perpetual Dissident* (Cambridge: Cambridge University Press, 1992). Heym wrote a memoir in German entitled *Nachruf* (Munich, 1988). Thomas C. Fox considers the relationship between Heym and his Jewishness in "Stefan Heym and the Negotiation of Socialist-Jewish Identity," in *Stefan Heym: Socialist — Dissenter — Jew* [*Stefan Heym: Sozialist — Dissident — Jude*], ed. Peter Hutchinson and Reinhard K. Zachau (Oxford: Peter Lang, 2003), 145–60.

33. The only book on the Ritchie Boys is the German work by Christian Bauer and Rebekka Göpfert, *Die Ritchie Boys: Deutsche Emigranten beim US-Geheimdienst* (Hamburg: Hoffmann und Campe, 2005).

34. For an overview of Heym's rebellious role in East Germany, see Hutchinson, *Stefan Heym*.

35. Hutchinson describes how Heym also had success dropping leaflets over enemy lines. Ibid., 44.

36. While in the States, Heym was very concerned with American racism and wrote his longest poem about the lynching of a black man. See Hutchinson, *Stefan Heym*, 23.

37. Where reviewers described the other books as overplaying the Jewish story, reviews of *The Crusaders* do not mention anything Jewish about the book, even that the protagonist Bing is a Jew, instead calling him merely "German-born." The novel thus successfully sublimated any Jewish readings of it. See Richard Plant's review "A Study of GI Good and Evil," *New York Times* (September 12, 1948), 37.

38. Fox, "Stefan Heym," 148.

39. The novel, entitled *Der Bittere Lorbeer* in German, was also a huge best seller in East Germany.

40. The biographical information on Gellhorn came from Moorehead, *Martha Gellhorn*, and Carl Rollyson's *Beautiful Exile: The Life of Martha Gellhorn* (London: Aurum, 2001). There is also biographical information in Kate McLoughlin's *Martha Gellhorn: The War Writer in the Field and in the Text* (Manchester: Manchester University Press, 2007).

41. *Point of No Return* came out around the same time as that of Gellhorn's close friend Irwin Shaw's *The Young Lions* and the two competed for readers. See Moorehead, *Martha Gellhorn*, 310.

42. As quoted in Rollyson, *Beautiful Exile*, 8.

43. For a succinct account of Gellhorn's war accounts, see William E. Deibler's "Dateline: D-Day: Ernest Hemingway Reported on Ernest Hemingway, Martha Gellhorn Reported on the War, Both Were Searching for the Truth," *North Dakota Quarterly* 68, nos. 2–3 (2001): 297–98.

44. For an account of Gellhorn's trip to Dachau, see Moorehead, *Martha Gellhorn*, 283–86.

45. Martha Gellhorn, "Dachau: Experimental Murder," in *Collier's* (June 23, 1945): 16, 28, 39.

46. McLoughlin discusses in detail how the account of Dachau in *Point of No Return* was based on Gellhorn's *Collier's* essay. See *Martha Gellhorn*, 80–82.

47. See Giovanna Dell'Orto, "Memory and Imagination Are the Great Deterrents: Martha Gellhorn at War as Correspondent and Literary Author," *Journal of American Culture* 27, no. 3 (September 2004): 310.

48. Martha Gellhorn, *Wine of Astonishment* (New York, 1949), 215.

49. From a January 15, 1971, letter to Betsy Drake as found in *The Selected Letters of Martha Gellhorn*, ed. Caroline Moorehead (New York: Henry Holt, 2006), 378.

50. Martha Gellhorn, "Afterword" to *Point of No Return* (Lincoln: University of Nebraska Press, 1995), 328.

51. Ibid.

52. See Moorehead, *Martha Gellhorn*, 284.

53. Ibid., 284–85.

54. Gellhorn, "Afterword," 331.

55. As quoted in Moorehead, *Martha Gellhorn*, 424.

56. For an interesting evaluation of the differences between the D-Day reports of Hemingway and Gellhorn, see Deibler, "Dateline: D-Day," 295–302.

57. See Rollyson, *Beautiful Exile*, 165–76.

58. See Dell'Orto, "Memory and Imagination," 306.

59. See Myles Green's review "Taut, Tender, Tough" in the *New York Times* (October 17, 1948), Book Review Section, 44. Rollyson outlines Hemingway's jealousy and competitive rage toward Gellhorn for "the advance praise accorded Gellhorn's war novel" in *Beautiful Exile*, 174–76.

60. See Moorehead, *Martha Gellhorn*, 307.

61. Gellhorn, "Afterword," 331.

62. Ibid., 332.

63. Ibid.

64. See Laura Nazimek, "An Undiscovered Jewish American Novel: Martha Gellhorn's *Point of No Return*," in *Studies in American Jewish Literature* 20 (2001): 71.

65. Ibid., 73.

66. See James Dawes, "The American War Novel," in *The Cambridge Companion to the Literature of World War II*, ed. Marina Mackay (Cambridge: Cambridge University Press, 2009), 63.

67. Gellhorn, "Afterword," 330.

68. Rollyson, *Beautiful Exile*, 178.

69. Martha Gellhorn, *The Wine of Astonishment* (New York: Bantam Books, 1949), 10.

70. As quoted in Moorehead, *Martha Gellhorn*, 283.

71. Thanks to Julian Levenson for his useful suggestion of this term. For a discussion of nonfiction "Holocaust pulp" published right after the war, see Rabinowitz, *American Pulp*, 215–18.

72. See the *Jewish Book Annual*, vol. 7 (1948/1949): 19 and vol. 8 (1949/1950): 4.

73. See Goren's "A 'Golden Decade' for American Jews: 1945–1955," 298.

74. Derek Penslar outlines the interrelation between Zionist and American Jewish soldiers in "the conceptualization and implementation of a global Jewish world war that blended Allied and Jewish, especially Zionist, interests into a seamless whole" in the chapter "The World Wars as Jewish Wars" in *Jews and the Military: A History* (Princeton, N.J.: Princeton University Press, 2013), 195–224.

75. See Beth Wenger's *History Lessons: The Creation of American Jewish Heritage* (Princeton, N.J.: Princeton University Press, 2011), 98–100 and 105–6.

76. By contrast, American Yiddish writers wrote about the destruction of the Jews of Europe earlier than English writers, detailing the story while it was happening. And after the war, their responses shifted, as Anita Norich documents, turning inward to "Jewish" modes or in the case of Sholem Asch, looking outward to Christological imagery. For a study of Yiddish American literary responses to the Holocaust, see Anita Norich's *Discovering Exile: Yiddish and Jewish American Culture during the Holocaust* (Stanford, Calif.: Stanford University Press, 2007).

77. The translation of *Night* into English was a much edited, shortened version of the original Yiddish manuscript that was over 800 pages. It was first cut down to 250 pages for publication in Yiddish in 1954, followed by a French version of 178 pages in 1958. With each transformation, the book's focus and tone shifted from a Jewish-centric vision to a more "universalist" one. For a discussion of this, see Ruth Wisse's *The Modern Jewish Canon: A Journey through Language and Culture* (New York: Free, 2000), 212–16. See also Ellen Fine's *Legacy of Night: The Literary Universe of Elie Wiesel* (Albany: SUNY Press, 1982).

78. See S. Lillian Kremer, *Witness through the Imagination: Jewish American Holocaust Literature* (Detroit: Wayne State University Press, 1989), 63.

79. J. D. Salinger's autobiographical 1950 story "For Esmé — With Love and Squalor" depicts the unusual friendship that developed between two servicemen, a New York intellectual and a not very clever American-type jock.

80. See, for instance, my essay on this topic, "Just One of the Goys," 171–94.

81. See Harold U. Ribalow's essay "The Jewish GI in American Fiction," in *The Menorah Journal* 37 (Spring 1949): 266–67.

82. See Isa Kapp's review "An Act of Love," in *Commentary* 7 (1949): 198–99.

83. Brandel, "Three Men in the War," 5.

84. "The Young Lions," *Time* (October 11, 1948): 40.

85. Diana Trilling, "Fiction in Review," *The Nation* (October 9, 1948): 409–10.

86. John W. Aldridge, *After the Lost Generation: A Critical Study of the Writers of Two Wars* (New York: McGraw-Hill, 1951), 102. As late as 1975, Peter Aichinger in his study *The American Soldier in Fiction, 1880–1963: A History of Attitudes toward Warfare and the Military Establishment* was suggesting that Jewish war novelists overrepre-

sented the antisemitism among the troops since "the Jew had this inherent tendency to be at odds with military life." See the chapter "The Jew in the American War Novel" (Ames: Iowa State University Press, 1975), 55–59.

87. Aldridge, *After the Lost Generation*, 104.

88. The two Jewish characters that Aldridge views positively are James Joyce's Leopold Bloom and Ernest Hemingway's Robert Cohn, because they are "presented as human beings caught up in a concrete human dilemma and not merely as Jews reacting only when the forces of discrimination are in play." Aldridge, *After the Lost Generation*, 156.

89. See Rontch, ed., *Jewish Youth at War: Letters from American Soldiers*, 1.

90. Undated letter by Capt. Albert Eisen in *Jewish Youth at War*, 43.

91. Dec. 16, 1943, letter by Cpl. Leon H. Becker, in *Jewish Youth at War*, 22.

92. See Moore's *GI Jews*, 104.

93. September 18, 1944, letter by Capt. Emanuel M. Asen in *Jewish Youth at War*, 14–15.

94. For instance, see the letters found on pp. 14–15, 49, 113, and 139 in *Jewish Youth at War*.

95. The original essays are housed at YIVO. The analysis of the contest is given by Moses Kligsberg in the *Yivo-bleter* 31, no. 32 (1948). The English translation "American Jewish Soldiers on Jews and Judaism: A Report of a Contest" is found in the *YIVO Annual of Jewish Social Science* 5 (1958): 256–65.

96. See Hutner, *What America Read: Taste, Class, and the Novel 1920–1960*, 249.

97. See Joshua Bloch, "A Survey of American Jewish Books in English for 1947–1948," *Jewish Book Annual*, vol. 7 (1948/1949): 3.

98. See John Berryman, "The State of American Writing, 1948: Seven Questions," *Partisan Review* 15 (1948): 857.

99. See Malcolm Cowley's detailed consideration of World War II novels in the chapter "War Novels: After Two Wars" in his book *The Literary Situation* (New York: Viking, 1955). This quote is from page 26.

100. See Dickstein, *Leopards in the Temple*, 24–25.

101. The paradigmatic example is Sholem Asch's popular 1946 novel *East River* about the relationship between an Irish Catholic girl and a Jewish boy. The trend was so widespread that the *Jewish Book Annual* devoted an entire section to it in its review of the trends of Jewish American writing that year. See the section "Novels of Intermarriage" in Joshua Bloch's "A Survey of American Jewish Books in English for 1947–1948," *Jewish Book Annual*, vol. 7 (1948/1949): 24–25.

102. Alfred Kazin, "The Mindless Young Militants: The Hero-Victims of the American War Novels," in *Commentary* 6 (1948): 499.

103. Ibid., 498.

104. We see this trend as well in the Jewish creation of the Superman hero who saves the world from tyranny.

105. Alan Mintz discusses these two type of "endings" in *Popular Culture and the Shaping of Holocaust Memory in America* (Seattle: University of Washington Press, 2001), 5.

106. For a discussion of the censorship of war information, as well as the general sanitizing done about the realities of war, see Michael C. C. Adam's *The Best War Ever: America and World War II* (Baltimore: Johns Hopkins University Press, 1994), 9–19.

(Although Adam gets it wrong when he notes [p. 14] that *The Naked and the Dead* was an exception to the trend of cleaning up the war although it [and *The Thin Red Line*] were "not read by the mainstream." In fact, Mailer's book was a major best seller across America.)

107. See "The Jew as a Soldier," in *Collier's* (April 22, 1944): 11, 28, 30, 32. Although the essay is uncredited, Kate McLoughlin states that it was by Frank Gervasi, a prominent journalist who wrote Zionist books such as *The Case for Israel*. See her book *Martha Gellhorn*, 192–93.

108. Gellhorn, *The Wine of Astonishment*, 24.

109. Deborah Dash Moore pointed this out to me.

Chapter 4

The chapter epigraph can be found in container 136.9, Leon Uris Archive, Harry Ranson Center, University of Texas at Austin.

1. "Our Country and Our Culture" is found in the *Partisan Review* 19, 2 vols. (1952): 282–597.

2. Pells, *The Liberal Mind in a Conservative Age*, 72.

3. Statement by William Phillips in "Our Country and Our Culture," *Partisan Review* 19 (1952): 2: 586.

4. "Editorial Statement" in "Our Country and Our Culture," *Partisan Review* 19 (1952): 2: 284.

5. Leerom Medovoi discusses the forum and how it marked a new shift to "identity exploration" in the 1950s and 1960s in *Rebels: Youth and the Cold War Origins of Identity* (Durham, N.C.: Duke University Press, 2005), 53–55.

6. For an overview of the manner in which McCarthyism affected all aspects of American cultural, political, and intellectual life, see the chapter "Are You Now, Have You Ever Been . . ." in Pells's *The Liberal Mind in a Conservative Age*, 262–343. For a discussion of the postwar decline of leftward tendencies with the New York intellectuals, see Wald's *The New York Intellectuals*, 226–343.

7. Murray Friedman discusses the evolution of liberal anti-Communism in *The Neoconservative Revolution: Jewish Intellectuals and the Shaping of Public Policy* (Cambridge: Cambridge University Press, 2005), 62–79.

8. Statement by Norman Mailer in "Our Country and Our Culture," *Partisan Review* 19 (1952): 2: 301.

9. Michael Kimmage outlines the many twists and turns of *Partisan Review* ideology in the postwar era in *The Conservative Turn: Lionel Trilling, Whittaker Chambers, and the Lessons of Anti-Communism*.

10. Wouk's first novel, *City Boy: The Adventures of Herbie Bookbinder* was published in 1948 but made no mark on the best seller lists, which were dominated by Mailer's *The Naked and the Dead*. Perhaps this led to a feeling of personal animosity toward Mailer and his work.

11. See Pells, *The Liberal Mind*, 202.

12. However, the shift to middle-class norms did not mean the complete loss of the liberal ethos made dominant with first-generation Eastern European immigrants who had used socialist platforms to fight for workers' rights. It did mean, though, having to renegotiate one's liberalism in an increasingly conservative country. For discussions of Jewish alignment with liberalism in the postwar era, see, for instance, Marc Dollinger's

Quest for Inclusion: Jews and Liberalism in Modern America (Princeton, N.J.: Princeton University Press, 2000); Eric L. Goldstein's *The Price of Whiteness* (Princeton, N.J.: Princeton University Press, 2006), 189–208; and Diner, *We Remember with Reverence and Love*, 273–76.

13. As quoted in Sloan Wilson's introduction to his novel *The Man in the Gray Flannel Suit* (New York: Arbor House, 1955), ii. James Gilbert's *Men in the Middle: Searching for Masculinity in the 1950s* (Chicago: University of Chicago Press, 2005), challenges the idea that men of the era readily accepted the conformist pressures and instead sought out their own forms of rebellion. For a discussion of the role the novel played in conceptualizing American suburban life, see Catherine Jurca, *White Diaspora: The Suburb and the Twentieth-Century American Novel* (Princeton, N.J.: Princeton University Press, 2001), 133–62.

14. See William H. Whyte's *The Organization Man* (Philadelphia: University of Pennsylvania Press, 2002).

15. Ibid., 243.

16. Ibid., 247.

17. Ibid., 244.

18. Malcolm Cowley, *The Literary Situation* (New York: Viking, 1955), 39.

19. See Ray Falktokyo's "What the GI's in Korea Are Reading," *New York Times* June 27, 1954, Book Review Section, 19. Also, the popularity of these books in Korea may have come about because there was almost no literature produced about the Korean War, so soldiers sought out books from the previous war to understand the current situation. See David Halberstam's *The Fifties* (New York: Random House, 1993), 73.

20. In a March 30, 1953, letter Wouk downplayed the impact of his huge fame, writing: "I don't think that it upset or paralyzed me; I went on working more or less as planned." As found in the Herman Wouk Papers; Series I, Box 3 Folder 4; Rare Book and Manuscript Library, Columbia University Library. Most of the material related to *The Caine Mutiny* in the Herman Wouk archives at Columbia University is restricted to public access until 2035.

21. Biographical information on Wouk can be found in *Herman Wouk* by Laurence Mazzeno (New York: Twayne, 1994). Mazzeno's book also has the most extensive consideration of critical responses to Wouk's work. However, as Mazzeno discusses in the book's preface, there has been remarkably little critical consideration of Wouk's work, considering what a major best seller he is and how much he "shaped the reading habits of middle-class generations." There is also biographical information in Arnold Beichman's *Herman Wouk: The Novelist as Social Historian* (New Brunswick, N.J.: Transaction Books, 1984), 9–42. A good overview of Wouk's particular vision of Jewish American identity can be found in Edward S. Shapiro's "The Jew as Patriot: Herman Wouk and American Jewish Identity," in *American Jewish History* 84, no. 4 (1996): 333–51.

22. For a full consideration of Edman's conservative philosophy and how it appealed to Wouk, see *Herman Wouk* by Mazzeno, 8–15.

23. See Herman Wouk's "The Stage and the Drama," *New Scientist* (April 17, 2012): 46.

24. See Mazzeno, *Herman Wouk*, 10.

25. See "Publishers Weekly Interviews: Herman Caine," in *Publishers Weekly* (February 7, 1972): 44.

26. As found in the Herman Wouk Papers; Series I, Box 3 Folder 4; Rare Book and Manuscript Library, Columbia University Library.

27. "The Wouk Mutiny," *Time* magazine cover story (September 5, 1955).

28. Of Betty he wrote in regards to her and his 1971 novel *Winds of War*: "I have read aloud this work, like all my other works, chapter by chapter to my wife. She has done two careful editorial readings. She is a brilliant, self-effacing woman, whose critical and creative suggestions are imbedded in all my books and plays beyond disentanglement." As quoted in Beichman's *Herman Wouk: The Novelist as Social Historian*, 18.

29. For sales numbers, see Mazzeno, *Herman Wouk*, 29.

30. Wouk wrote that "I didn't know that THE CAINE MUTINY was being considered for the award until the day I found out I had received it." From a January 20, 1956, letter to Reed Painter. As found in the Herman Wouk Papers; Series I, Box 2 Folder 3; Rare Book and Manuscript Library, Columbia University Library.

31. See his interview "Herman Wouk" in *Publishers Weekly* 44 (February 7, 1972): 44. When I wrote to Wouk in late October 2012, he responded to me within ten days.

32. Mazzeno, *Herman Wouk*, 9.

33. See Wouk's preface to the 2003 Little, Brown edition to the book (from which all the quotes in this chapter will be taken).

34. This incident mimics Wouk's own life when he too jumped ship after a kamikaze attack and he also had a book manuscript with him (*Aurora Dawn*). See Frederic Carpenter's "Herman Wouk," *The English Journal* (January 1956): 1. Moreover, there are many other biographical similarities with *The Caine Mutiny*. For instance, Wouk, like Smith, at the end of the war was going to become his ship's captain, although in Wouk's case the ship was destroyed by a typhoon (the one that was avoided in *The Caine Mutiny*). See Beichman, *Herman Wouk*, 14–15.

35. Waldmeir, *American Novels of the Second World War*, 125. See also Spencer Brown's review essay for *Commentary* entitled "A Code of Honor for a Mutinous Era: Herman Wouk on the Problems of Responsibility" (*Commentary* 13 [1952]: 595–99), where he asserts the book is "ahead of the intellectuals. If it cannot teach them their own business, it at least points to where an important part of their present business lies." This quote is from page 599.

36. Wouk was aware of this when in the 2003 preface he called the ending "overly happy?"

37. Wouk's letter to me was dated November 1, 2012.

38. "The Wouk Mutiny."

39. In a November 1, 2012, letter to me, Wouk wrote, "I perceived in the Navy's traditions some parallels to my Jewish life which I discuss in *This Is My God*."

40. Wouk's faith in the officer corps may have come about for two reasons. First, he had served as an officer himself during his three-year stint. Also, his own command officer had deeply appreciated and respected the men who served under him. This is evident in a moving, gratitude-filled February 6, 1944, dispatch from the commander of his group, Rear Admiral Turner, to his men thanking them for their bravery and service and stating "it is an honor to have been designated to lead you." As found in the Herman Wouk Papers; Series I, Box 2 Folder 6; Rare Book and Manuscript Library, Columbia University Library.

41. Shapiro, "World War II," 76.

42. Mazzeno, *Herman Wouk*, 40. In a November 1, 2012, letter from Wouk, in re-

sponse to my query about the impact of McCarthyism on his novel, he wrote "My novel *Youngblood Hawke* has much to say about HUAC and the McCarthy time. They have no relevance to the *Mutiny*."

43. "The Wouk Mutiny."

44. See, for instance, Joseph Waldmeir, who wrote that Wouk's novel showed that he was "little more than [an] ideological neo-Fascist." Waldmeir, *American Novels*, 137. Frederic Carpenter takes a slightly more nuanced view of things, by viewing Willie Keith as a protagonist who challenges simplistic black-and-white notions about good and evil. See his essay "Herman Wouk," *The English Journal* (January 1956): 1.

45. See Harvey Swados's "Popular Taste and *The Caine Mutiny*, *Partisan Review* (March–April 1953): 248–56.

46. Ibid., 253.

47. Ibid., 255.

48. Waldmeir, *American Novels*, 130.

49. As quoted in Manso's *Mailer: His Life and Times*, 202.

50. See W. J. Stuckey, *The Pulitzer Prize Novels: A Critical Backward Look* (Norman: University of Oklahoma Press, 1981), 157–58. A similar thing occurred with the 1947 Pulitzer Prize, when it was awarded to James Michener's crowd-pleasing *Tales of the South Pacific* over John Horn Burns's much more complex and cynical war novel *The Gallery*.

51. Uris's letter is found in Rontch, ed., *Jewish Youth at War: Letters from American Soldiers*, 223.

52. Uris's positive take on Guadalcanal could not have been more different from the general view that the campaign was a poorly led nightmare for the men who participated in it. This perspective is for instance put forth in James Jones's semiautobiographical 1962 novel *The Thin Red Line*, which employs a polyphonic narrative structure where a range of men from all rungs of military service speak of the campaign as an ineptly led horrific mess. Uris's positive take on Guadalcanal, and all the U.S. Marine campaigns he participated in, evinces his idealization of his war service and his desire to assert throughout his own toughness and bravery.

53. January 23, 1943, letter, Container 136, Leon Uris Archive, Harry Ransom Center, University of Texas at Austin.

54. Photo dated October 17, 1943. Leon wrote to his sister Essie on November 9, 1943, of the letter, "I think Dad spread it on a bit thick about the Battle flag. I didn't like it. But it's past and no more to be said." Leon Uris Papers, Container 136.9, Harry Ransom Center, University of Texas at Austin.

55. These letters are found in *Jewish Youth at War*, 223–25. In an April 15, 1945, letter from Uris to his sister Essie, Leon joked about the letters in the volume: "Dad sent me a book Jewish Youth at War in which there are three pages of my letter [*sic*] — I must say that the Uris kid is talented — great writer just ask him." Found in the Container 136.8, Leon Uris Archive, Harry Ransom Center, University of Texas at Austin.

56. See, for instance, the review in *The Monthly Film Bulletin* 22, nos. 252/263 (1955): 83.

57. As quoted in George McMillan's review "Tension Never Eases," *New York Times*, April 26, 1953, Book Review Section, 5.

58. April 13, 1942, letter, Container 126.8, Leon Uris Archive, Harry Ransom Center, University of Texas at Austin.

59. Uris is quoted saying this in Merle Miller's essay "The Backdrop Is Victory," *Saturday Review of Literature*, April 25, 1953, 16.

60. All the biographical information comes from Ira B. Nadel's *Leon Uris: Life of a Best Seller* (Austin: University of Texas Press, 2010). There is also a bit of biographical information in *Leon Uris: A Critical Companion*, ed. Kathleen Shine Cain (Westport, Conn.: Greenwood, 1998). In my research in the Leon Uris Archive, Harry Ransom Center, University of Texas at Austin, I could find no hint of Uris's bad feeling toward his father as all his letters home were gracious and without any signs of resentment toward his father.

61. See, for instance, George McMillan's review "Tension Never Eases," *New York Times*, April 26, 1953, Book Review Section, 5; and Orville Prescott's discussion in "Books of the Times," *New York Times*, May 20, 1953, 27. Harvey Breit gives a detailed breakdown of the book's publisher, Putnam's, assertion that the novel was "the first book they have published that failed to bring in one unfavorable book review," saying that "of sixty three reviews, a little over 50 percent negatively compared "Battle Cry" to "The Caine Mutiny," "The Naked and the Dead" or "From Here to Eternity." See "In and Out of Books," in the *New York Times*, June 28, 1953, Book Review Section, 8. Clearly Uris's publishers sought to position his novel as one of the great classic World War II novels, although all the reviews that I saw were extremely mixed and few hailed the book as a literary masterpiece.

62. Nadel, *Leon Uris*, 64.

63. Ibid., 35.

64. Uris's view of the situation can be seen in a letter he wrote in 1949 about the War for Independence when he wrote that "You can bet your bottom dollar if I weren't married, I'd be over there shooting A-rabs." As quoted in Nadel, *Leon Uris*, 53.

65. Ibid., 1.

66. Stephen J. Whitfield describes the strange neglect of Leon Uris in American Jewish studies considering the massive impact of his novel *Exodus*, in his essay "Necrology: Leon Uris (1924–2003)," *Jewish Quarterly Review* 94, no. 4 (Fall 2004): 666–71. Since Whitfield's 2004 essay, Uris has been included in the most recent survey of Jewish American literature, Josh Lambert's Jewish Publication Society Guide *American Jewish Fiction*, which has an entry on *Exodus* (Philadelphia: Jewish Publication Society, 2009), 74–75. The only critical collection on his work, *Leon Uris: A Critical Companion*, ed. Kathleen Shine Cain (Westport, Conn.: Greenwood, 1998) came out in a series devoted to best-selling American authors according to the suggestions of high school teachers and librarians. The recent biography by Nadel, *Leon Uris*, contains a good deal of critical analysis, reversing the neglect of this major American best seller.

67. As found in *Jewish Youth at War*, 225.

68. As quoted in Nadel, *Leon Uris*, 43. While Uris would depict the marines as "brothers" in his novel, he was nevertheless nervous about letting them know he was Jewish, and for the most part "kept quiet about it." Ibid.

69. Without his permission, Uris's publisher Putnam cut out the double narrative device in the galleys that they sent him. Uris was outraged and told Putnam he would not agree to such a shift in the narrative. It was a brave move on Uris's part since he was a first-time novelist with no sales record. Nevertheless, Putnam backed down and agreed to reinsert the dual narration. See Nadel, *Leon Uris*, 58.

70. See Merle Miller's article "The Backdrop Is Victory," *Saturday Review of Literature*, April 25, 1953, 16.

71. For an analysis of the theme of tough Jews in *Exodus*, see Henry Gonshak's "'Rambowitz' versus the 'Schlemiel' in Leon Uris' Exodus," *Journal of American Culture*, 22, no. 1 (Spring 1999): 9–16.

72. Leon Uris managed a Native American soldier boxer, Johnny Gates, while in Wellington, New Zealand, who may have been the inspiration for this character. See Nadel, *Leon Uris*, 40.

73. For a discussion of this trend, see Dollinger, *Quest for Inclusion*, 16–18.

74. Nadel, *Leon Uris*, 61.

Chapter 5

The chapter epigraph appears as quoted in "Catching Heller" by David Nathan in *Conversations with Joseph Heller*, ed. Adam J. Sorkin (Jackson: University Press of Mississippi, 1993), 294. Heller's acknowledgment near the end of his life of Yossarian's Jewishness mimics Arthur Miller's assertion, fifty years after the publication of *Death of a Salesman*, that in fact the Lomans were Jewish. Perhaps both authors at the end of their lives finally felt comfortable acknowledging the Jewishness of their first major works. Both had written their literature as young men seeking to be great universal or American writers rather than specifically Jewish ones, and neither wanted the protagonists to be read as Jewish types since it would limit their aims of creating non-ethnically limited types. See Arthur Miller's preface, "Salesman at Fifty," in *Death of a Salesman: Fiftieth Year Edition* (New York: Penguin Books, 1999), ix–xiv.

1. The Joseph Heller Archive at Brandeis University has the originals of all the versions of *Catch-22* where one can see the many changes that Heller made between the different editions. The main changes that Heller made, besides renaming this chapter, were to switch "Catch-18" to "Catch-22" and to have the base be on the imaginary island of Pianosa rather than the real one of Corsica (where Heller was stationed). Heller outlines all the main changes he made for the final manuscript in a January 19, 1961, document found in the Joseph Heller collection, 1945–1969, Robert D. Farber University Archives and Special Collections Department, Brandeis University, Series 1, Box 10, Folder 5.

2. Critical sources on *Catch-22* include Harold Bloom, ed., *Bloom's Guides: Joseph Heller's Catch-22* (New York: Infobase Publishing, 2009); Sanford Pinsker, *Understanding Joseph Heller* (University of South Carolina Press, 1991); James Nagel, ed., *Critical Essays on Catch-22* (Encino, Calif.: Dickenson, 1974); *A "Catch-22" Casebook*, ed. Frederick Kiley and Walter McDonald (New York: Thomas Y. Crowell, 1973); Robert Merrill, *Joseph Heller* (Boston: Twayne, 1987); and Judith Ruderman, *Joseph Heller* (New York: Continuum, 1991).

3. See Pells, *The Liberal Mind in a Conservative Age*, 404.

4. See Kirsten Fermaglich's *American Dreams and Nazi Nightmares: Early Holocaust Consciousness and Liberal America, 1957–1965* (Hanover, N.H.: Brandeis University Press, 2006), 6–7.

5. Ibid., 8–9.

6. Tracy Daugherty notes the following in *Just One Catch* (New York: St. Martin's, 2011): "In November 1962, *Esquire*'s editor, Arnold Gingrich, said, 'The young

people . . . tell me that the college students are still reading 'Catcher in the Rye' . . . [but] coming up fast is 'Catch-22,'" 239.

7. As quoted in "A Word to Our Readers," in *Dissent* 1, no. 1 (Winter 1954): 3. For a discussion of the journal, see Kimmage's *The Conservative Turn: Lionel Trilling, Whittaker Chambers, and the Lessons of Anti-Communism*, 269–70; and Pells's *The Liberal Mind*, 380–84.

8. Jack Kerouac, *On the Road* (New York: Penguin Books, 2008), 169.

9. See Alfred Kazin's essay "Psychoanalysis and Literary Culture Today," *Partisan Review* (Fall 1958): 46.

10. See Norman Mailer's "The White Negro: Superficial Reflections on the Hipster" in his essay collection *Advertisements for Myself* (New York: Berkley Medallion, 1959), 314.

11. Dickstein, *Leopards in the Temple*, 150.

12. Andrew Hoberek discusses this trend in his book *The Twilight of the Middle Class: World War II American Fiction and White-Collar Work* (Princeton, N.J.: Princeton University Press, 2005), 70–94.

13. For a discussion of this, see Dickstein, *Leopards in the Temple*, 145.

14. See Halberstam, *The Fifties*, 509.

15. Joseph Heller would in the early 1960s become a scriptwriter for *McHale's Navy*, another comedy about the military.

16. Stephen J. Whitfield, *The Culture of the Cold War* (Baltimore: Johns Hopkins University Press, 1996), 214.

17. Mark Harris, *Something about a Soldier* (New York: Signet, 1957), 24.

18. Quote found in Philip Roth's "Defender of the Faith," in *Goodbye Columbus and Five Short Stories* (New York: Vintage, 1987), 174.

19. Dickstein discusses the relationship between these three novels in *Leopards in the Temple*, 40–48. Pynchon sent Heller's agent a fan letter about *Catch-22* in which he wrote "You thought I'd LIKE it. Jesus. I love it. I won't tell you how much, or why, because I always sound phony whenever I start running off at the mouth like a literary critic. But it is close to the finest novel I've ever read." As found in the Joseph Heller collection, 1945–1969, Robert D. Farber University Archives and Special Collections Department, Brandeis University, Box 10, Folder 15.

20. Alfred Kazin, *Bright Book of Life: American Novelists and Storytellers from Hemingway to Mailer* (Boston: Little, Brown, 1973), 82.

21. Dawes, *The Language of War*, 157.

22. Heller wrote the book in a pastiche-type style which was like a jigsaw puzzle that would be put together later with the help of his trusted editor, Robert Gottlieb. For an account of his writing process, see Daugherty, *Just One Catch*, 209–14.

23. Harold Bloom, who considers the novel to be an overrated period piece, views the huge praise, and often obsessed readership, as having "a "cultish" type of response. See *Bloom's Guides*, 13.

24. Heller mentioned the poor review in many interviews such as in "An Interview with Joseph Heller Conducted by Charlie Reilly" in *Contemporary Literature* 39, no. 4 (1998): 511 and in "An Interview with Joseph Heller" by Richard B. Sale in *Conversations with Joseph Heller*, ed. Adam J. Sorkin (Jackson: University Press of Mississippi, 1993), 82.

25. Richard G. Stern, "Bombers Away," *New York Times Book Review* (October 22, 1961), 50.

26. Orville Prescott, "Books of the Times," *New York Times* (October 23, 1961), 27.

27. Biographical information on Heller came from the following sources: his autobiography *Now and Then: From Coney Island to Here* (New York: Alfred A. Knopf, 1998); Tracy Daugherty's *Just One Catch*; and his daughter Erica Heller's memoir *Yossarian Slept Here: When Joseph Heller Was Dad, the Apthorp Was Home, and Life Was a Catch-22*, coauthored with Karen White (New York: Simon and Schuster, 2011).

28. Tracy Daugherty discusses the strange fact that Heller was allowed to return home after sixty runs, when the rest of the men were required to complete seventy, in *Just One Catch*, 93.

29. As quoted in Heller, *Now and Then*, 170.

30. As quoted in *The Sixties*, ed. Lynda Rosen Obst (New York: Random House/Rolling Stone, 1977), 50.

31. Sanford Pinsker fleshes out how the two novels relate to each other, and why the latter one is less successful than the first in his essay "Once More into the Breach: Joseph Heller Gives *Catch-22* a Second Act," In *Topic: A Journal of the Liberal Arts* 50 (2000): 28–39.

32. I am using the 2004 paperback edition of *Catch-22* published by Simon and Schuster (New York) for all my quotes.

33. Heller's annotated copy of *Catch-22* is found in the Joseph Heller collection, 1945–1969, Robert D. Farber University Archives and Special Collections Department, Brandeis University, Subseries 2, Box 10, Folder 15. This quote is from page 162.

34. Heller argued that the events in the novel, including this one, were all plausible in "An Impolite Interview with Joseph Heller" by Paul Krassner, in *Conversations with Joseph Heller*, ed. Adam J. Sorkin (Jackson: University Press of Mississippi, 1993), 14.

35. See Bloom, *Bloom's Guides: Joseph Heller*, 76.

36. Ruderman, *Joseph Heller*, 31.

37. See the chapter "Catch-22 and the Language of Deficiency," in Ruderman, *Joseph Heller*, 30–48. This quote is from page 42.

38. As quoted in Sam Merrill's 1975 *Playboy* interview with Joseph Heller, in *Conversations with Joseph Heller*, 150. Yet all the things that Heller lists as giving his book a contemporary feel were in existence during World War II.

39. As quoted in Daugherty, *Just One Catch*, 219.

40. Malcolm Cowley, *The Literary Situation* (New York: Viking, 1955), 38.

41. The Jewish conservative critic Norman Podhoretz attacked this stance, and how the novel wipes out the notion of the Nazis as the real enemies of the war, in his essay "Looking Back at Catch-22" in *Commentary* (February 2008): 32–38. This essay is also in part a response to an essay Podhoretz published in his 1964 *Doings and Undoings* (New York: Farrar, Straus and Giroux, 1964), 228–35. In his original essay Podhoretz gives the novel a mixed review, both calling it "one of the bravest and most nearly successful attempts we have yet had to describe and make credible the incredible reality of American life in the middle of the 20th century" (228), while at the same time criticizing Yossarian's change of heart in the end when he asserts that he had fought for his country.

42. Michael C. Scoggins outlines the many ways that the novel was based on Heller's own wartime experiences in his essay "Joseph Heller's Combat Experiences in *Catch-22*," in *War, Literature & the Arts* 15 (2003): 213–27. Daugherty also shows all the similarities between Heller's life and the novel in *Just One Catch*, 80–95. My discussion is based on these two sources.

43. Heller, *Now and Then*, 169–90.

44. In a 1962 interview Heller stated "Oh, yes — I'm a terrible coward. I'm just like Yossarian, you know." As quoted in "An Impolite Interview with Joseph Heller," by Paul Krassner, in *Conversations with Joseph Heller*, 9. Heller's discomfort with being viewed as the basis for Yossarian, and his inability to fully deny this, is evident in his response to Barbara Gelb in an interview about his follow-up novel to *Catch-22, Closing Time*, when she asks him "Are Yossarian and Sammy — the two conflicting sides of Joseph Heller?" "No . . . Yes. This is not autobiography." See "Catch-22 Plus: A Conversation with Joseph Heller," *New York Times Book Review* (August 28, 1994): 3. Michael C. Scoggins outlines how autobiographical the novel was, and how much Heller sought to deny this, in his essay "Joseph Heller's Combat Experiences in Catch-22," 213–27. See also Merrill, *Joseph Heller*, 10–11.

45. Twenty-three years after returning to the States from his military service, Heller traveled back to Italy with his wife and two pre-teen children to revisit where he had served. He wrote up the trip in an essay for the populist travel magazine *Holiday*. Written in a straight prose style, the unsettling and strange essay combines standard travelogue fare (e.g., what they ate in different restaurants) with an antiwar ideology, all of which is illuminated with dark and moody watercolor stills of Italians and Italian sites by John Groth. The piece stands in stark contrast with *Catch-22* with its whirlwind and often absurdist account of the war from the perspective of a young single American man. In the *Holiday* essay, Heller is now married and juggling the needs of his kids, who are bored and just want to return to New York, with his own nostalgic longing to reconnect with his past. Heller finds, to his dismay, that there is nothing whatsoever to mark his air base nor where his encampment was. However, he does discover that there are still scars on the landscape from his runs, such as a hole in a mountain he mistakenly bombed when he should have been knocking out a bridge. Whereas in *Catch-22* Yossarian is the one who deserts and leaves, in the *Holiday* piece, Heller is "the only American from the air base who had ever returned" (51). In the end, what Heller finds is not his own World War II, since there are now so few traces of it, but the horror of the current-day Vietnam War. This occurs in an emotional meeting with a Frenchman who is in deep mourning for his brain-damaged hospitalized son who was wounded in the Indochina war (142). See "'Catch-22' Revisited," *Holiday* 41, no. 4 (April 1967): 45–60, 120, 140–42.

46. Heller discusses the real events that were the basis for the scene with Snowden's death in his autobiography *Now and Then*, 177–81. This quote is from page 181.

47. As quoted in Merrill's 1975 *Playboy* interview with Joseph Heller, in *Conversations with Joseph Heller*, 153.

48. As quoted in Rosen, *The Sixties*, 50, 52.

49. Heller describes in a 1975 interview with Sam Merrill for *Playboy Magazine* how when he was a nineteen-year-old recruit, he "actually hoped" he would get into combat since the war "seemed so dramatic and heroic . . . I felt like I was going to Hollywood." After being nearly shot down in Avignon, this changed when he realized that "They're

trying to kill me, too! War wasn't much fun after that." In *Conversations with Joseph Heller*, 148–49.

50. In "An Interview with Joseph Heller Conducted by Charlie Reilly," in *Contemporary Literature* 39, no. 4 (1998): 521.

51. Critics who read Yossarian as a type of Jewish schlemiel include Dickstein, who finds the novel redolent with "schlemiel humor" in *Leopards in the Temple*, 47. Dickstein also notes that he has "descended from the schlemiel of the Jewish novel but finally [is] an inversion of that passive and unhappy figure." See Morris Dickstein, *Gates of Eden: American Culture in the Sixties* (New York: Basic Books, 1977), 113. See also Ruderman, *Joseph Heller*, 143.

52. Ruderman, *Joseph Heller*, 141. Daniel Walden gives a Jewish reading of the novel in his essay "'Therefore Choose Life': A Jewish Interpretation of Heller's *Catch-22*," In *Critical Essays on Catch-22*, ed. James Nagel (Encino, Calif.: Dickenson, 1974), 57–63. Ruderman wrote a book chapter on the subject entitled "What to Do with 'A Jew Like That'?: Defining Joseph Heller as a Jewish-American Writer," in *Joseph Heller*, 135–66. Dickstein discusses how the novel was grounded in Heller's "Jewish outlook and upbringing" in *Leopards in the Temple*, 47. Joseph Lowin published an essay on the Jewish aspects of Heller's writings: "The Jewish Art of Joseph Heller," in the *Jewish Book Annual* 43 (1985/1986): 141–53.

53. As quoted in Ruderman, *Joseph Heller*, 135.

54. From an interview with Krassner, "An Impolite Interview," 22.

55. Ibid.

56. As quoted in James Nagel's "Two Brief Manuscript Sketches: Heller's *Catch-22*," *Modern Fiction Studies* 20, no. 2 (Summer 1974): 222.

57. James Nagel believes that the "Jew like that" refers to Yossarian and this sketch shows that Heller played with the idea of making Yossarian overtly a Jew. See Nagel, "Two Brief Manuscript Sketches." Ruderman, by contrast, believes that the "Jew like that" is the Robert Cohn figure and Nagel is incorrect to believe the sketch shows that Yossarian for a time was Jewish. See *Joseph Heller*, 138–39. I would agree with Ruderman's interpretation since the grammatical logic of the paragraph points toward Yossarian being separate from the "Jew like that" who is the Cohn-type figure.

58. This is surprising considering Heller's long-standing admiration of Irwin Shaw — whom he labeled one of his earliest inspirations — whose Jewish protagonist in *The Young Lions* is not a "sensitive Jew" but more in the tough ilk of Robert Cohn. Heller discusses having Shaw as a major literary inspiration in *Conversations with Joseph Heller*, 83 and 160.

59. As quoted in Nagel, "Two Brief Manuscript Sketches," 222. By using the term "some of those best friends would be Jews" he is at the same time making fun of the statement often used by haters to justify their actions.

60. Ibid.

61. Ibid., 223.

62. See Fermaglich's *American Dreams and Nazi Nightmares*, 8–9.

63. Sanford Pinsker, "Reassessing *Catch-22*," *Sewanee Review* 108, no. 4 (Fall 2000), 609.

64. Wayne Charles Miller reads the Assyrian symbolism differently: "Just as the Assyrians were a threat to the Hebrew nation, the source of western world religious belief and of the God Yossarian calls 'a country bumpkin,' so too Yossarian is a threat to the

power morality embodied in the military structure of the United States." See his book *An Armed America: Its Face in Fiction: A History of the American Military Novel*, 224.

65. Josh Greenfeld, "22 Was Funnier than 14," *New York Times Book Review* (March 3, 1968), 1. According to Heller's biographer, Tracy Daugherty, we see in "Yossarian's profound, *unstated* Judaism: his sense of worldly exile and intimation of connection to something ancient, even if that something survives only in an instinctual personal ritual." See *Just One Catch*, 223.

66. Alfred Kazin, *Bright Book of Life: American Novelists and Storytellers from Hemingway to Mailer*, 83.

67. Ruderman, *Joseph Heller*, 138.

68. Pinsker, "Reassessing *Catch-22*," 603.

69. Morris Dickstein, *Gates of Eden: American Culture in the Sixties* (New York: Basic Books, 1977), 115.

70. See Fred Fetrow's "Joseph Heller's Use of Names," in *Studies in Contemporary Satire* 1 (1975), 36. Heller claimed that Yossarian's first name John is "so typically nebbish, you know?" From an interview with Paul Krassner, "An Impolite Interview," *The Realist* 39 (November 1962): 23.

71. As quoted in "Catching Heller" by David Nathan, in *Conversations with Joseph Heller*, ed. Adam J. Sorkin (Jackson: University Press of Mississippi, 1993), 294.

72. Harold Bloom finds it troubling that the novel "isolates the reader from the historical reality of Hitler's evil, yet nevertheless the war against the Nazis was also Yossarian's war." See his edited volume *Bloom's Guides: Joseph Heller's "Catch-22"* (New York: Infobase, 2009), 8. In the walk through Rome we see the submerged topic of the Nazi war threatening to emerge.

73. Dickstein, *Gates of Eden: American Culture in the Sixties*, 14.

74. Kazin, *Bright Book of Life*, 85.

75. Minna Doskow offers an interesting interpretation of the "Eternal City" as Yossarian's journey through the "underworld" as occurs in *The Odyssey, The Aeneid*, and *The Divine Comedy*, in her essay "The Night Journey in 'Catch-22,'" *Twentieth Century Literature* 12 (January 1967): 186–93. The chapter also resonates with the "Circe" chapter in James Joyce's *Ulysses*, which covers the nightmarish walk of Stephen Dedalus and Leopold Bloom through the red-light district of Dublin.

76. More than ten thousand Roman Jews successfully hid from the Nazis and were protected by Italians who opposed the deportations.

77. For a discussion of this, see Joseph Heller's interview as found in *Catch as Catch Can*, ed. Matthew J. Bruccoli and Park Bucker (New York: Simon and Schuster, 2003), 302.

78. Heller's annotated copy of *Catch-22* is found in the Joseph Heller collection, 1945–1969, Robert D. Farber University Archives and Special Collections Department, Brandeis University, Subseries 2, Box 9, File 264.

79. Joseph Heller collection, 1945–1969, Robert D. Farber University Archives and Special Collections Department, Brandeis University, Subseries 2, Box 9, File 264. The third mention of his guilt is found on Heller's notes to page 400.

80. In Heller's notes, he asserts that the chapter alludes to Dostoevsky's novel *Crime and Punishment*. See his notes to page 405, in his annotated copy of *Catch-22* found in the Joseph Heller collection, 1945–1969, Robert D. Farber University Archives and Special Collections Department, Brandeis University, Subseries 2, Box 9, File 264. It

is interesting that for Heller this chapter resonates with *Crime and Punishment*, where Dostoevsky's protagonist, Raskolnikov, murders an old woman and then suffers anguish over the pointless act. This suggests that Yossarian's unwillingness to intervene therefore makes him as guilty of evil as if he had actually done the act himself.

81. Fred Fetrow argues in his essay "Joseph Heller's Use of Names" that whereas previously in the novel those who were most victimized remain unnamed (the man in white in the hospital, Nately's whore's sister), "the naming of the most overtly victimized character, a character otherwise insignificant, shows that the victims by this point in the novel have become "real" to Yossarian." In *Studies in Contemporary Satire* 1 (1975): 32.

82. David Garroich suggested this idea to me.

83. See, for instance, Waldmeir, *American Novels of the Second World War*, 164–65; and Dickstein, *Gates of Eden: American Culture in the Sixties*, 116.

84. See Fermaglich's *American Dreams and Nazi Nightmares*, 14–15.

85. This stress is evident in his statement that he had deliberately seeded his book with contemporary aspects, when in reality, those things existed during the war. It points toward Heller's lack of clarity about the time when the novel is really set.

Conclusion

1. January 22, 1945, letter from Luzon to Bea Silverman Mailer, Container 517.5, Norman Mailer Archive, Harry Ransom Center, University of Texas at Austin.

2. Saul Bellow, "Notes of a Dangling Man," *Partisan Review* 11 (1944): 348–50.

3. See Kenneth Fearing's *New York Times* review "Man Versus Man" (March 26, 1944): 5, 15. There was a second positive review in the *New York Times* by John Chamberlain in his "Books of the Times" (March 25, 1944): 13.

4. All quotes from *Dangling Man* are found in the following edition: *Bellow: Novels 1944–1953* (New York: Library of America, 2003), 1–141.

5. For a compelling comparison of *Dangling Man* as a Jewish literary take on the Dostoevskian novel of alienation in contrast with Chester Himes's *If He Hollers Let Him Go* as an African American take on the same theme, see Dickstein, *Leopards in the Temple*, 54–59.

6. Ada Aharoni notes that in this novella "we feel Bellow is investigating what happens when the woman in the family becomes the breadwinner, and he is critically weighing the repercussions." In "Women in Saul Bellow's Novel," as found in *Saul Bellow in the 1980s: A Collection of Critical Essays*, ed. Gloria L. Cronin and L. H. Goldman (East Lansing: Michigan State University Press, 1989), 96. This essay is found on pages 95–112.

7. Dickstein gives an illuminating examination of how Dostoevsky's dangling man appealed deeply to Jewish and black writers (Bellow and Ellison) in *Leopards in the Temple*, 56–59. For a detailed comparison of Bellow's and Dostoevsky's dangling men, see Jean-François Leroux's "Exhausting Ennui: Bellow, Doestoevsky, and the Literature of Boredom," *College Literature* 35, no. 1 (Winter 2008): 1–15.

8. James Atlas sees this as an ironic ending. See *Bellow: A Biography* (New York: Random House, 2000), 93. While there may be a touch of irony, the whole novella suggests that the Dangling Man has failed at finding the unregimented, free-floating life fulfilling. A better way to understand it is how Mark Weinstein describes the ending: "Although there is irony in his final exclamations, it is a simple irony directed against his own failure to use his freedom." As quoted in "Bellows Endings," in *Saul Bellow:*

A *Mosaic*, ed. L. H. Goldman, Gloria L. Cronin, and Ada Aharoni (New York: Peter Lang, 1992), 88.

9. As Andrew Hoberek noted in *The Twilight of the Middle Class* "*Dangling Man* poses one form of modernism (Dostoyevskyan self-exposure) against another (the minimalism Hemingway learned from Stein)." See also Michael K. Glenday's *Macmillan Modern Novelists: Norman Mailer* (London: Macmillan, 1995), 49.

10. See Dickstein, *Leopards in the Temple*, 59.

11. For a good discussion of the history of these terms, see Shachar Pinsker's *Literary Passports: The Making of Modernist Hebrew Fiction in Europe* (Stanford, Calif.: Stanford University Press, 2010), 169–258. Yuri Slezkine in *The Jewish Century* (Princeton, N.J.: Princeton University Press, 2004) notes that because "the most important institution in Israel was the Army" one of the most popular books of the 1940s was a Soviet war novel (329).

12. For a study of the development of the tough Jew trope in America, see Paul Breines's *Tough Jews: Political Fantasies and the Moral Dilemma of American Jewry* (New York: Basic Books, 1990).

13. See "The Jew as a Soldier" in *Collier's* (April 22, 1944), 11, 28, 30, 32.

14. As quoted in Manso's *Mailer: His Life and Times*, 203–4.

15. See Michael Shnayerson's *Irwin Shaw: A Biography* (New York: Putnam's Sons, 1989), 263–65.

16. Mailer stated this in an essay "Evaluations — Quick and Expensive Comments on the Talent in the Room" in his *Advertisements for Myself* (New York: Berkley Publishing, 1959), 426. Mailer follows this statement with a mean description of how Jones has now "sold out." Jones was deeply wounded by this unexpected attack from a man he considered a close friend, whose novel *Deer Park* he had even tried to help Mailer get published. For a discussion of the evolution of the Jones/Mailer friendship, see Manso's *Mailer: His Life and Times*, 275–79, 401, 578.

17. Dickstein, *Leopards in the Temple*, 35.

18. Ibid.

19. As quoted in Daugherty's *Just One Catch*, 150.

20. As stated in a telegram from Buckwald to Heller's press in "The War for Catch-22" by Tracy Daugherty in *Vanity Fair* (August 2011): 11.

21. James Jones, *From Here to Eternity* (New York: Delta, 1998), 560.

22. See Merle Miller, "What It Means to Be a Homosexual," *Sunday New York Times Magazine*, January 17, 1971.

23. James Jones interview with Nelson Aldrich, "The Art of Fiction No. 22," *Paris Review* 20 (Autumn–Winter 1958–1959): 13.

24. Ibid.

25. For an exhaustive survey of World War II combat films, see Jeanine Basinger's *The World War II Combat Film: Anatomy of a Genre* (New York: Columbia University Press, 1986).

26. Thomas Doherty's *Projections of War: Hollywood, American Culture, and World War II* (New York: Columbia University Press, 1993), 139.

27. For analysis of the role of the government in terms of influencing the representation of the war in Hollywood films, see Doherty's *Projections of War*.

28. See Patricia Erens, *The Jew in American Cinema* (Bloomington: Indiana University Press, 1984), 171.

29. The negation of antisemitism in the military and the deracination of the Jewish characters continues to this day. For instance, in Steven Spielberg's 2001 miniseries *Band of Brothers*, David Schwimmer plays the inept and cowardly officer Herbert Sobel. Yet no matter how poorly he leads, the other men never respond with antisemitic slurs against him, directly contradicting the reality of how endemic antisemitism was in the armed services during World War II.

30. See Erens, *The Jew in American Cinema*, 173–81.

31. Hana Wirth-Nesher, "What Is Jewish Literature: Defining the Undefinable," in *What Is Jewish Literature*, ed. Hana Wirth-Nesher (New York: Jewish Publication Society, 1994), 16.

32. See Ruth Wisse, *The Modern Jewish Canon: A Journey through Language and Culture* (Chicago: University of Chicago Press, 2003), 8.

33. See Ben Schrier's polemical essay that argues that Ruth Wisse's views about what makes texts "Jewish" are motivated by her conservative beliefs: "New York Intellectual/Neocon/Jewish; or, How I Learned to Stop Worrying and Ignore Ruth Wisse," *Studies in American Jewish Literature* 31, no. 1. (2012): 85–108.

34. See Josh Lambert's *American Jewish Fiction (JPS Guide)* (Philadelphia: Jewish Publication Series Guide, 2009), 10; *The Cambridge Companion to Jewish American Literature*, ed. Michael P. Kramer and Hana Wirth-Nesher (Cambridge: Cambridge University Press, 2003), 9; and *A Norton Anthology of Jewish American Literature*, ed. Jules Chametzky, John Felstiner, Hilene Flanzbaum, and Kathryn Hellerstein (New York: W. W. Norton, 2001), 4.

35. Jan Gorak discusses this way of looking at canons in his *The Making of the Modern Canon: Genesis and Crisis of a Literary Idea* (New Jersey: Athlone, 1992).

36. For a survey of this topic, see my essay "Just One of the Goys."

37. A recent issue of the journal *Melus: Multi-Ethnic Literature of the United States* was devoted to questioning and challenging "why such a potentially vibrant field of study was being neglected" by American literary studies. The introduction to the volume argues that the neglect of Jewish American literary studies is compounded by the field being viewed as too "ethnic" for American literary studies and too "white" for ethnic studies. The introduction also has an excellent bibliography of sources on the topic. See the guest editors' introduction "Finding Home: The Future of Jewish American Literary Studies," by Lori Harrison-Kahan and Josh Lambert in *Melus* 37, no. 2 (Summer 2012): 6–18. Also, a recent edition of *Studies in American Jewish Literature* 31, no. 1 (2012) contains a number of interesting essays that reflect on the role of Jewish American literature in American literary studies.

38. For analysis of this tradition, see Beth S. Wenger's chapter "War Stories: Jewish Patriotism on Parade" in her book *History Lessons: The Creation of American Jewish Heritage* (Princeton, N.J.: Princeton University Press, 2011), 96–134.

39. This trope is of course as old as the hills. Famously it was the trickster, Odysseus, who broke the siege of Troy, not the war general Agamemnon or the best fighter of the day, Achilles.

40. John T. Matthews, "American Writing of the Great War," in *The Cambridge Companion to the Literature of the First World War*, ed. Vincent Sherry (Cambridge: Cambridge University Press, 2005), 217.

BIBLIOGRAPHY

Abbott, H. Porter. "The 'Lost Cause' of Character." In *Saul Bellow in the 1980s: A Collection of Critical Essays*, edited by Gloria L. Cronin and L. H. Goldman, 113–36. East Lansing: Michigan State University Press, 1989.

Abzug, Robert H. *Inside the Vicious Heart: Americans and the Liberation of Nazi Concentration Camps*. Oxford: Oxford University Press, 1987.

Adam, Michael C. C. *The Best War Ever: America and World War II*. Baltimore: Johns Hopkins University Press, 1994.

Aharoni, Ada. "Women in Saul Bellow's Novel." In *Saul Bellow in the 1980s: A Collection of Critical Essays*, edited by Gloria L. Cronin and L. H. Goldman, 95–111. East Lansing: Michigan State University Press, 1989.

Aichinger, Peter. *The American Soldier in Fiction, 1880–1963: A History of Attitudes toward Warfare and the Military Establishment*. Ames: Iowa State University Press, 1975.

Aldridge, John W. *After the Lost Generation: A Critical Study of the Writers of Two Wars*. New York: McGraw-Hill, 1951.

Ambrose, Stephen E. *The Victors: Eisenhower and His Boys: The Men of World War II*. New York: Simon and Schuster, 1999.

Atlas, James. *Bellow: A Biography*. New York: Random House, 2000.

"A Word to Our Readers." *Dissent* 1, no. 1 (Winter 1954): 1–9.

Band, Arnold. *Studies in Modern Jewish Literature: JPS Scholar of Distinction Series*. New York: The Jewish Publication Society, 2003.

Basinger, Jeanine. *The World War II Combat Film: Anatomy of a Genre*. New York: Columbia University Press, 1986.

Bauer, Christian and Rebeka Göpfert. *Die Ritchie Boys: Deutsche Emigranten beim US-Geheimdienst*. Hamburg: Hoffmann und Campe, 2005.

Baumgarten, Jean. *Introduction to Old Yiddish Literature*. Translated and edited by Jerold C. Frakes. Oxford: Oxford University Press, 2005.

Beichman, Arnold. *Herman Wouk: The Novelist as Social Historian*. New Brunswick, N.J.: Transaction Books, 1984.

Bellow, Saul. *Dangling Man*. In *Bellow: Novels 1944–1953*, 1–141. New York: Library of America, 2003.

———. "Notes of a Dangling Man." *Partisan Review* 11 (1944): 348–50.

———. *Saul Bellow: Letters*, edited by Benjamin Taylor. New York: Viking, 2010.

Berger, Alan L. and Gloria L. Cronin, eds. *Jewish American and Holocaust Literature*. Albany, N.Y.: SUNY Press, 2004.

Berkowitz, Henry J. *Boot Camp*. Philadelphia: The Jewish Publication Society, 1948.

Berryman, John. "The State of American Writing, 1948: Seven Questions." *Partisan Review* 15 (1948): 857.

Bloch, Joshua. "A Survey of American Jewish Books in English for 1947–1948." *Jewish Book Annual* 6 (1947/1948): 4.

———."A Survey of American Jewish Books in English for 1948–1950." *Jewish Book Annual* 8 (1949/1950): 4.

Bloom, Harold, ed. *Bloom's Guides: Joseph Heller's Catch-22*. New York: Infobase Publishing, 2009.

Bluemel, Kristen, ed. *Intermodernism: Literary Culture in Mid-Twentieth Century Britain*. Edinburgh: Edinburgh University Press, 2009.

Brandel, Marc. "Catharsis of Fear." *New York Times*, January 9, 1949, Book Review Section, 10.

———. "Three Men in the War." *New York Times*, October 3, 1948, Book Review Section, 9.

Breines, Paul. *Tough Jews: Political Fantasies and the Moral Dilemma of American Jewry*. New York: Basic Books, 1990.

Breit, Harvey. "An Interview with Ira Wolfert." *New York Times*, February 6, 1949, Book Review Section, 16.

Brown, Harry. *A Walk in the Sun*. New York: Signet, 1957.

Brown, Spencer. "A Code of Honor for a Mutinous Era: Herman Wouk on the Problems of Responsibility." *Commentary* 13 (1952): 595–99.

Bruccoli, Matthew J. and Park Bucker, eds. *Catch as Catch Can*. New York: Simon and Schuster, 2003.

Budick, Emily Miller. "The Holocaust in the Jewish American Literary Imagination." In *The Cambridge Companion to Jewish American Literature*, edited by Hana Wirth-Nesher and Michael Kramer, 212–30. Cambridge: Cambridge University Press, 2003.

Buhle, Paul. *From the Lower East Side to Hollywood: Jews in American Popular Culture*. New York: Verso, 2004.

———, ed. *Jews and American Popular Culture*. Vol. 2. Westport, Conn.: Praeger, 2007.

Burns, John Hurn. *The Gallery*. New York: Harper and Brothers, 1947.

Cain, Kathleen Shine, ed. *Leon Uris: A Critical Companion*. Westport, Conn.: Greenwood, 1998.

Carpenter, Frederic. "Herman Wouk and the Wisdom of Disillusion." *The English Journal* (January 1956): 1–6.

Cesarani, David and Eric J. Sundquist, eds. *After the Holocaust: Challenging the Myth of Silence*. New York: Routledge, 2012.

Chametzky, Jules, John Felstiner, Hilene Flanzbaum, and Kathryn Hellerstein, eds. *A Norton Anthology of Jewish American Literature*. New York: W. W. Norton, 2001.

Cowley, Malcolm. *The Literary Situation*. New York: Viking, 1955.

Crane, Stephen. *The Red Badge of Courage*. New York: W. W. Norton, 2007.

Cronin, Gloria L. and L. H. Goldman, eds. *Saul Bellow in the 1980s: A Collection of Critical Essays*. East Lansing: Michigan State University Press, 1989.

Cummings, E. E. *The Enormous Room*. New York: Dover, 2002.

Dauber, Jeremy. *Antonio's Devils: Writers of the Jewish Enlightenment and the Birth of*

Modern Hebrew and Yiddish Literature. Stanford, Calif.: Stanford University Press, 2004.

Daugherty, Tracy. *Just One Catch*. New York: St. Martin's, 2011.

Davidson, Michael. *Guys like Us: Citing Masculinity in Cold War Poetics*. Chicago: University of Chicago Press, 2004.

Davis, Kenneth C. *Two-Bit Culture: The Paperbacking of America*. Boston: Houghton Mifflin, 1984.

Dawes, James. "The American War Novel." In *The Cambridge Companion to the Literature of World War II*, edited by Marina Mackay, 56–66. Cambridge: Cambridge University Press, 2009.

——. *The Language of War: Literature and Culture in the U.S. from the Civil War through World War II*. Cambridge, Mass.: Harvard University Press, 2002.

Deibler, William E. "Dateline: D-Day: Ernest Hemingway Reported on Ernest Hemingway, Martha Gellhorn Reported on the War, Both Were Searching for the Truth." *North Dakota Quarterly* 68, nos. 2–3 (2001): 297–98.

Dell'Orto, Giovanna. "Memory and Imagination Are the Great Deterrents: Martha Gellhorn at War as Correspondent and Literary Author." *The Journal of American Culture* 27, no. 3 (September 2004): 303–14.

Dickstein, Morris. *Gates of Eden: American Culture in the Sixties*. New York: Basic Books, 1977.

——. *Leopards in the Temple: The Transformation of American Fiction, 1945–1970*. Cambridge, Mass.: Harvard University Press, 2002.

Diner, Hasia. *The Jews of the United States 1654–2000*. Berkeley: University of California Press, 2004.

——. *We Remember with Reverence and Love: American Jews and the Myth of Silence after the Holocaust, 1945–1962*. New York: New York University Press, 2009.

Dinnerstein, Leonard. *Anti-Semitism in America*. New York: Oxford University Press, 1994.

Doherty, Thomas. *Projections of War: Hollywood, American Culture, and World War II*. New York: Columbia University Press, 1993.

Dollinger, Marc. *Quest for Inclusion: Jews and Liberalism in the Modern Era*. Princeton, N.J.: Princeton University Press, 2000.

Doskow, Minna. "The Night Journey in 'Catch-22.'" *Twentieth Century Literature* 12 (January 1967): 186–93.

Dos Passos, John. *Three Soldiers*. New York: Dover, 2004.

Dubin, Louis I. and Samuel C. Kohs, eds. *American Jews in World War II: The Story of 550,000 Fighters for Freedom*, vol. 2. New York: Dial, 1947.

Eidelman, Jay M., ed. *Ours to Fight For: American Jewish Voices from the Second World War*. New York: Museum of Jewish Heritage — A Living Memorial to the Holocaust, 2003.

Erens, Patricia. *The Jew in American Cinema*. Bloomington: Indiana University Press, 1984.

Falktokyo, Ray. "What the GI's in Korea Are Reading." *New York Times*, June 27, 1954, Book Review Section, 19.

Fermaglich, Kirsten. *American Dreams and Nazi Nightmares: Early Holocaust Consciousness and Liberal America, 1957–1965*. Hanover, N.H.: Brandeis University Press, 2006.

Fetrow, Fred. "Joseph Heller's Use of Names." *Studies in Contemporary Satire* 1 (1975): 28–38.

Fiedler, Leslie A. "Archetype and Signature: A Study of the Relationship between Biography and Poetry." *The Sewanee Review* 60, no. 2 (April–June).

——. "Irwin Shaw: Adultery, the Last Politics." *Commentary* 22, no. 1 (July 1956): 71–74.

——. "The State of American Writing, 1948: Seven Questions." *Partisan Review* 15 (1948): 872–73.

Filreis, Alan. Introduction to *Tucker's People* by Ira Wolfert, xv–xliv. Urbana: University of Illinois Press, 1997.

Fine, Ellen. *Legacy of Night: The Literary Universe of Elie Wiesel*. Albany, N.Y.: SUNY Press, 1982.

Ford, Nancy Gentile. *Americans All! Foreign-Born Soldiers in World War I*. Houston: Texas A & M University Press, 2001.

Fox, Thomas C. "Stefan Heym and the Negotiation of Socialist-Jewish Identity." In *Stefan Heym: Socialist — Dissenter — Jew*, edited by Peter Hutchinson and Reinhard K. Zachau, 145–60. Oxford, Eng.: Peter Lang, 2003.

Freedman, Jonathan. *The Temple of Culture: Assimilation and Anti-Semitism in Literary Anglo-America*. New York: Oxford University Press, 2000.

Friedman, Murray. *The Neoconservative Revolution: Jewish Intellectuals and the Shaping of Public Policy*. Cambridge: Cambridge University Press, 2005.

Fussell, Paul. *Wartime: Understanding and Behavior in the Second World War*. Oxford: Oxford University Press, 1990.

Gabler, Neal. *An Empire of Their Own: How the Jews Invented Hollywood*. New York: Anchor Books, 1989.

Garrett, Leah. "Just One of the Goys: Salinger's, Miller's and Malamud's Hidden Jewish Heroes." *AJS Review* 34, no. 2 (2010): 171–94.

Gellhorn, Martha. "Dachau: Experimental Murder." *Collier's* (June 23, 1945): 16, 28, 39.

——. *Point of No Return*. Lincoln: University of Nebraska Press, 1995.

——. *The Wine of Astonishment*. New York: Bantam Books, 1949.

Gilbert, James. *Men in the Middle: Searching for Masculinity in the 1950s*. Chicago: University of Chicago Press, 2005.

Giles, James R. "Interviews with Irwin Shaw: Summer 1980." *Resources for American Literary Study* 18, no. 1 (1992): 10–11.

Glenday, Michael K. *Macmillan Modern Novelists: Norman Mailer*. London: Macmillan, 1995.

Goldman, L.H., Gloria L. Cronin, and Ada Aharoni, eds. *Saul Bellow: A Mosaic*. New York: Peter Lang, 1992.

Goldstein. Eric L. *The Price of Whiteness*. Princeton, N.J.: Princeton University Press, 2006.

Gonshak, Henry. " 'Rambowitz' versus the 'Schlemiel' in Leon Uris' *Exodus*." *Journal of American Culture* 22, no. 1 (Spring 1999): 9–16.

Gorak, Jan. *The Making of the Modern Canon: Genesis and Crisis of a Literary Idea*. New Jersey: Athlone, 1992.

Goren, Arthur A. " 'A Golden Decade' for American Jews: 1945–1955." In *The American Jewish Experience*, edited by Jonathan D. Sarna, 294–311. New York: Holmes and Meier, 1997.

Greenberg, Clement. "The Plight of Culture." *Commentary* (June–July 1951): 28–30.

——."The State of American Writing, 1948: Seven Questions." *Partisan Review* 15 (1948): 879.

Greenfeld, Josh. "22 Was Funnier than 14." *New York Times Book Review*, March 3, 1968, 1.

Halberstam, David. *The Fifties*. New York: Random House, 1993.

Hargrove, Marion. *See Here, Private Hargrove*. New York: Pocket Books, 1943.

Harris, Mark. *Something about a Soldier*. New York: Signet, 1957.

Harrison-Kahan, Lori and Josh Lambert. "Guest Editors' Introduction Finding Home: The Future of Jewish American Literary Studies." *Melus* 37, no. 2 (Summer 2012): 6–18.

Heggan, Thomas. *Mister Roberts*. Annapolis, Md.: Naval Institute Press, 2009.

Heller, Erica and Karen White. *Yossarian Slept Here: When Joseph Heller Was Dad, the Apthorp Was Home, and Life Was a Catch-22*. New York: Simon and Schuster, 2011.

Heller, Joseph. *Catch-22*. New York: Simon and Schuster, 2004.

——. " 'Catch-22' Revisited." *Holiday* 41, no. 4 (April 1967): 45–60, 120, 140–42.

——. Annotated copy of *Catch-22*. Joseph Heller collection, 1945–1969. Robert D. Farber University Archives and Special Collections Department, Brandeis University, Subseries 2, Box 10, Folder 15.

——. Correspondence and documents. Joseph Heller collection, 1945–1969. Robert D. Farber University Archives and Special Collections Department, Brandeis University, Box 10, Folder 15.

——. *Now and Then: From Coney Island to Here*. New York: Alfred A. Knopf, 1998.

Hemingway, Ernest. *A Farewell to Arms*. New York: Scribner, 2014.

——. *For Whom the Bell Tolls*. New York: Scribner, 1995.

——. Introduction to *Men at War: An Anthology*, edited by Ernest Hemingway, 7–19. London: Fontanta Books, 1966.

——. *The Sun Also Rises*. New York: Scribner, 2006.

Hendin, Josephine. *Vulnerable People: A View of American Fiction since 1945*. New York: Oxford University Press, 1978.

Heym, Stefan. *The Crusaders*. New York: Signet, 1970.

Hoberek, Andrew. *The Twilight of the Middle Class: World War II American Fiction and White-Collar Work*. Princeton, N.J.: Princeton University Press, 2005.

Hoberman, J. and Jeffrey Shandler, eds. *Entertaining America: Jews, Movies, and Broadcasting*. Princeton, N.J.: Princeton University Press, 2003.

Hölbling, Walter. "The World War: American Writing." In *The Cambridge Companion to War Writing*, edited by Kate McLoughlin. Cambridge: Cambridge University Press, 2009.

Humble, Nicola. *The Feminine Middlebrow Novel, 1920s to 1950s: Class, Domesticity, and Bohemianism*. New York: Oxford University Press, 2004.

Hutchinson, Peter. *Stefan Heym: The Perpetual Dissident*. Cambridge: Cambridge University Press, 1992.

Hutner, Gordon. *What America Read: Taste, Class, and the Novel, 1920–1960*. Chapel Hill: University of North Carolina Press, 2009.

"The Jew as a Soldier." Uncredited essay. *Collier's*, April 22, 1944, 11, 28, 30, 32.

Jones, James. *From Here to Eternity*. New York: Delta, 1998.

———. "Interview with Nelson Aldrich: The Art of Fiction No. 22." *Paris Review* 20 (Autumn–Winter, 1958–1959).

———. *The Thin Red Line*. New York: Delta, 1998.

Jones, Peter G. *War and the Novelist: Appraising the American War Novel*. Columbia: University of Missouri Press, 1976.

Jurca, Catherine. *White Diaspora: The Suburb and the Twentieth-Century American Novel*. Princeton, N.J.: Princeton University Press, 2001.

Kazin, Alfred. *Bright Book of Life: American Novelists and Storytellers from Hemingway to Mailer*. Boston: Little Brown, 1973.

———. "The Mindless Young Militants: The Hero-Victims of the American War Novels." *Commentary* 6 (1948): 493–505.

———. "Psychoanalysis and Literary Culture Today." *Partisan Review* (Fall 1958): 45–55.

Kerouac, Jack. *On the Road*. New York: Penguin Books, 2008.

Kiley, Frederick and Walter McDonald, eds. *A "Catch-22" Casebook*. New York: Thomas Y. Crowell, 1973.

Kimmage, Michael. *The Conservative Turn: Lionel Trilling, Whittaker Chambers, and the Lessons of Anti-Communism*. Cambridge, Mass.: Harvard University Press, 2009.

Kimmel, Michael S. *Manhood in America: A Cultural History*. New York: Oxford University Press, 2009.

Kligsberg, Moses. "American Jewish Soldiers on Jews and Judaism: A Report of a Contest." *YIVO Annual of Jewish Social Science* 5 (1958): 256–65. The Yiddish original is found in the *Yivo-bleter* 31, 32 (1948).

Kohs, S. C. "Jewish War Records of World War II." *American Jewish Yearbook* 47 (1946): 153.

Kramer, Michael P. and Hana Wirth-Nesher, eds. *The Cambridge Companion to Jewish American Literature*. Cambridge: Cambridge University Press, 2003.

Kremer, Lillian. *Witness through the Imagination: Jewish American Holocaust Literature*. Detroit: Wayne State University Press, 1989.

Kushner, Tony. *The Holocaust and the Liberal Imagination: A Social and Cultural History*. Oxford: Blackwell, 1994.

Lambert, Josh. *American Jewish Fiction: A JPS Guide*. Philadelphia: The Jewish Publication Society, 2009.

Lassner, Phyllis. " 'Camp Follower of Catastrophe': Martha Gellhorn's World War II Challenge to the Modernist War." *Modern Fiction Studies* 44, no. 3 (1998): 792–812.

Lee, Charles. *The Hidden Public: The Story of the Book-of-the-Month Club*. New York: Doubleday, 1958.

Leigh, Nigel. *Radical Fictions and the Novels of Norman Mailer*. New York: Macmillan, 1990.

Leroux, François. "Exhausting Ennui: Bellow, Dostoevsky, and the Literature of Boredom." *College Literature* 35, no. 1 (Winter 2008): 1–15.

Levine, Lawrence W. *Highbrow/Lowbrow: The Emergence of Cultural Hierarchy in America*. Cambridge, Mass.: Harvard University Press, 1988.

Levitas, Louise. "The Naked Are Fanatics and the Dead Don't Care." *New York Star*, August 22, 1948, M5.

Limon, John. *Writing after War: American War Fiction from Realism to Postmodernism.* New York: Oxford University Press, 1994.

Lowen, Joseph. "The Jewish Art of Joseph Heller." *Jewish Book Annual* 43 (1985/1986): 141–53.

Mailer, Norman. *Advertisements for Myself.* New York: Putnam, 1959.

———. Correspondence and documents. Norman Mailer Archive. Harry Ransom Center, University of Texas at Austin.

———. Interview by Glenn T. Johnston. August 25, 2004. Interview #OH 1560. Transcribed. University of North Texas Oral History Program, University of North Texas, Denton, Texas.

———. *The Naked and the Dead.* New York: Picador, 1998.

———. *The Spooky Art: Some Thoughts on Writing.* New York: Little Brown, 2003.

Manso, Peter. *Mailer: His Life and Times.* New York: Simon and Schuster, 1985.

Margolick, David. "The Great (Gay) Novelist You've Never Heard Of." *New York Times Magazine,* June 11, 2013.

Matthews, John T. "American Writing of the Great War." In *The Cambridge Companion to the Literature of the First World War,* edited by Vincent Sherry, 217–20. Cambridge: Cambridge University Press, 2005.

May, Elaine Tyler. *Homeward Bound: American Families in the Cold War Era.* New York: Basic Books, 1988.

Mazzeno, Lawrence. *Herman Wouk.* New York: Twayne, 1994.

McLoughlin, Kate. *Martha Gellhorn: The War Writer in the Field and in the Text.* Manchester: Manchester University Press, 2007.

Medovoi, Leerom. *Rebels: Youth and the Cold War Origins of Identity.* Durham, N.C.: Duke University Press, 2005.

Merrill, Robert. *Joseph Heller.* Boston: Twayne, 1987.

———. *Norman Mailer Revisited.* New York: Twayne, 1992.

Michener, James A. *Tales of the South Pacific.* New York: Fawcett, 1973.

Miller, Arthur. "Concerning Jews Who Write." *Jewish Life* 2, no. 5 (1948): 7–8.

———. "Preface: 'Salesman at Fifty.' " In *Death of a Salesman: Fiftieth Anniversary Edition,* ix–xiv. New York: Penguin Books, 1999.

Miller, Merle. "Mission's End in the Marshalls." In *Yank: The Story of World War II as Written by Soldiers,* by the staff of *Yank,* 26–28. New York: Brassey's US, 1984.

———. *That Winter.* New York: Popular Library, 1948.

———. "What It Means to Be a Homosexual." *Sunday New York Times Magazine,* January 17, 1971.

Miller, Wayne Charles. *An Armed America: Its Face in Fiction: A History of the American Military Novel.* New York: New York University Press, 1970.

Mills, Hilary. *Mailer: A Biography.* New York: Empire Books, 1982.

Mintz, Alan. *Popular Culture and the Shaping of Holocaust Memory in America.* Seattle: University of Washington Press, 2001.

Miron, Dan. *A Traveler Disguised: The Rise of Modern Yiddish Fiction in the Nineteenth Century.* Syracuse, N.Y.: Syracuse University Press, 1996.

Moore, Deborah Dash. *GI Jews: How World War II Changed a Generation.* Cambridge, Mass.: Harvard University Press, 2004.

Moorehead, Caroline. *Martha Gellhorn.* London: Chatto and Windus, 2003.

———, ed. *The Selected Letters of Martha Gellhorn.* New York: Henry Holt, 2006.

Motley, Mary Penick. *The Invisible Soldier: The Experience of the Black Soldier, World War II*. Detroit: Wayne State University Press, 1987.

Muste, John M. "Norman Mailer and John Dos Passos: The Question of Influence." *Modern Fiction Studies* 17, no. 3 (Fall 1971): 361–74.

Nadel, Ira B. *Leon Uris: Life of a Best Seller*. Austin: University of Texas Press, 2010.

Nagel, James, ed. *Critical Essays on "Catch-22."* Encino, Calif.: Dickenson, 1974.

———. "Two Brief Manuscript Sketches: Heller's *Catch-22*." *Modern Fiction Studies* 20, no. 2 (Summer 1974): 221–24.

Nathan, David. "Catching Heller." In *Conversations with Joseph Heller*, edited by Adam J. Sorkin, 294. Jackson: University Press of Mississippi, 1993.

Nazimek, Laura. "An Undiscovered Jewish American Novel: Martha Gellhorn's *Point of No Return*." *Studies in American Jewish Literature* 20 (2001): 69–80.

Norich, Anita. *Discovering Exile: Yiddish and Jewish American Culture during the Holocaust*. Stanford, Calif.: Stanford University Press, 2007.

Norris, Margot. *Writing War in the Twentieth Century*. Charlottesville: University Press of Virginia, 2000.

Obst, Lynda Rosen, ed. *The Sixties*. New York: Random House/Rolling Stone, 1977.

"Our Country and Our Culture: Literary Symposium." *Partisan Review* 19, 2 vols. (1952): 282–597.

Passos, John Dos. *Three Soldiers*. New York: Modern Library, 1949.

Patterson, James T. *Grand Expectations: The United States, 1945–1974*. New York: Oxford University Press, 2002.

Pells, Richard H. *The Liberal Mind in a Conservative Age: American Intellectuals in the 1940s and 1950s*. New York: Harper and Row, 1985.

Penslar, Derek. *Jews and the Military: A History*. Princeton, N.J.: Princeton University Press, 2013.

Pinsker, Sanford. "Once More into the Breach: Joseph Heller Gives *Catch-22* a Second Act." *Topic: A Journal of the Liberal Arts* 50 (2000): 28–39.

———. "Reassessing 'Catch-22.' " *The Sewanee Review* 108, no. 4 (Fall 2000), 602–10.

———. *Understanding Joseph Heller*. Columbia: University of South Carolina Press, 1991.

Pinsker, Schacher. *Literary Passports: The Making of Modernist Hebrew Fiction in Europe*. Stanford, Calif.: Stanford University Press, 2010.

Pizer, Donald. *Twentieth-Century American Literary Naturalism: An Interpretation*. Carbondale: Southern Illinois University Press, 1982.

Podhoretz, Norman. *Doings and Undoings*. New York: Farrar, Straus and Giroux, 1964.

———. "Looking Back at *Catch-22*." *Commentary* (February 2008): 32–38.

Poore, Charles. "For the Reader's Christmas List: A Retrospective Look at the Results of a Prolific Year along Publishers' Row." *New York Times*, December 5, 1948.

Prigozy, Ruth. "The Liberal Novelist in the McCarthy Era." *Twentieth-Century Literature* 21, no. 3 (October 1973): 253–64.

Pyle, Ernie. *Brave Men*. New York: Henry Holt, 1944.

Rabinowitz, Paula. *American Pulp: How Paperbacks Brought Modernism to Main Street*. Princeton: Princeton University Press, 2014.

Reich, Nathan. "The Year in Retrospect." *American Jewish Yearbook* 50 (1948–49): 115.

Remarque, Erich Maria. *All Quiet on the Western Front* (no translator listed). London: Triad/Grenada, 1982.

Ribalow, Harold U. "The Jewish GI in American Fiction." *Menorah Journal* 37 (Spring 1949): 266–67.

Rollyson, Carl. *Beautiful Exile: The Life of Martha Gellhorn*. London: Aurum, 2001.

——. *The Lives of Norman Mailer: A Biography*. New York: Paragon House, 1991.

Rontch, Isaac, ed. *Jewish Youth at War: Letters from American Soldiers*. New York: Marstin, 1945.

Rosenthal, Raymond. "Underside of War." *Commentary* 6 (1948): 91–92.

Roth, Lawrence. *Inspecting Jews: American Jewish Detective Stories*. New Brunswick, N.J.: Rutgers University Press, 2004.

Roth, Philip. "Defender of the Faith." In *Goodbye Columbus and Five Short Stories*, 161–200. New York: Vintage, 1987.

Rubin, Joan Shelley. *The Making of Middlebrow Culture*. Chapel Hill: University of North Carolina Press, 1992.

Ruderman, Judith. *Joseph Heller*. New York: Continuum, 1991.

Salinger, J. D. "For Esmé–With Love and Squalor." *New Yorker*, April 8, 1950.

Sandrow, Edward T. "Jews in the Army: A Short Study." *The Reconstructionist*, March 17, 1944, 16.

Schrier, Ben. "New York Intellectual/Neocon/Jewish; or, How I Learned to Stop Worrying and Ignore Ruth Wisse." *Studies in American Jewish Literature* 31, no. 1 (2012): 85–108.

Scoggins, Michael. "Joseph Heller's Combat Experiences in Catch-22." *War, Literature & the Arts* 15 (2003): 213–27.

Shandler, Jeffrey. *While America Watches: Televising the Holocaust*. New York: Oxford University Press, 1999.

Shapiro, Edward S. "The Jew as Patriot: Herman Wouk and American Jewish Identity." *American Jewish History* 84, no. 4 (1996): 333–51.

——. *A Time for Healing: American Jewry since World War II*. Baltimore: Johns Hopkins University Press, 1992.

Shaw, Irwin. "The Art of Fiction: Irwin Shaw: Interview with George Plimpton and John Phillips." *The Paris Review* 4 (Winter, 1953).

——. *The Young Lions*. Chicago: University of Chicago Press, 2000.

Sherry, Vincent. Introduction to *The Cambridge Companion to the Literature of the First World War*, edited by Vincent Sherry, 1–11. Cambridge: Cambridge University Press, 2005.

Shnayerson, Michael. *Irwin Shaw: A Biography*. New York: Putnam's Sons, 1989.

Slezkine, Yuri. *The Jewish Century*. Princeton, N.J.: Princeton University Press, 2004.

Sorkin, Adam J. ed. *Conversations with Joseph Heller*. Jackson: University Press of Mississippi, 1993.

Startt, William. "Irwin Shaw: An Extended Talent." *Midwest Quarterly* 2 (1961): 325–37.

Staub, Michael E. *Torn at the Roots: The Crisis of Jewish Liberalism in Postwar American*. New York: Columbia University Press, 2002.

Stuckey, W. J. *The Pulitzer Prize Novels: A Critical Backward Look*. Norman: University of Oklahoma Press, 1981.

Svonkin, Stuart. *Jews against Prejudice: American Jews and the Fight for Civil Liberties*. New York: Columbia University Press, 1997.

Swados, Harvey. "Popular Taste and *The Caine Mutiny*." *Partisan Review* (March–April 1953): 248–56.

Tobin, James. *Ernie Pyle's War: America's Eyewitness to World War II*. New York: Free Press, 1999.

Travis, Trysh. "Print and the Creation of Middlebrow Culture." In *Perspectives on American Book History: Artifacts and Commentary*, edited by Scott Evan Casper, Joanna D. Chaison, and Jeffrey David Groves, 338–57. Amherst: University of Massachusetts Press, 2002.

Trilling, Diana. "Fiction in Review." *The Nation*, October 9, 1948, 409–10.

Uris, Leon. *Battle Cry*. New York: Avon Books, 2005.

———. Correspondence. Leon Uris Archive. Harry Ranson Center, University of Texas at Austin.

Wald, Alan M. *The New York Intellectuals: The Rise and Decline of the Anti-Stalinist Left from the 1930s to the 1980s*. Chapel Hill: University of North Carolina Press, 1987.

Walden, Daniel. " 'Therefore Choose Life': A Jewish Interpretation of Heller's *Catch-22*." In *Critical Essays on "Catch-22"* edited by James Nagel, 57–63. Encino, Calif.: Dickenson, 1974.

Waldmeir, Joseph. *American Novels of the Second World War*. Paris: Mouton, 1969.

Wallant, Edward Lewis. *The Pawnbroker*. New York: Harcourt Brace Jovanovich, 1978.

Walsh, Jeffrey. *American War Literature: 1914 to Vietnam*. New York: St Martin's, 1982.

Weber, Donald. *Haunted in the New World: Jewish American Culture from Cahan to the Goldbergs*. Bloomington: Indiana University Press, 2005.

Wenger, Beth. *History Lessons: The Creation of American Jewish Heritage*. Princeton, N.J.: Princeton University Press, 2011.

Whitfield, Stephen J. *The Culture of the Cold War*. Baltimore: Johns Hopkins University Press, 1996.

———. "Necrology: Leon Uris (1924–2003)." *Jewish Quarterly Review* 94, no. 4 (Fall 2004): 666–71.

Whyte, William H. *The Organization Man*. Philadelphia: University of Pennsylvania Press, 2002.

Wiesel, Elie. *Night*. Translated by Marion Wiesel. New York: Hill and Wang, 2006.

Wilson, Sloan. *The Man in the Gray Flannel Suit*. New York: Arbor House, 1955.

Wisse, Ruth. *The Modern Jewish Canon: A Journey through Language and Culture*. New York: Free, 2000.

Wolfert, Ira. *An Act of Love*. New York: Simon and Schuster, 1945.

Wouk, Herman. *The Caine Mutiny*. New York: Little Brown and Company, 2003.

———. Correspondence. Herman Wouk Papers. Rare Book and Manuscript Library, Columbia University Library, New York. Series I, Boxes 2–3.

INDEX

Dempsey, David, 238n2
Diary of Anne Frank, The, 12
Dickstein, Morris, 32, 126–27, 171, 208, 212, 221, 255nn51–52, 257n7
Diner, Hasia, 14, 78, 80, 228n12
Dinnerstein, Leonard, 45
displaced persons issue, 46, 47, 78, 237n69
Dissent, 169–70
Dollinger, Marc, 228n12, 228n14
Doskow, Minna, 256n75
Dos Passos, John, 33–34, 35, 45, 51, 74
Dostoevsky, Fyodor, 173, 206, 208, 256n80, 257n5, 257n7
Duncan, Robert, 174

Edman, Irwin, 138
Eidelman, Jay M., 28
Erens, Patricia, 219

Farrell, James, 27, 51
Faulkner, William, 16, 27, 59, 155
Fermaglich, Kirsten, 169, 201
Fetrow, Fred, 257n81
Fiedler, Leslie, 15, 16, 17–18, 94, 120, 221, 231n48
Fitzgerald, F. Scott, 16, 196
Fox, Thomas C., 105
Freedman, Jonathan, 15
From Here to Eternity (film), 218
Fuller, Robert, 174
Fussell, Paul, 51

Gellhorn, Martha, 7, 79, 106–9, 116, 221, 224, 235n46, 241n19; Hemingway and, 81, 108–9, 235n46, 243n59; *Point of No Return* (aka *The Wine of Astonishment*), 3, 79, 106–14, 130, 172, 230n39
Gentleman's Agreement, 112, 119
Gervasi, Frank, 129, 246n107, 258n13
GI Bill, 6, 179, 226
Gilbert, James, 229nn25–27, 230n30
Giles, James P., 92
Glatstein, Jacob, 70
Gogol, Nikolai, 208
Gottlieb, Robert, 179, 186, 252n22
Grade, Chaim, 196
Great Dictator, The, 175
Greenberg, Clement, 16–18, 231n51
Greenfield, Josh, 194
Gwaltney, Francis Irby, 28, 59, 153

Hammett, Dashiell, 96, 206
Hargrove, Marion, 33, 42–44, 174, 236nn61–62
Harris, Mark, 174–76, 178
Heggen, Thomas, 33, 37–38, 45, 145, 174
Heller, Joseph, 11, 179, 188–89, 212, 254n45, 254n49, 255n58
  WORKS: *Catch-22*, 4, 8, 14, 21, 33, 39–40, 45, 167–69, 172–73, 175, 176, 178–202, 210–11, 220, 224, 225, 251n1, 252n19, 252nn22–24, 253n34, 253n38, 253–54nn41–42, 254n44–46, 256n72, 256n75, 256–57nn80–81, 257n85; "'Catch-22' Revisited," 254n45; *Closing Time*, 180, 253n31, 254n44
Hemingway, Ernest, 17, 18, 34–35, 50, 74, 116, 165, 185, 196, 206, 209, 223, 258n9; Crane and, 34, 235n44; *A Farewell to Arms*, 33, 34; Gellhorn and, 81, 108–9, 235n46, 243n59; Heller and, 185, 191–92; Mailer and, 24, 27, 235n46, 238n8; Miller and, 100; Shaw and, 81, 235n46; *The Sun Also Rises*, 100, 192, 214, 235n46, 236n53, 245n88
Hersey, John, 116–17
Heym, Stefan, 7, 101–2, 242n32, 242n36; *The Crusaders*, 3, 102–6, 118, 242n37
Hicks, Granville, 240n35
Himes, Chester, 257n5
Hitler, Adolf, 47, 70, 71, 88, 105, 109, 175
Hoberek, Andrew, 258n9
Hölbling, Walter, 231n54,
Holocaust, 4, 11–14, 37, 46, 77–80, 113–18, 123, 124–25, 128, 165–66, 205, 222, 225, 240n3; in Gellhorn, 79, 106–8, 111, 113–14; in Heller, 168, 187, 196–98, 200–202, 220; in Heym, 103, 105–6; in Mailer, 59; in Miller, 99; in Roth, 177; in Shaw, 79, 91–93; in Uris, 164; in Wouk, 143–44, 151, 164, 165–66; Yiddish authors on, 244n76
"Holocaust Literature" genre, 79, 115, 116–18, 237n69, 244n71
homosexuality, 11, 30, 33, 40, 55, 72, 95, 99, 149, 213–15
House Un-American Activities Committee (HUAC), 7, 130, 219, 237n75, 249n42
Howe, Irving, 169
Hutner, Gerald, 232n60
Hyman, Mac, 174

individualism, 7, 8, 18, 21, 26, 32, 35, 134, 144, 150–51, 153, 168–69, 172, 208
Israel, establishment of, 45, 47, 116, 126, 129, 156, 236n66

Japanese soldiers in fiction, 14, 38–39, 49, 53–54, 66, 68–69, 71, 74–75, 148–49
"Jewish American novel" term, 20, 219–22
Jewish intellectuals in fiction, 10, 209–10; in Bellow, 205–6, 208–9; in Gellhorn, 112; in Harris, 174; in Heller, 181, 185, 194, 210, 223; in Heym, 105; in Jones, 215; in Mailer, 51, 56, 57–58, 66; in Salinger, 42; in Shaw, 87, 93, 127, 148; in Wolfert, 71; in Wouk, 135, 136, 141, 143–44, 148–50, 152, 154
"Jewishness" in fiction, 8–9, 13, 17, 20, 171–72
Jewish postwar life, 5–9, 12, 19–20, 45–47, 86–87, 94–95, 118–19, 152–53, 162, 168, 171, 225, 228n12; popularity of Jewish American fiction, 171–72; reading habits, 15–16, 128
Jewish soldiers: as characters in fiction, 4, 5, 10, 13, 20–21, 40–45, 80, 99, 117, 119–28, 137, 172, 209–11, 217, 221–23, 225–26, 228n8, 230n41; in films, 218–19, 234nn18, 241n20; in Gellhorn, 79, 110–16; in Harris, 175–76; in Heller, 167–68, 172, 190–200, 209–10, 217, 251 (headnote), 255n51, 255n57, 255n59, 256n65; in Hemingway, 192, 214, 236n53, 245n88, 255nn57–58; in Heym, 104–6, 242n37; in Jones, 211–18, 221, 236n53; in Mailer, 51, 55–60, 63–66, 131, 165, 209–10, 212, 239n13; in Miller, 99–101; in Roth, 176–77; in Shaw, 87–95, 116, 255n58; in Uris, 158–65; in Wolfert, 67, 69–75; World War I avoidance, 26, 234nn18–19; World War II service, 25–31, 37, 77–78, 122–24, 128–30, 157, 233n14, 234n16; in Wouk, 144–48, 165, 210
Jewish stereotypes, 4, 27–28, 56, 110, 116, 163, 192–93
Jews in movie industry, 4, 219, 227n4
Jones, James, 139, 211–18, 220, 258n16; *From Here to Eternity*, 211–15; *The Thin Red Line*, 211, 215–18, 225, 238n8, 249n52
Joyce, James, 88, 191, 245n88, 256n75

Judaism, 6, 26, 86–87, 90, 93, 120, 121, 123, 138, 149–50

Kafka, Franz, 173, 200–201, 205, 220
Kapp, Isa, 120
Kazin, Alfred, 15, 94, 120, 127–28, 170, 178, 196, 202
Kerouac, Jack, 170, 184
Kimmel, Michael S., 229n25
Kinsey Report, 10–11
Korean War, 136–37, 144, 158, 162, 164, 225, 247n19
Kremer, Lillian, 13
Kunitz, Stanley, 172
Kushner, Tony, 237n69

Lassner, Phyllis, 79
Lazarus, Emma, 11
Leigh, Nigel, 55
liberalism, 5–8, 18, 46, 55, 80, 121, 126, 130, 133–34, 143, 151, 153, 169, 176, 193, 199–200, 223–24, 228n12, 246n12
Lucy Show, The, 172

Mailer, Norman, 5, 11, 20, 23–25, 26–29, 49, 158, 184, 203–5, 208–9, 224, 232n2, 233n4, 233n11, 236n55, 236n57, 237n1, 238nn12–13; Hemingway and, 24, 27, 235n46, 238n8; Jones and, 211–12, 258n16; Wolfert and, 66, 240n32; Wouk and, 134, 153, 246n10
  WORKS: *Barbary Shore*, 7; college fiction, 239n20; *The Naked and the Dead*, 3, 8, 14, 19, 21, 28, 31, 33, 45, 50–68, 74–75, 81–82, 89, 92, 127, 130–31, 135, 162, 165, 184–85, 203, 210–12, 214, 234n25, 238n2, 238n4, 246n106; "The White Negro," 169–71, 191
Malamud, Bernard, 3, 171
Malick, Terrence, 217–18
Margolin, Anna, 11
Marine Corps, 154–58, 174, 250n68
Marotznik, Meyer, 28, 60–61
Marshall Plan, 8, 130
Marx Brothers, 194
masculinity, 5, 9–10, 32, 34, 116, 118–19, 126–2, 164–65, 223, 229nn25–27; in Bellow, 206–9; in Gellhorn, 209; in Heym, 209; in Mailer, 65–66, 82, 127; in Miller, 100; in Shaw, 81, 89, 95, 127, 209, 211; in Uris, 160, 164–65, 209; in Wolfert, 209

Thin Red Line, The (film), 217–18
training camp. *See* boot camp
Trilling, Diana, 121
Trilling, Lionel, 16, 179

universalism, 69, 172–75, 116, 169, 193, 202. *See also* pluralism
Updike, John, 184
Uris, Leon, 5, 19, 133, 154–57, 224, 234n26, 236n61, 249nn52–55, 250n60, 250n64, 250n66
  WORKS: *Battle Cry*, 8, 21, 134–35, 137, 155–66, 184–85, 216, 250n61, 250nn68–69; *Exodus*, 5, 156–57, 160, 224, 250n66; *Mila 18*, 116–17, 186

Vietnam War, 167, 170, 189, 254n45
Vonnegut, Kurt, 178

Wald, Alan M., 228n12
Waldmeir, Joseph, 143, 153, 249n44
Wallant, Edward Lewis, 117–18
war novel genre, 4, 7, 9–10, 18–19, 32–33, 130–31, 223–24; comedic treatments, 173–78; Heller's subversion of, 184–85, 192–93
WASPs (white Anglo-Saxon Protestants), 54–55, 70–71, 87, 98, 118–19, 144–45, 148, 150–51, 154, 184, 195, 199, 215
Weinstein, Mark, 257n8
Wenger, Beth S., 116, 227n6, 228n8
White Christmas, 227n4
Whitfield, Stephen, 173
Whyte, William H., 136, 169
Wiesel, Elie, 117, 244n77

Wilson, Sloan, 135–36, 247n13
Wirth-Nesher, Hana, 220
Wisse, Ruth, 220, 259n33
Wolfert, Ira, 7, 66–67; *An Act of Love*, 3, 21, 66–75, 82, 112, 120, 149, 240n32, 240n35; *Married Men*, 67; *Tucker's People*, 67
women in war novels, 10–11, 82, 126–27, 146–47, 159, 182, 185, 223
Woolf, Virginia, 19
World War I, 26, 33–37, 50, 223
World War II: apocalyptic nature, 178; Guadalcanal Campaign, 66–67, 154–57, 159, 211, 215, 249n52; middle-class attitudes toward, 152–54, 164–66; Pacific vs. European theaters, 49–50, 59, 75. *See also* Holocaust
Wouk, Herman, 5, 20, 137–40, 171–72, 247nn20–21, 248n34, 248nn39–40
  WORKS: *Aurora Dawn*, 139; *The Caine Mutiny*, 3–4, 8, 21, 37, 38, 134–54, 164–65, 168, 216, 223, 224, 248n34, 249n42, 249n44; *City Boy*, 246n10; *Marjorie Morningstar*, 5, 139, 147, 168, 224; *This Is My God*, 138, 248n39; *The Winds of War*, 139, 248n28; *Youngblood Hawke*, 249n42

Yank, 50, 95
Yezierska, Anzia, 11
Yiddish language, 6, 43, 87, 99, 123, 173, 175; literature, 9, 194, 196, 229n18, 231nn49–50, 244n76
Young Lions, The (film), 218, 241n18

Zionism, 93, 108, 116, 157, 241n19, 244n74